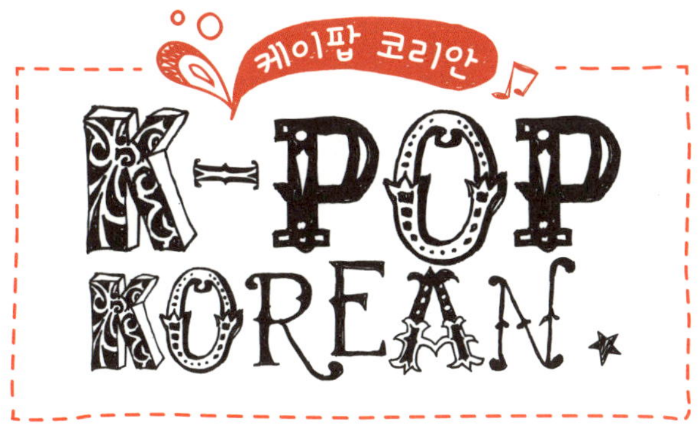


**DARAKWON**

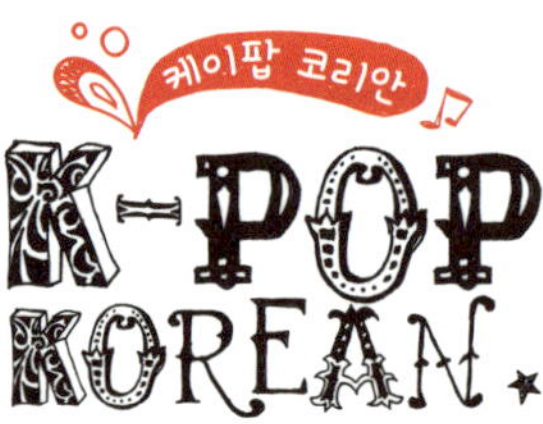

**Written by** Park Sunyoung, Ahn Yongjun
**Translated by** Jane Lee Perry
**First Published** August, 2016
**Publisher** Chung Kyudo
**Editor** Lee Suk-hee, Kim Sook-hee, Baek Da-heuin, Sohn YeoRam
**Cover design** Kim Na-kyung
**Interior design** Kim Na-kyung, Yoon Hyun-ju
**Proofread by** Michael Putlack
**Illustrated by** Cha Sang-mi

**DARAKWON**

Darakwon Bldg., 211 Munbal-ro, Paju-si
Gyeonggi-do, 10881 Republic of Korea
**Tel** : 02-736-2031 **Fax** : 02-732-2037
(Marketing Dept. ext.: 250~252 Editorial Dept. ext.: 420~426)



**Price: 14,000 won**
**ISBN: 978-89-277-3158-0  13710**

http://www.darakwon.co.kr
http://www.darakwon.co.kr/koreanbooks

Visit the Darakwon homepage to learn about our other publications and promotions and to download the contents of the CD in MP3 format.

# K-POP KOREAN

Park Sunyoung | Ahn Yongjun

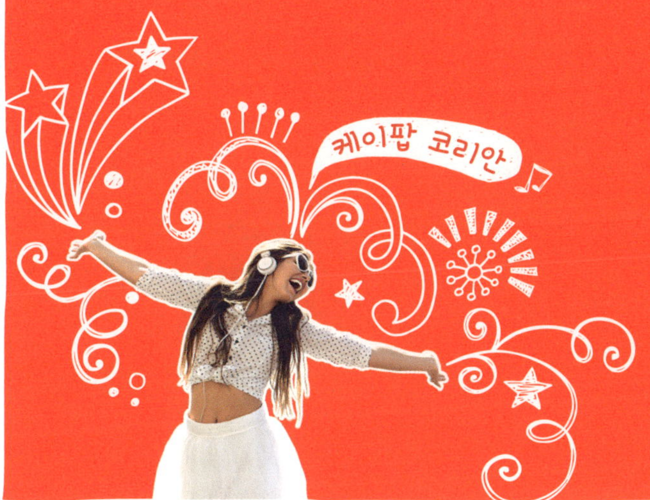


DARAKWON

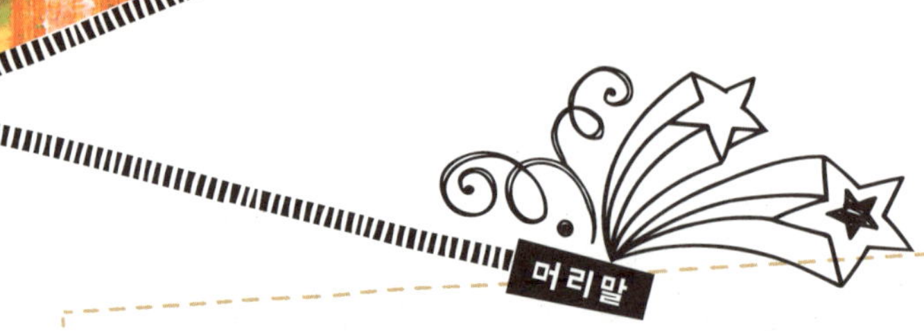


2000년대 중반 이후로 K-POP은 아시아를 시작으로 전 세계적으로 빠르게 확산되면서 많은 인기를 얻고 있습니다. K-POP의 인기는 한국어와 한국 문화에 대한 관심으로 이어져 많은 외국인들이 한국어를 학습하는 계기가 되고 있지만 아쉽게도 K-POP을 활용해 한국어를 학습할 수 있는 교재는 많지 않습니다. K-POP을 이해하고 즐기면서 이를 바탕으로 한국어 학습에 도움을 줄 수 있는 책이 있다면 좋겠다는 생각에 이 책을 기획하게 되었습니다.

본 교재는 기본적인 한국어 문법 체계에 대한 이해를 가지고 있는 TOPIK 1~2급 수준의 외국인 학습자를 비롯하여 한국어와 K-POP에 관심이 많은 일반인들을 대상으로 하고 있습니다.

최근 10년간 발표된 K-POP 곡들 중에서 초·중급 학습자가 한국어를 학습하기에 적합하면서도 대중적으로 인기를 끌었던 대표곡을 선정하여 교재에 실었습니다.

번역과 삽화를 활용하여 학습자가 학습에 대한 부담 없이 한국어에 흥미를 가지고 스스로 학습할 수 있도록 구성하였습니다. 또한 문법에 중점을 두기보다는 일상생활에서 바로 쓸 수 있는 주요 표현을 실어 실제 회화에서의 활용도를 높였습니다.

이 책을 통해 많은 외국인 학습자들이 자신이 좋아하는 K-POP의 가사를 보면서 그 내용을 이해하고, 더 나아가 가사를 외우듯이 자연스럽게 한국어 문장을 외우고 익히며 좀 더 재미있고 쉽게 한국어를 공부할 수 있기를 바랍니다.

박선영, 안용준

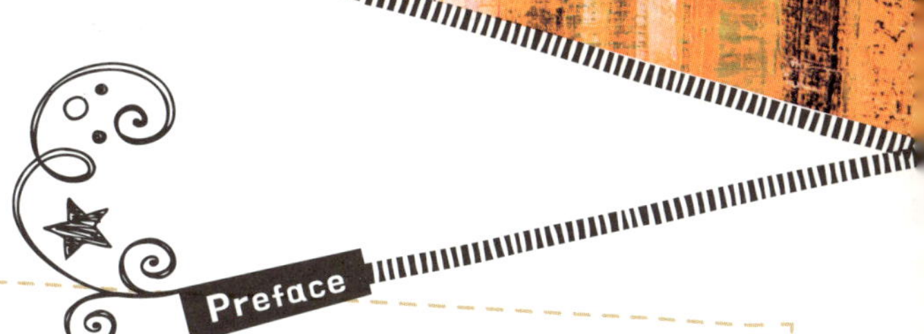



The boom started in Asia and spread all over the world in the mid-2000s. As K-Pop has grown popular, more attention has been drawn to the Korean language and culture. Naturally, lots of foreigners who are interested in K-Pop are studying Korean these days. However, there are few books out there that suggest a guideline to study Korean through K-Pop. This book is published to help students enjoy learning Korean by understanding K-Pop better.

The main target of this book is foreign learners who have achieved TOPIK level 1~2 with a basic understanding of Korean grammar. It is also written for people who are interested in K-Pop and learning Korean.

In addition, the songs selected in the book are some of the most widely loved K-Pop songs in the past decade. The lyrics are also appropriate for beginners and intermediate learners who are studying Korean.

To enhance learners' understanding of the dialogues and other contents in the book, images and translations are included. The book also contains lots of practical expressions that can be used in everyday life.

We hope that all the foreign learners who study with this book may gain a better understanding of Korean while studying their favorite K-Pop lyrics. Furthermore, we hope that the learners will be able to pick up Korean easier by simply practicing the K-Pop lyrics.

Park Sunyoung, Ahn Yongjun

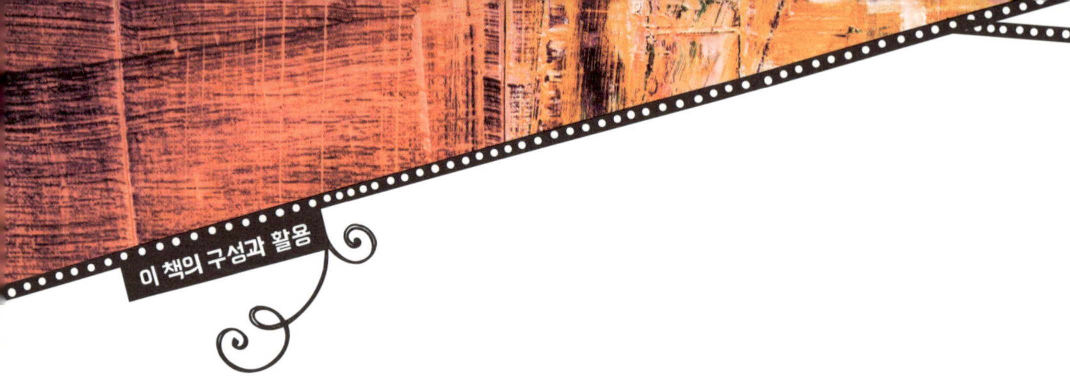


## 가사

전체 가사 중에서 각 과에서 배우게 될 표현이 들어 있는 부분을 실었습니다. 노래에서 반복적으로 들리는 후렴구와 노래의 상징적인 의미를 담고 있는 부분, 실제로 자주 사용되는 표현이 담긴 부분 등을 종합적으로 고려하여 선택하였습니다.

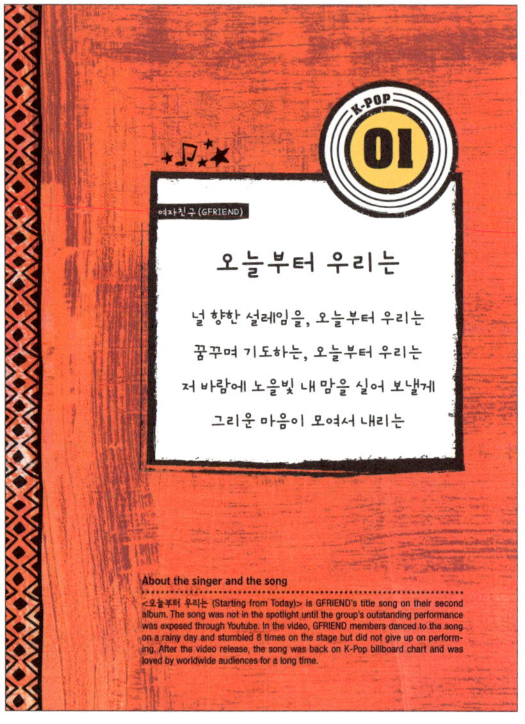


## 가수와 노래 설명

본격적으로 노래를 배우기 전에 가수와 노래에 대한 배경지식을 쌓을 수 있도록 가수와 노래에 대한 기본적인 소개와 재미있는 이야기들을 담았습니다.

## 표현

해당 단원에서 배우게 되는 대표적인
표현을 가사에서 선별하고 다양한 상
황별 문장들을 함께 제시하였습니다.
실제 대화에서 바로 사용할 수 있을
만큼 활용도가 높고 유용한 예문들로
구성되어 있습니다.

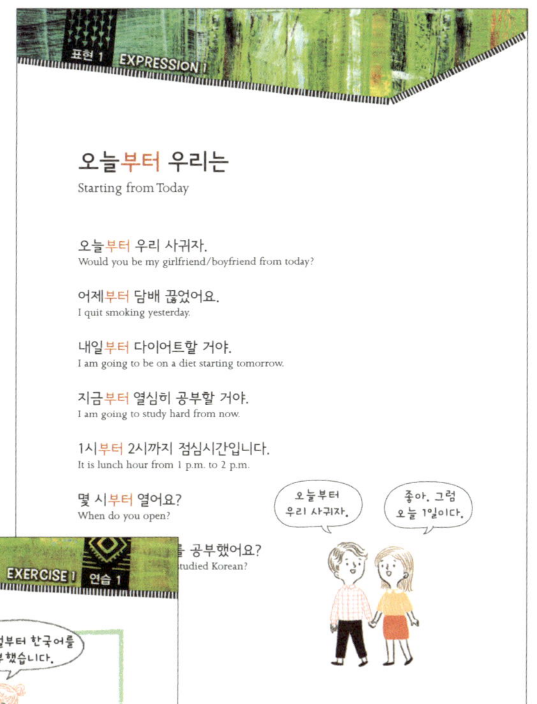



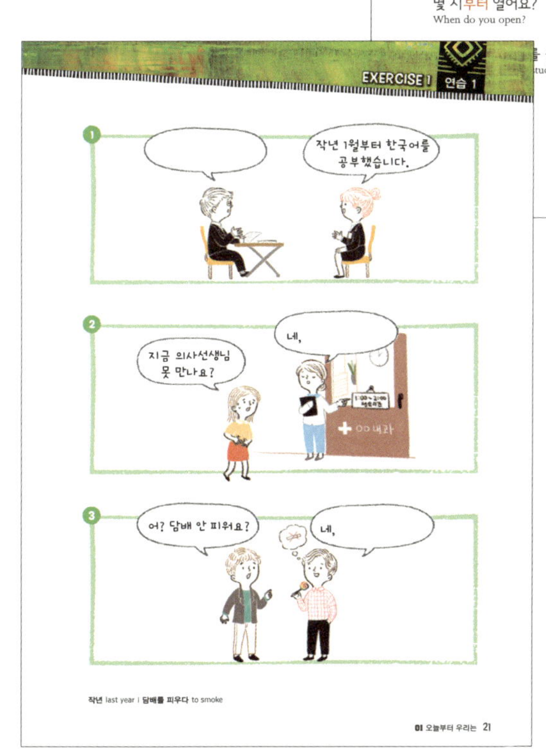



## 연습

표현 에서 배운 예문들을 그대로 적용
하여 연습 문제를 풀 수 있도록 하였습
니다. 삽화와 함께 제시된 연습 문제
를 통해 앞서 배운 문장들을 어떤 상
황에서 사용할 수 있는지 자연스럽게
이해하면서 문제를 풀 수 있습니다.

## 문법 및 표현 설명

해당 단원의 문법과 표현을 자세한 설명과 예문을 보면서 다시 한 번 확인할 수 있습니다. 문법 설명 부분에서는 편의를 위해 몇 가지 약어를 사용하고 있으며 사용 약어의 표기는 다음과 같습니다.

### 약어

※ N-noun / V-verb /
   A-adjective / Ad-adverb

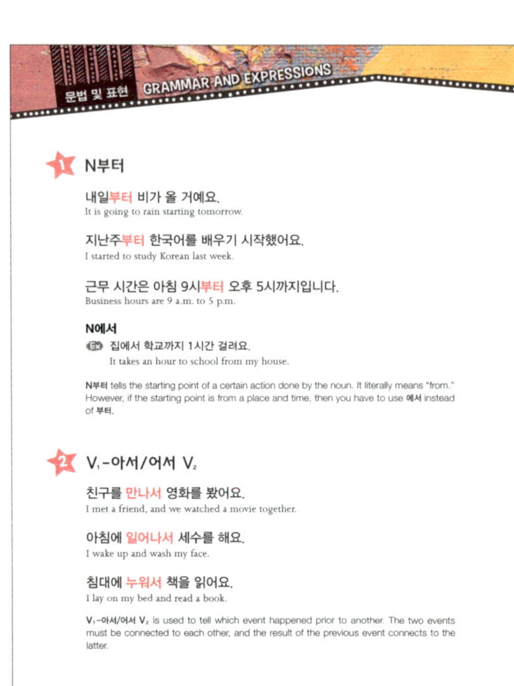


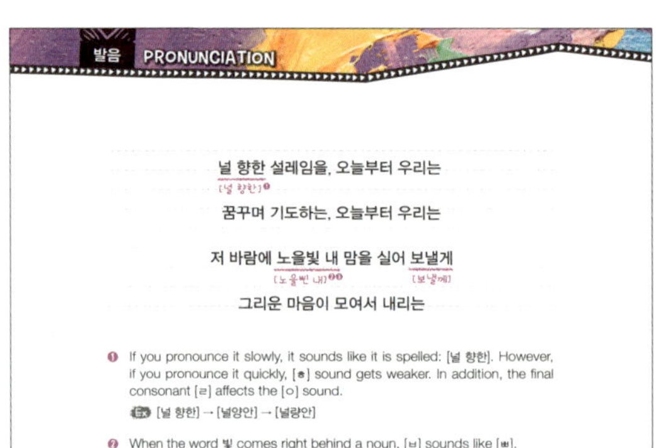


## 발음

노래 가사의 주요 부분을 중심으로 한국어 발음의 특징을 알아봅니다. 한국어의 발음 규칙에 대한 구체적인 설명과 예문을 통해 자연스럽게 한국어를 듣고 이해하며 발음할 수 있도록 돕습니다.

## 한국어 활용 TIP

노래 가사에서 잘못 사용된 한국어의 올바른 맞춤법과 발음상의 이유로 줄여 쓰는 줄임말, 그리고 현재 한국에서 많이 사용되는 유행어나 재미있는 한국어 표현 등을 실었습니다



### 맞춤법

안타깝게도 한국 노래 가사에는 잘못된 한국어 표현이 많이 사용되고 있습니다. 이는 실제 생활에서 한국 사람들도 한국어를 잘못 사용하는 경우가 많기 때문입니다. 여기에서는 이러한 표현의 올바른 표기를 알 수 있도록 했습니다.

### 어순

노래 가사에서는 특정 부분을 강조하거나 시적인 느낌을 주기 위해 일반적으로 쓰이는 한국어와 달리 어순이 뒤바뀌어 있는 경우가 많습니다. 노래 가사에 쓰인 말들을 올바른 어순으로 제시하여 학습자가 노래 가사를 효율적으로 이해하고 자연스러운 어순으로 한국어를 말할 수 있도록 돕습니다.

### 유행어

한국에서 유행하고 있는 최신 유행어나 말투 등을 소개하여 한국어를 재미있게 공부할 수 있도록 돕습니다.

### 줄임말

한국어에는 발음의 편의상 줄여 쓰는 표현들이 많이 존재하는데 이러한 줄임말들은 사전에서도 찾을 수 없는 경우가 많아 그 의미를 알기가 어렵습니다. 이러한 줄임말들의 원래 형태를 소개하여 사전에서 찾기 쉽게 하고 한국어 줄임말에 대해 대략적으로 이해할 수 있게 돕습니다.

### 유용한 표현

한국어의 재미있는 표현이나 한국어 공부에 필요한 내용들을 소개합니다.

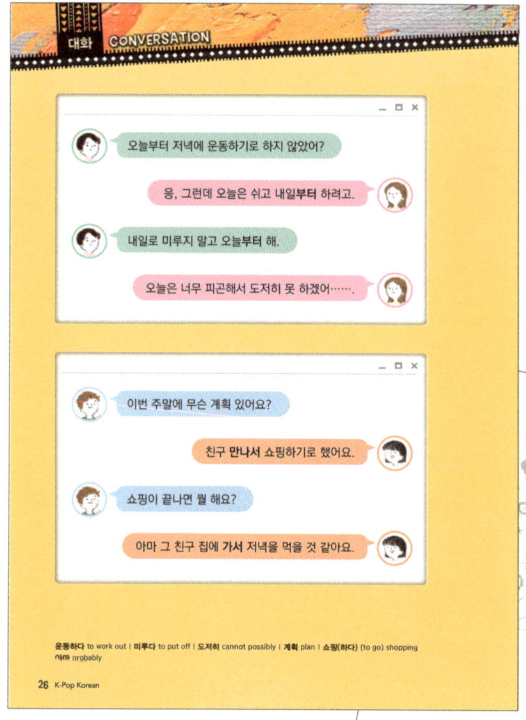



## 대화

자연스러운 대화 상황을 통해 배운 문법과 표현을 다시 한 번 확인해 봅니다. 한국에서는 말하는 상대방에 따라 반말과 존댓말을 구분하여 사용해야 하는데 여기에서는 각각의 상황에 익숙해질 수 있도록 인물 관계에 따라 대화체를 구분하여 제시하였습니다.



## 전체 가사

각 과에서 학습한 표현이 들어 있는 가사의 1절 부분을 매 과의 마지막 장에 수록했습니다.
한국어 가사와 영어 번역을 함께 수록하여 학습자가 따라 부르면서 의미를 쉽게 파악할 수 있도록 하였습니다.

★ 부록에서는 어휘 색인과 연습 문제 해답을 비롯하여 본문에서 나온 표현, 연습, 대화의 영어 번역이 수록되어 있습니다. 또한 가수와 노래 설명, 문법, 한국어 TIP에 대한 한국어 설명도 있습니다.

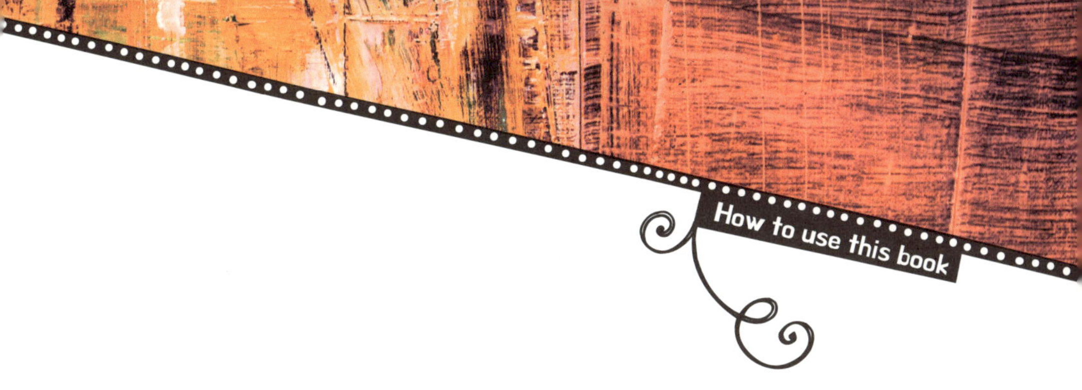


## Target Lyrics

The lyrics used on this page are from the selected expressions in each unit. The expressions are mainly from the chorus part of the song, symbolic lyrics, and the parts of the lyrics that are frequently used in daily conversations.

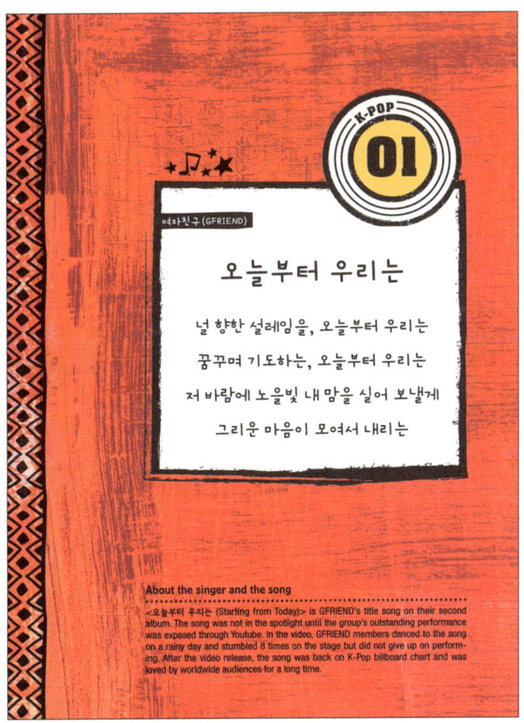


## About the singer and the song

This part briefly introduces the singer and the song in the unit so that learners will feel closer to the singer and have a better understanding of the song before they start the lesson.

## Expressions

The key expressions are sorted from the lyrics in the book. This part shows varied situations when you can use the expressions. In addition, the example sentences in the book are practical and frequently used in real conversations.

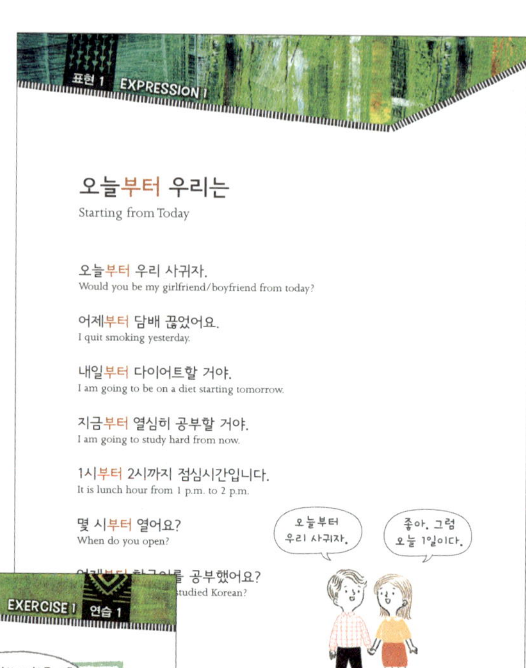


## Exercise

The exercise part is for learners to use the example sentences in the <Expressions> part and to apply them to the practice questions. The illustrations next to the exercise questions are there to help the learners understand.

## Grammar and Expressions

The grammar and expressions part explains the grammar rules and expressions used in the unit by giving example sentences. For convenience, abbreviations are used to explain the grammar rules. The abbreviations used in the book are as below.

### Abbreviations

※ N-noun / V-verb / A-adjective / Ad-adverb

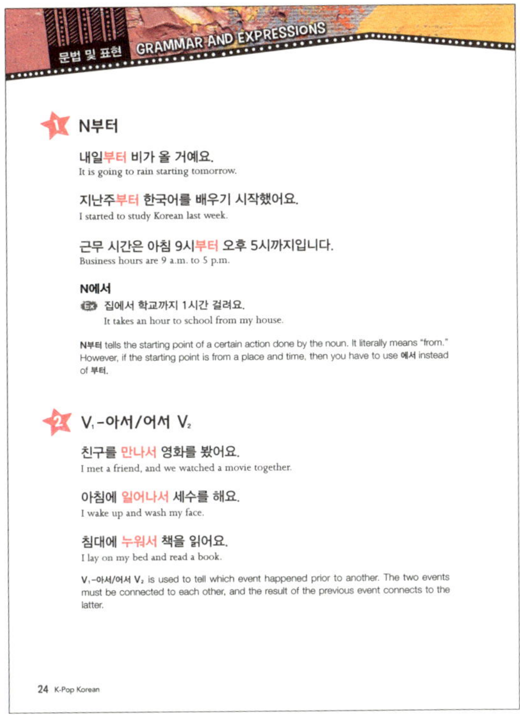


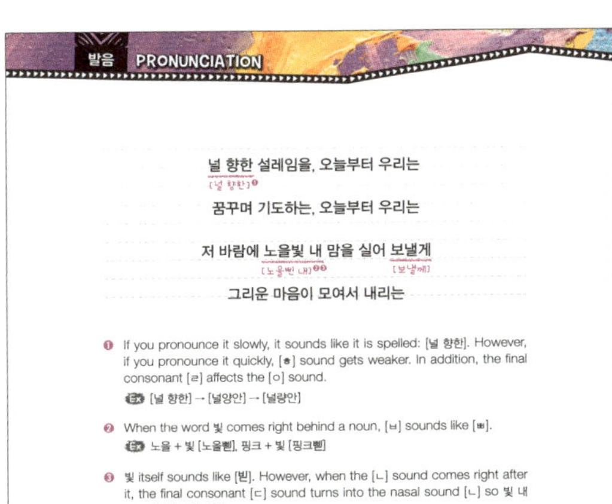


## Pronunciation

This part explains the characteristics of the Korean pronunciation rules by referring to the song lyrics. It has several example sentences to show how to apply the Korean pronunciation rules in various situations.

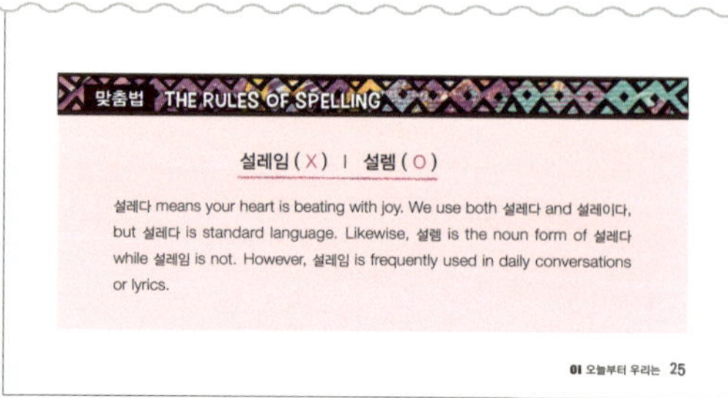


## TIPs on the Korean Language

This part of the book points out a few broken grammar rules in the lyrics and shows the correct forms. It also lists contractions, buzzwords, and some fun Korean expressions used in the lyrics.

## The Rules of Spelling

It is a shame that lots of Korean song lyrics use incorrect expressions. In fact, lots of Koreans use incorrect expressions in daily conversations. In this part of the book, learners will see the misused expressions in the lyrics and learn their correct forms.

## Order of Words

Lots of song lyrics change the order of words to emphasize certain messages or to make them sound poetic. This part of the book shows the correct order of words that are used in the lyrics. It helps learners understand the lyrics better and say the words in the correct order.

## Trendy Words

This part of the book introduces some of the latest Korean trendy words to get a glimpse at Korean culture.

## Contractions

Lots of Korean words are used in contracted forms for convenience. However, many of them are not listed in the dictionary, which may cause confusion. In this part of the book, learners will understand the original forms of the contracted words in the lyrics.

## Useful Expressions

This part introduces some fun and useful Korean expressions and also suggests useful ways to study Korean.

## Conversation

One of the best ways to review the expressions and grammar rules is to use them in real conversations. In this part of the book, learners will be able to naturally understand Korean honorific rules through example sentences that apply the rules.

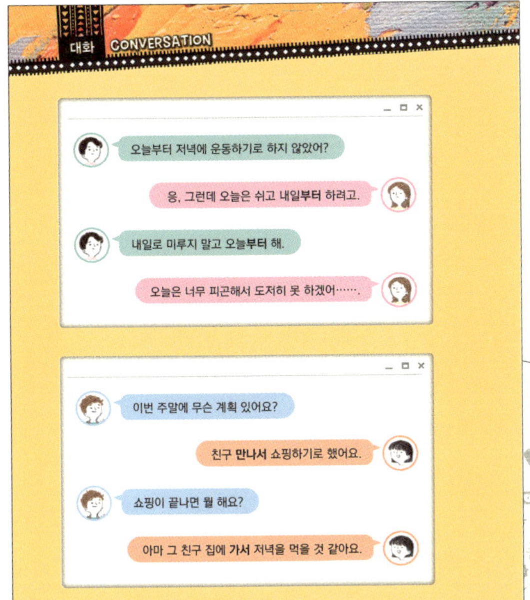



## Lyrics

The first verses of each song that include key expressions of the unit are attached on the last page of the unit. Both Korean and English lyrics are written in the book so that the readers may understand the lyrics while singing along with the songs.



★ The appendix includes a vocabulary index and answers for the exercise questions. In addition, English translations for the expressions, practice questions, and conversations are attached in the appendix. The Korean translations of the following sections have been added in appendix too: About the singers and the songs, grammar, and tips on the Korean language.

# 목차

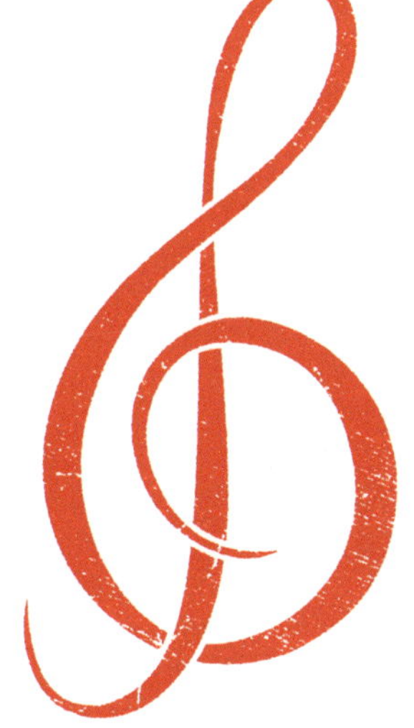

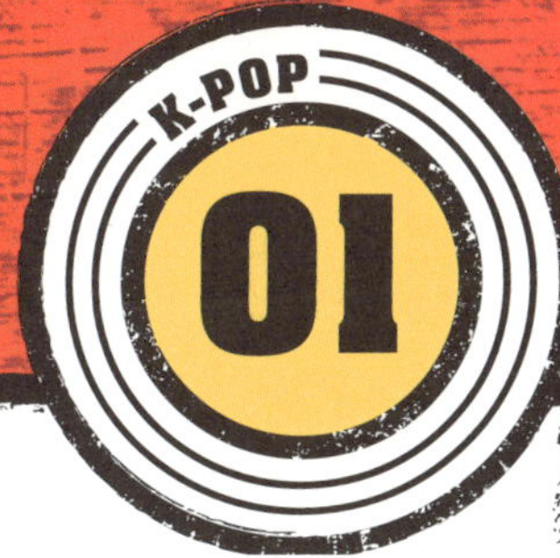


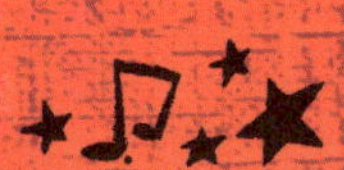

**여자친구 (GFRIEND)**

# 오늘부터 우리는

넬 향한 설레임을, 오늘부터 우리는
꿈꾸며 기도하는, 오늘부터 우리는
저 바람에 노을빛 내 맘을 실어 보낼게
그리운 마음이 모여서 내리는

## About the singer and the song

<오늘부터 우리는 (Starting from Today)> is GFRIEND's title song on their second album. The song was not in the spotlight until the group's outstanding performance was exposed through Youtube. In the video, GFRIEND members danced to the song on a rainy day and stumbled 8 times on the stage but did not give up on performing. After the video release, the song was back on K-Pop billboard chart and was loved by worldwide audiences for a long time.

# 오늘부터 우리는

Starting from Today


## 오늘부터 우리 사귀자.
Would you be my girlfriend/boyfriend from today?

## 어제부터 담배 끊었어요.
I quit smoking yesterday.

## 내일부터 다이어트할 거야.
I am going to be on a diet starting tomorrow.

## 지금부터 열심히 공부할 거야.
I am going to study hard from now.

## 1시부터 2시까지 점심시간입니다.
It is lunch hour from 1 p.m. to 2 p.m.

## 몇 시부터 열어요?
When do you open?

## 언제부터 한국어를 공부했어요?
Since when have you studied Korean?

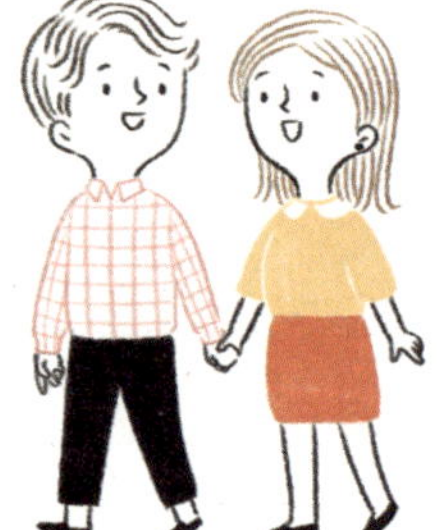

**1**

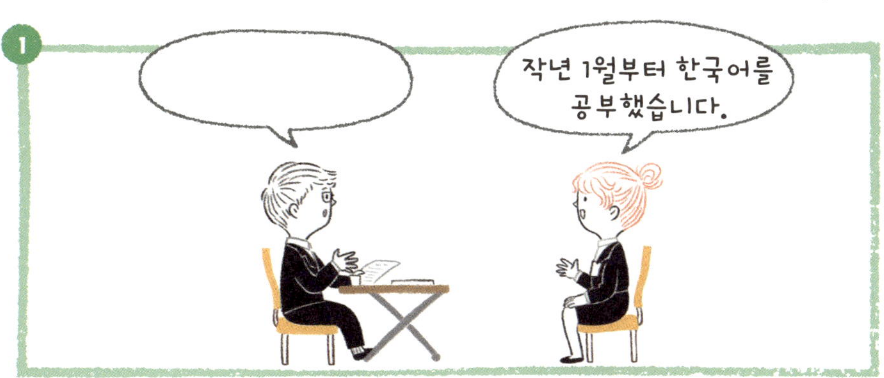


**2**

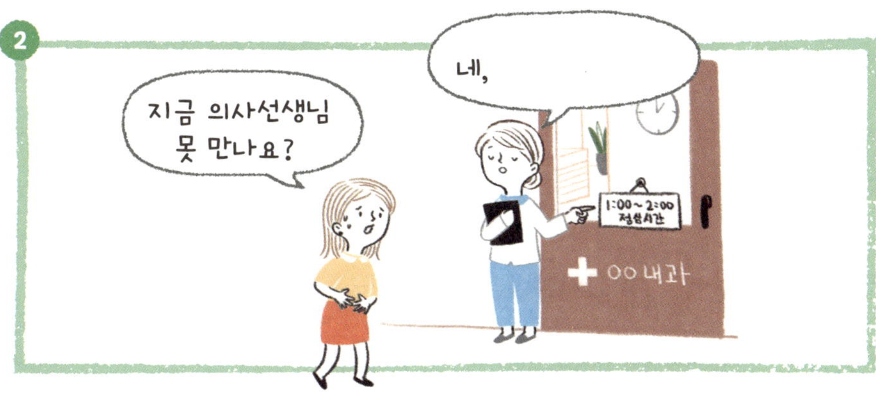


**3**

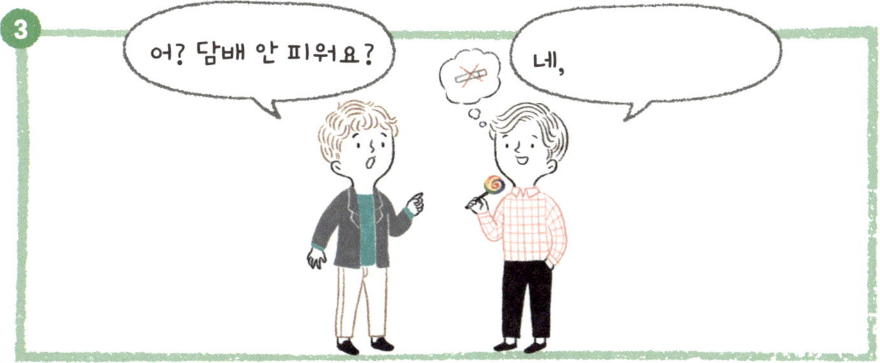


**작년** last year | **담배를 피우다** to smoke

# 그리운 마음이 모여서 내리는

I long for you like endless raindrops.


마트에 가서 우유를 샀어.
I got some milk at the store.


우유를 사서 집에 왔어.
I brought the milk home.


집에 와서 쉬고 있어.
I am resting at home.


소파에 누워서 텔레비전을 봐.
I am watching TV on the sofa.


하루 종일 서서 일해.
I work on my feet all day.


친구를 만나서 같이 쇼핑을 할 거야.
I am going shopping with my friend.


케이크를 만들어서 남자 친구에게 줄 거야.
I am going to bake a cake for my boyfriend.

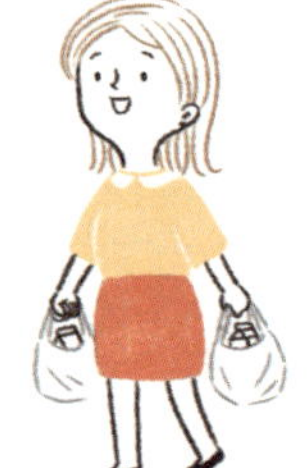

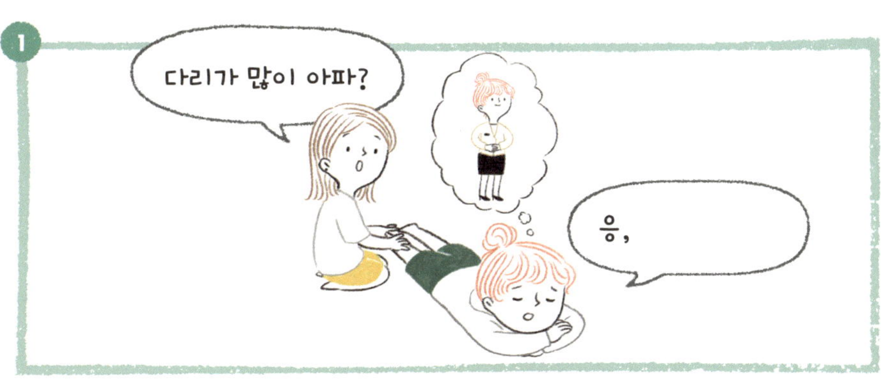
다리가 많이 아파?
응,

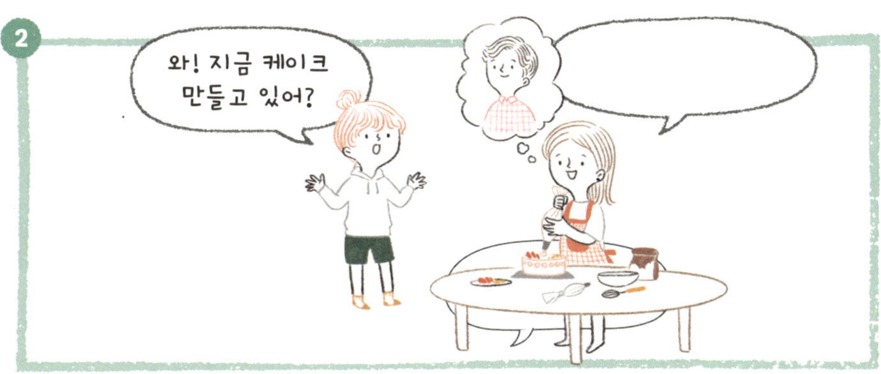
와! 지금 케이크 만들고 있어?

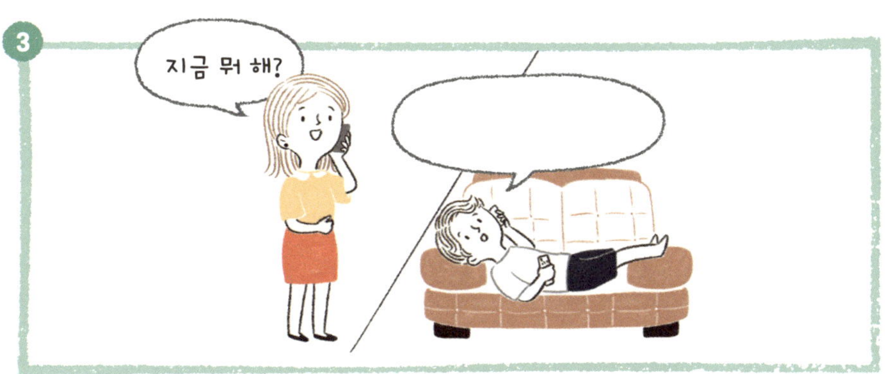
지금 뭐 해?

 **N부터**

**내일부터 비가 올 거예요.**
It is going to rain starting tomorrow.

**지난주부터 한국어를 배우기 시작했어요.**
I started to study Korean last week.

**근무 시간은 아침 9시부터 오후 5시까지입니다.**
Business hours are 9 a.m. to 5 p.m.

**N에서**

**Ex** 집에서 학교까지 1시간 걸려요.
It takes an hour to school from my house.

**N부터** tells the starting point of a certain action done by the noun. It literally means "from." However, if the starting point is from a place and time, then you have to use **에서** instead of **부터**.

 **V₁-아서/어서 V₂**

**친구를 만나서 영화를 봤어요.**
I met a friend, and we watched a movie together.

**아침에 일어나서 세수를 해요.**
I wake up and wash my face.

**침대에 누워서 책을 읽어요.**
I lay on my bed and read a book.

**V₁-아서/어서 V₂** is used to tell which event happened prior to another. The two events must be connected to each other, and the result of the previous event connects to the latter.

널 향한 설레임을, 오늘부터 우리는
[널 향한] ❶

꿈꾸며 기도하는, 오늘부터 우리는

저 바람에 노을빛 내 맘을 실어 보낼게
[노을삔 내] ❷❸          [보낼께]

그리운 마음이 모여서 내리는

❶ If you pronounce it slowly, it sounds like it is spelled: [널 향한]. However, if you pronounce it quickly, [ㅎ] sound gets weaker. In addition, the final consonant [ㄹ] affects the [ㅇ] sound.

**Ex** [널 향한] → [널양안] → [널량안]

❷ When the word 빛 comes right behind a noun, [ㅂ] sounds like [ㅃ].

**Ex** 노을 + 빛 [노을삔], 핑크 + 빛 [핑크삔]

❸ 빛 itself sounds like [빋]. However, when the [ㄴ] sound comes right after it, the final consonant [ㄷ] sound turns into the nasal sound [ㄴ] so 빛 내 sounds like [빈 내].

**Ex** 꽃나무 [꼳][나무] → [꼰나무], 옷냄새 [옫][냄새] → [온냄새]



## 설레임 ( X )  |  설렘 ( O )

설레다 means your heart is beating with joy. We use both 설레다 and 설레이다, but 설레다 is standard language. Likewise, 설렘 is the noun form of 설레다 while 설레임 is not. However, 설레임 is frequently used in daily conversations or lyrics.

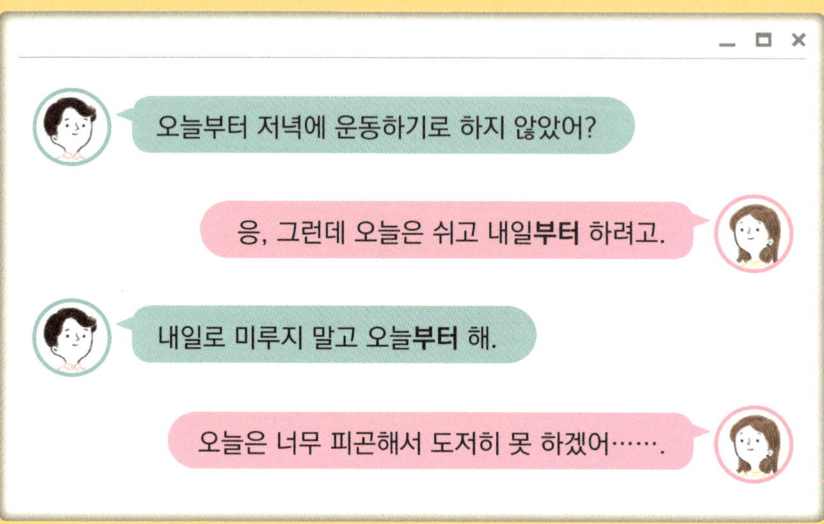


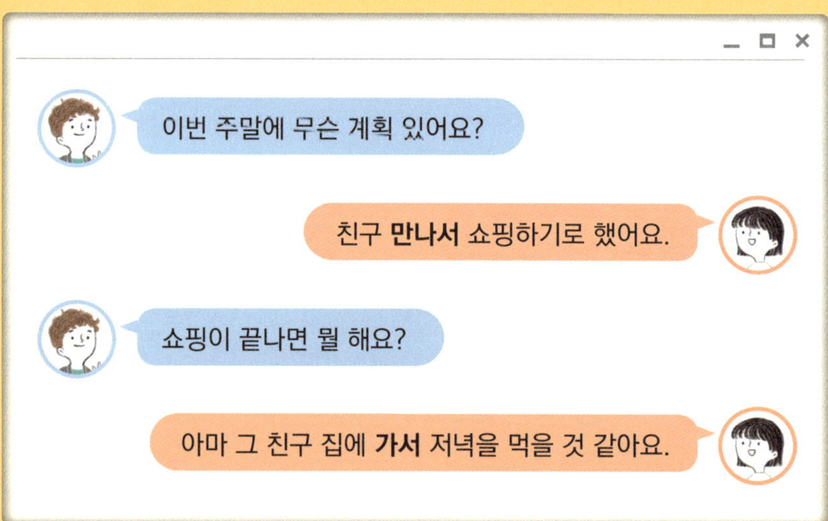


**운동하다** to work out | **미루다** to put off | **도저히** cannot possibly | **계획** plan | **쇼핑(하다)** (to go) shopping
**아마** probably

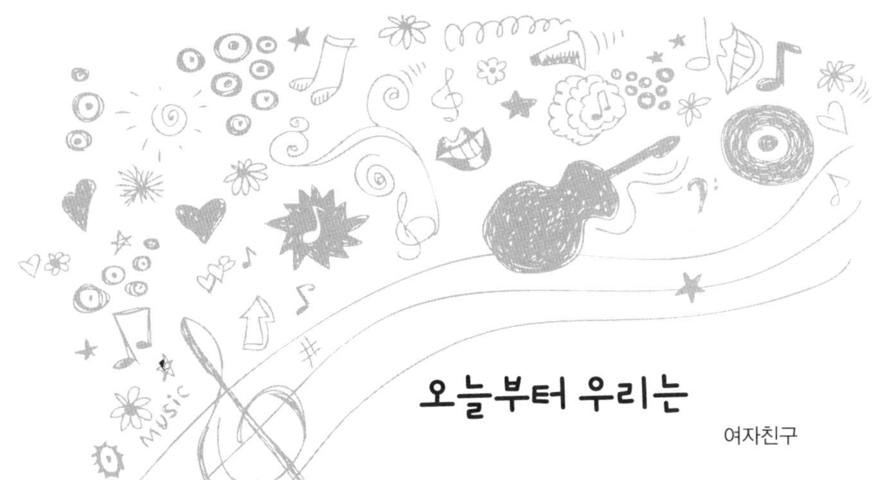

# 오늘부터 우리는

여자친구

널 향한 설레임을 오늘부터 우리는
꿈꾸며 기도하는 오늘부터 우리는
저 바람에 노을빛 내 맘을 실어 보낼게.
그리운 마음이 모여서 내리는

Me gustas tu gustas tu
su tu tu ru 좋아해요.
gustas tu su tu ru ru
한 발짝 뒤에 섰던 우리는
언제쯤 센치해질까요?
서로 부끄러워서 아무 말도 못하는
너에게로 다가가고 싶은데

바람에 나풀거리는 꽃잎처럼
미래는 알 수가 없잖아.
이제는 용기 내서 고백할게요.
하나보단 둘이서 서로를 느껴 봐요.
내 마음 모아서 너에게 전하고 싶어.

설레임을 오늘부터 우리는
꿈꾸며 기도하는 오늘부터 우리는
저 바람에 노을빛 내 맘을 실어 보낼게.
그리운 마음이 모여서 내리는

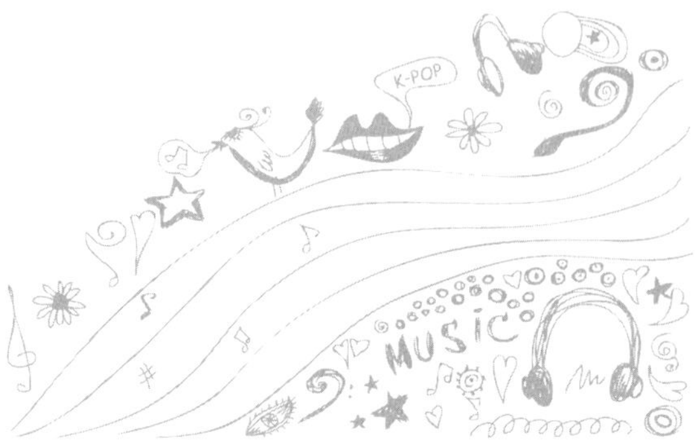

# Starting from Today

GFRIEND

My heart beats for you. Our love is starting from today.
I dream, and I pray. Our love is starting from today.
I'll send you my heart through the wind in the sunset.
I long for you like endless raindrops.

Me gustas tu gustas tu
su tu tu ru I like you.
gustas tu su tu ru ru
We are standing one step behind.
When will we get sentimental?
We are so shy. Can't even say a word to each other
But I want to get closer to you.

Like a flower fluttering in the wind,
We don't know about our future.
I'll be brave and confess my heart to you.
Two is better than one. We can feel each other.
I wish you could feel my love for you.

My heart beats, and we are starting from today.
I dream and I pray, our love is starting from today.
I'll send you my heart through the wind in the sunset.
I long for you like endless raindrops.

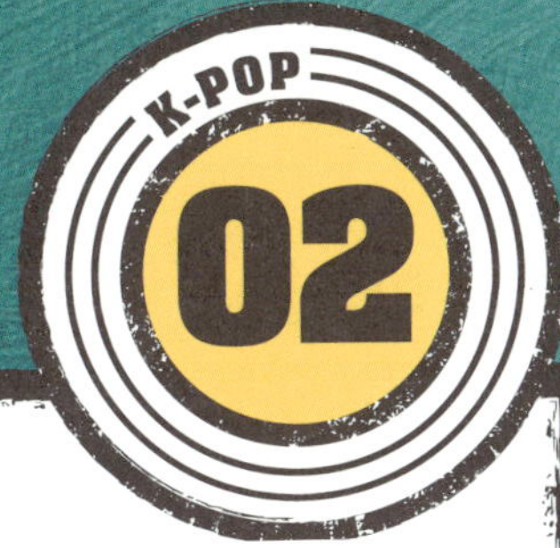


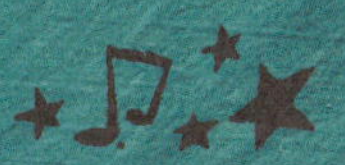


# Honey

나만의 허니 허니 허니

돌아서야 하니 하니 하니

언제나 난 너 하나만을 원하고 있는데

oh baby 허니 허니 허니

나의 맘의 허니 허니 허니

간절하게 너 하나만을 바라고 있잖아.

### About the singer and the song

KARA is one of Korea's top girl groups, but they were not in the spotlight in the first couple of years after their debut. Their song <Honey> is about a girl's shy love and was their first song to rank number one on a music show. You can check out KARA's early days in the <Honey> music video.

# 돌아서야 하니?

Are you turning back from me?

## 뭐 하니?

What are you doing?

## 언제 오니?

When are you coming?

## 잘 잤니?

Did you sleep well?

## 밥 먹었니?

Did you eat something?

## 다 했니?

Did you finish it?

## 재미있니?

Is it fun?

## 괜찮니?

Are you all right?

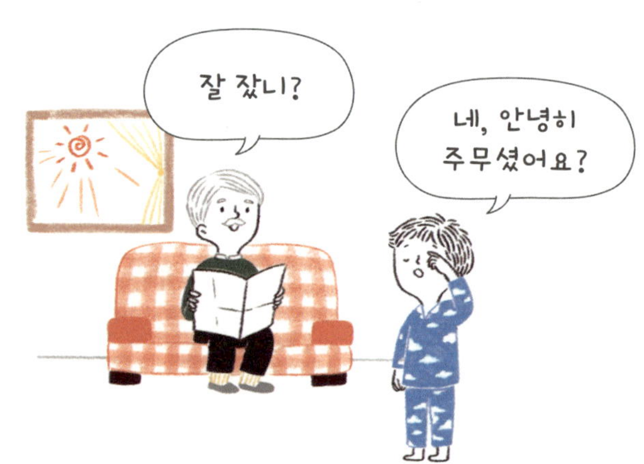

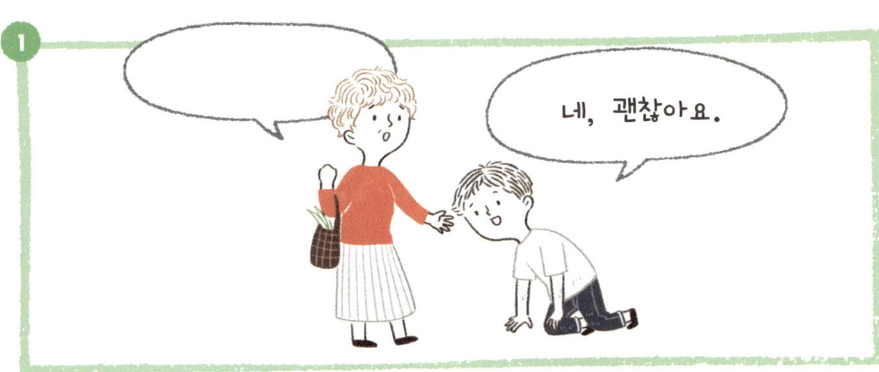
네, 괜찮아요.

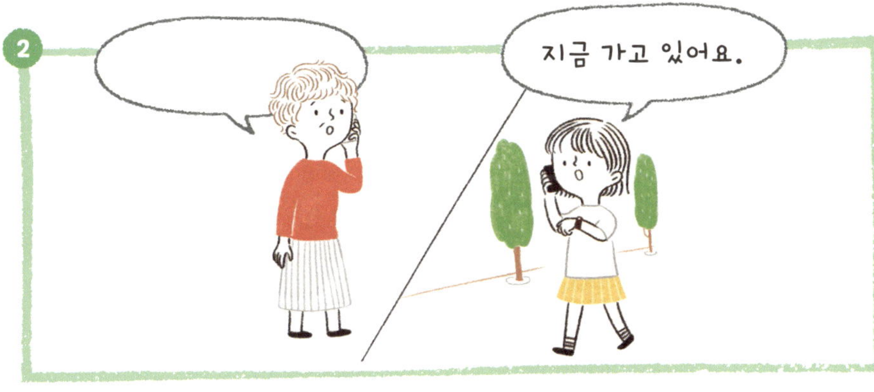
지금 가고 있어요.

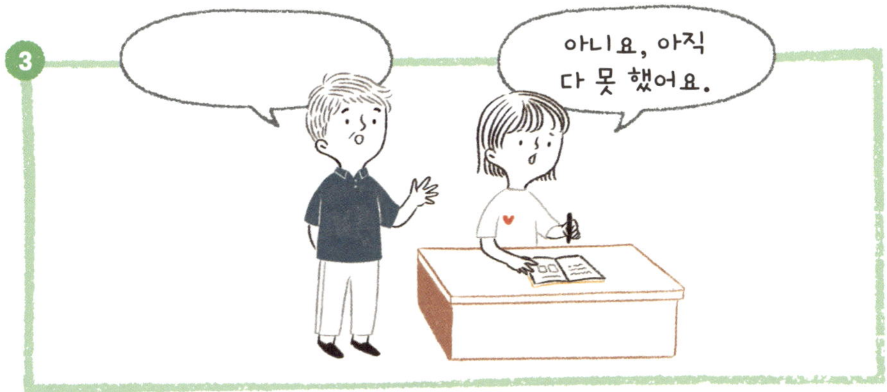
아니요, 아직
다 못 했어요.

# 난 너 하나만을 원하고 있는데

You are the only one I want

더 많은 것을 원해.
I want more.

네가 행복하기를 원해.
I want you to be happy.

건강하기를 원해.
I want you to be healthy.

뭘 더 원해?
What more do you want?

가벼운 노트북을 원해요.
I want a light laptop computer.

빠른 답변 원해요.
I want an answer soon.

가격이 저렴한 것을 원해요.
I want something cheaper.

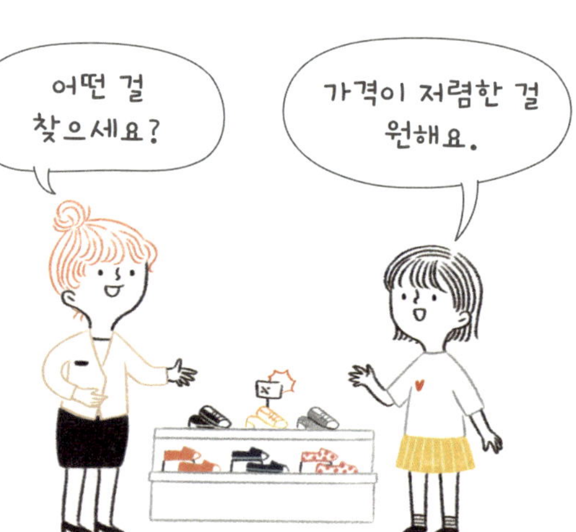

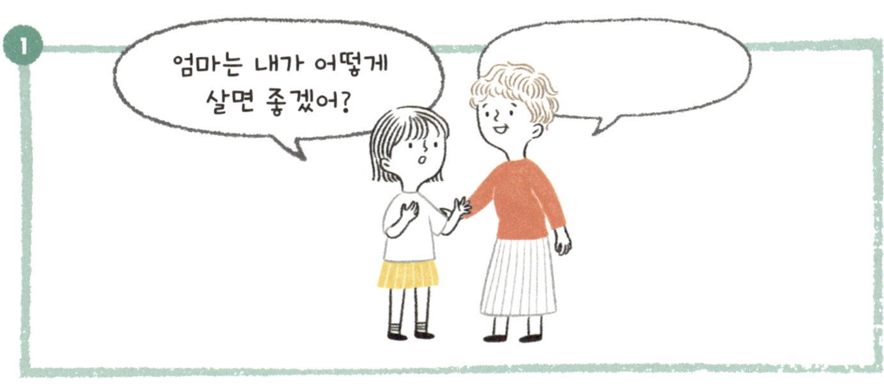


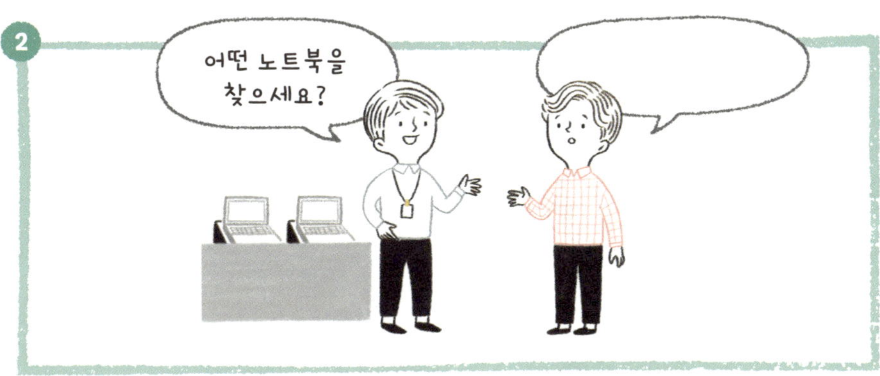


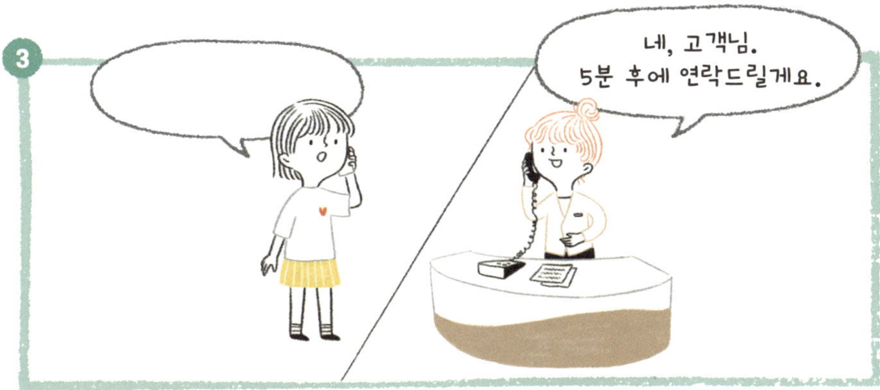


고객님 sir, ma'am, customer | 연락드리다 to get back to

## ⭐ A/V-니?

**밥 먹었니?**
Did you eat something?

**언제 일이 끝나니?**
How long will it take?

**교실이 춥지 않니?**
Isn't it cold in the classroom?

### A/V-냐?
**Ex** 밥 먹었냐? / 교실이 춥지 않냐?

**A/V-니?** is used when you ask another person a question. You use this expression to somebody close to you and a similar age or younger. **A/V-냐?** is a close expression to **A/V-니?**, but it has a stronger tone while **A/V-니?** has a softer tone.

## ⭐ N-을/를 원하다, A/V-기를 원하다

**저는 행복한 삶을 원해요.**
I want a happy life.

**나는 당신과 결혼하기를 원해요.**
I want to marry you.

**저는 동생이 빨리 집에 돌아오기를 원해요.**
I wish my younger sister/brother would come home soon.

**N을/를 원하다** means you want to possess something, and we literally translate this expression into "want." On the other hand, **A/V-기를 원하다** means that you "want" or "wish" that something would happen or that someone would do something that you want.

나만의 허니 허니 허니 돌아서야 하니 하니 하니
[나마네]❶

언제나 난 너 하나만을 원하고 있는데
[워나고]❷  [인는데]

oh baby 허니 허니 허니 나의 맘의 허니 허니 허니
[나에]❶  [마메]❶

간절하게 너 하나만을 바라고 있잖아
[간저라게]❷  [이짜나]

❶ 의 is a postposition, and it means "of." You generally read it like [에].

❷ When ㅎ comes after the final consonant [ㄴ] or [ㄹ] in the same word, the sound-linking between the final consonants and ㅎ occurs when you read it without a pause.

**Ex** 원하고 [워나고], 간절하게 [간저라게]

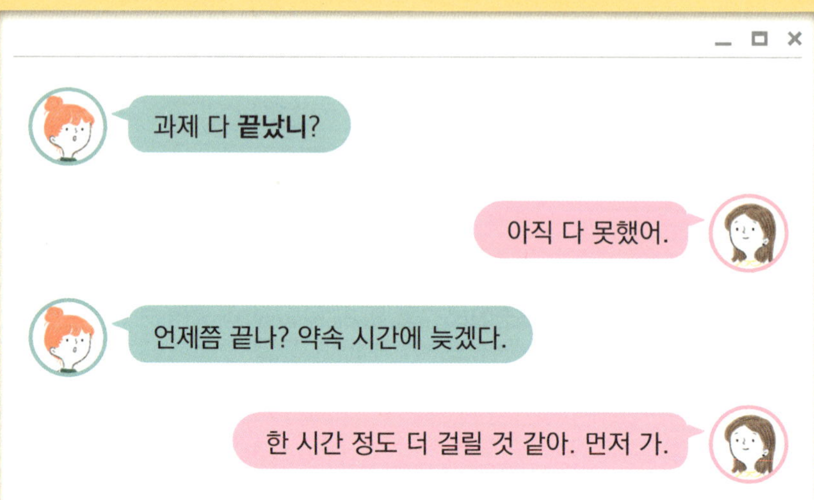


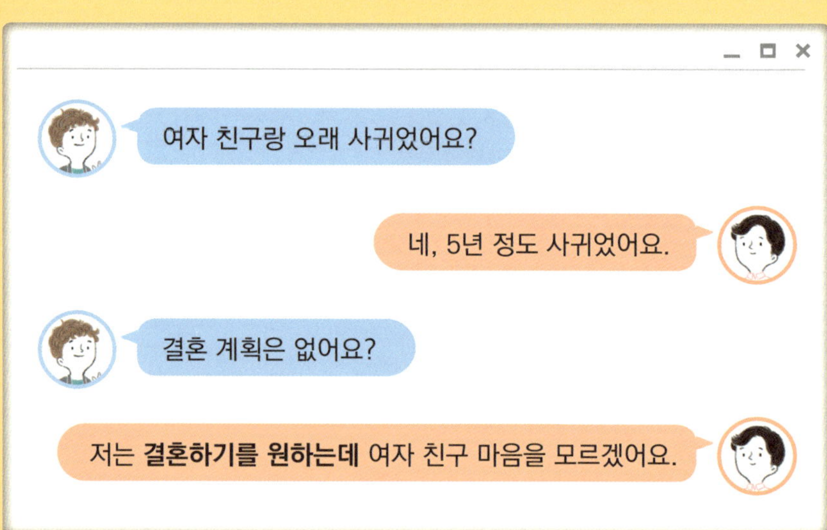


**과제** assignment | **끝나다** to finish | **약속 시간** appointed time | **정도** around | **걸리다** to take | **먼저** first
**사귀다** to go out | **마음** feel, heart

# Honey

카라

난난난 너 없으면 난난난 너 아니면
난난난 살 수 없잖아.

아직도 설레여 너만 보면은 떨려.
모른 척하고 난 싶어도 눈에 보이는 간절함
숨이 벅차서 슬퍼 와 병이 깊어져 아파 와.
너무 좋아서 그래 내 맘이 꼭 널 원해.

★ 나만의 허니 허니 허니 돌아서야 하니 하니 하니
언제나 난 너 하나만을 원하고 있는데
oh baby 허니 허니 허니 나의 맘의 허니 허니 허니
간절하게 너 하나만을 바라고 있잖아.

Hey, boy, my little honey
came from heaven right here to save me.
One touch, that's all it takes.
Complete with you no regrets.
I need you by my side.
I'll love you long through day andnight.
Deep inside I know you're mine.
No more words kiss me good night.

너무 좋아서 그랬어 바보 같이 나 변했어.
너만 바라봐 그래 내 맘이 꼭 널 원해.

★ 반복

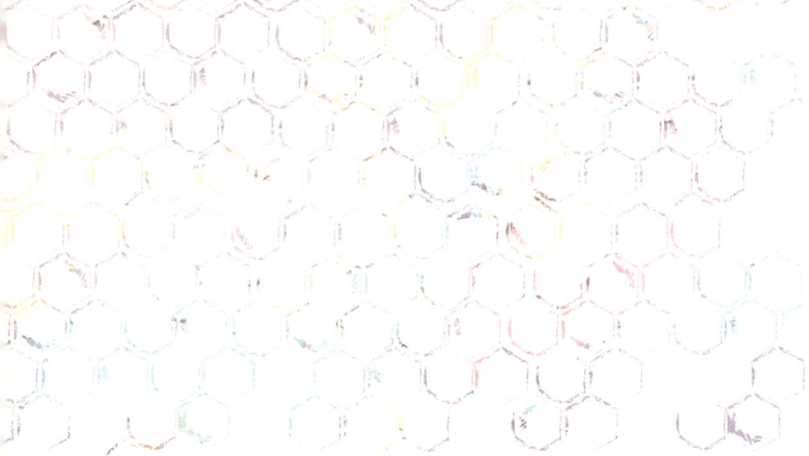

# Honey

KARA

I, I, I, without you I, I, I, if it's not you
I, I, I, cannot live.

My heart still flutters whenever I see you.
I want to deny but cannot hide it.
It's hard to breathe, and it saddens me. My heart is aching even more.
I long for you so much. My heart wants you so much.

★ My only honey, honey, honey. Are you turning back from me?
You are the only one I ever want.
oh baby, honey, honey, honey. My sweetheart honey, honey, honey.
Look how much I desire you.

Hey, boy, my little honey
Came from heaven right here to save me.
One touch that's all it takes.
Complete with you no regrets.
I need you by my side.
I'll love you long through day and night.
Deep inside I know you're mine.
No more words kiss me good night.

I just like you so much. Love made me a fool.
I only see you. My heart wants you so much.

★ Repeat

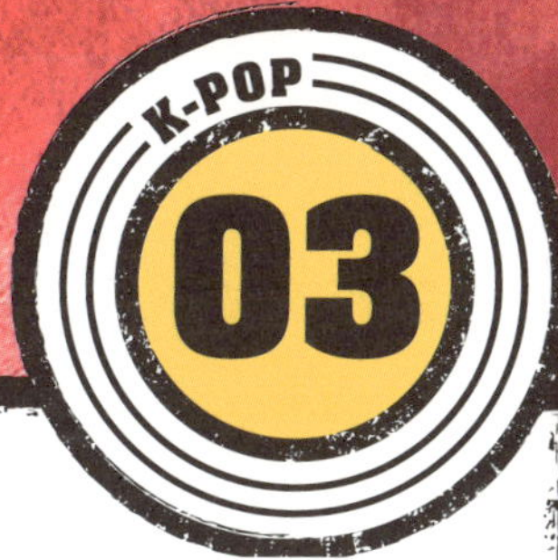


버스커 버스커(Busker Busker)

# 벚꽃 엔딩

오늘은 우리 같이 걸어요, 이 거리를

밤에 들려오는 자장노래 어떤가요?

몰랐던 그대와 단둘이 손잡고

알 수 없는 이 떨림과 둘이 걸어요.

**About the singer and the song**

Busker Busker is the runner-up of Korea's most popular reality TV audition *Super Star K* season 3. The group consists of three members and is well known for songs with cheerful melodies and lovely lyrics. Their song <벚꽃 엔딩 (Cherry Blossom Ending)> was on their first album, which was released in 2011. It is considered Korea's spring carol song since you can hear the song played on every street corner in March and April when the cherry blossoms are blooming.

# 우리 같이 걸어요.

Let's walk together.

## 우리 같이 놀아요.
Let's hang out together.

## 우리 같이 한국어 공부해요.
Let's study Korean together.

## 우리 같이 커피 마셔요.
Let's have coffee together.

## 우리 같이 사진 찍어요.
Let's take a photo together.

## 우리 같이 영화 봐요.
Let's watch a movie together.

## 우리 같이 점심 먹어요.
Let's have lunch together.

## 우리 같이 벚꽃놀이* 가요.
Let's go to the Cherry Blossom Picnic together.

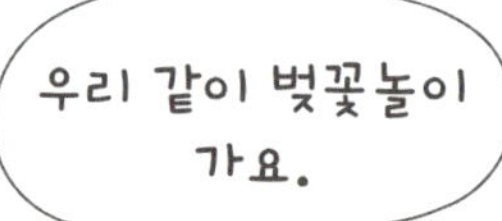


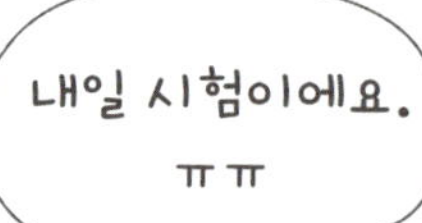


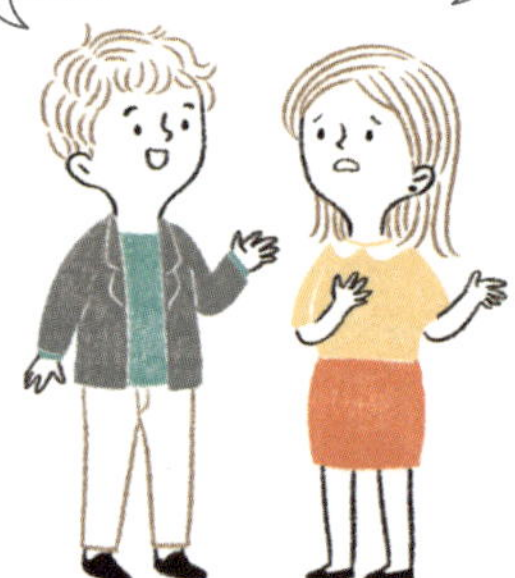

* Koreans go to see the cherry blossoms with their family members, friends, or dates in April. It's a nationwide activity during this time of the year. We call this activity '벚꽃놀이(Cherry Blossom Picnic)' in Korea.

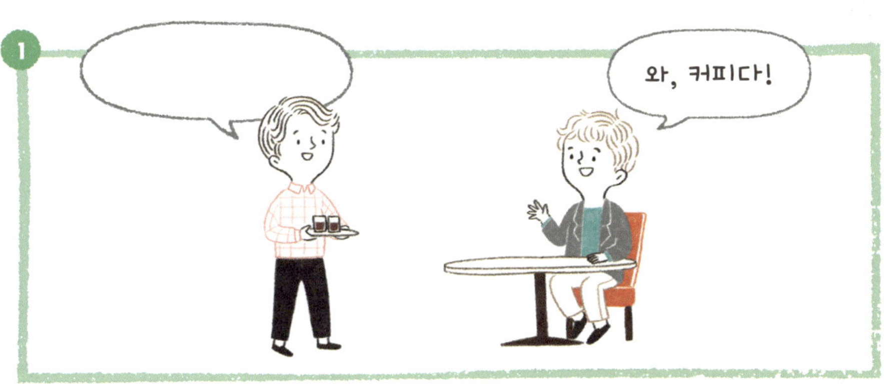


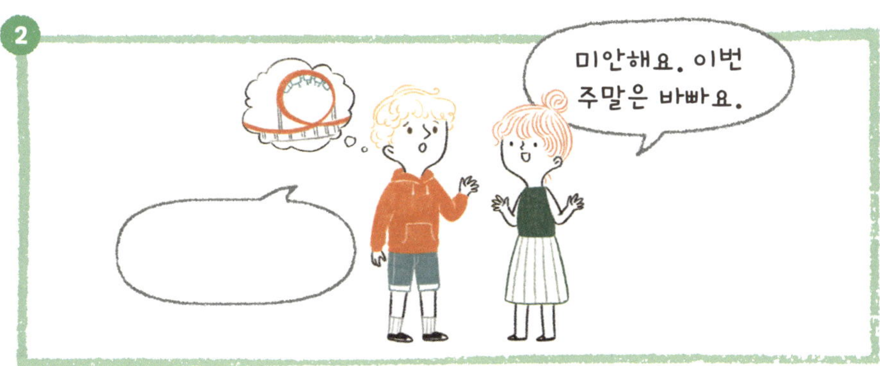


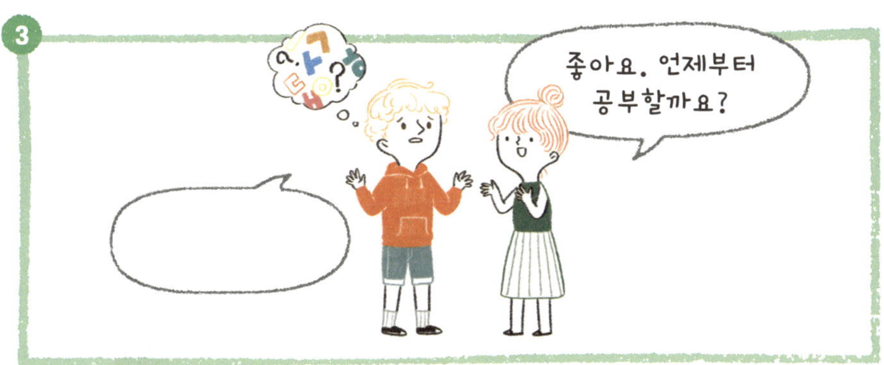


주말 weekend

# 밤에 들려오는 자장노래 어떤가요?

How do you like the lullaby at night?

## 이 식당 어떤가요?
What about this restaurant?

## 거기 날씨 어떤가요?
How's the weather there?

## 오늘 기분 어떤가요?
How do you feel today?

## 이 옷 어떤가요?
How do you like this clothing?

## 이 노래 어떤가요?
How do you like this song?

## 제 헤어스타일 어떤가요?
How do you like my hairstyle?

## 한국 음식 어떤가요?
How do you like Korean food?

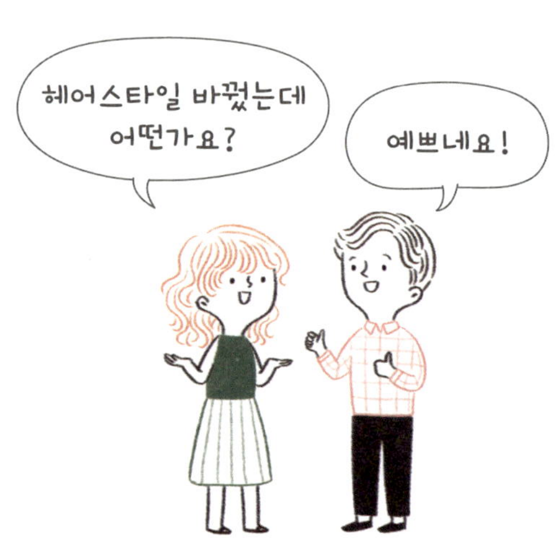

**1**

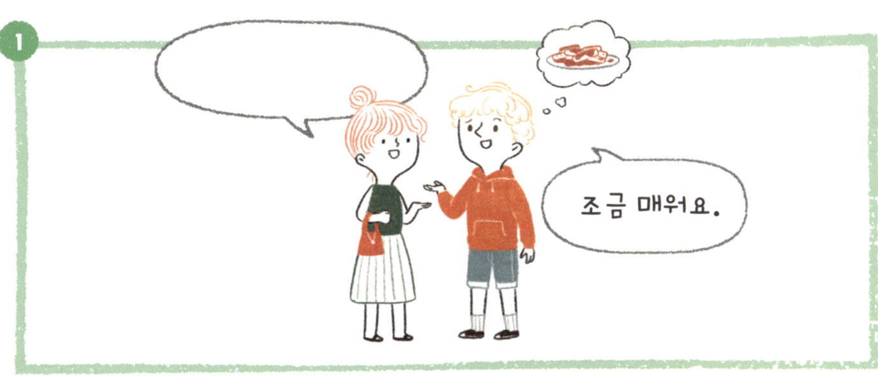


**2**

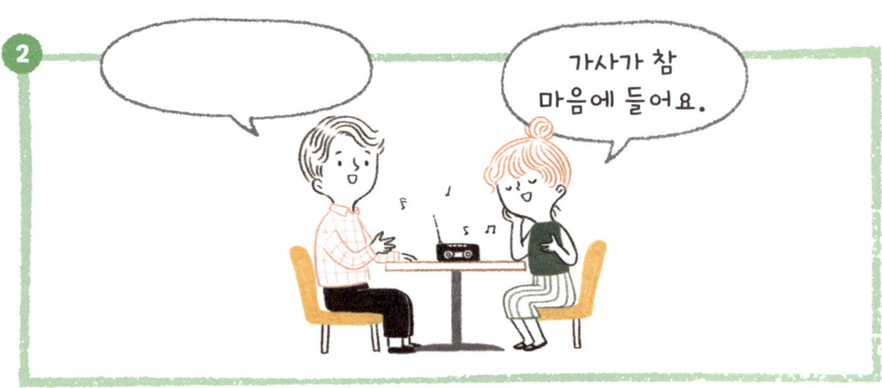


**3**

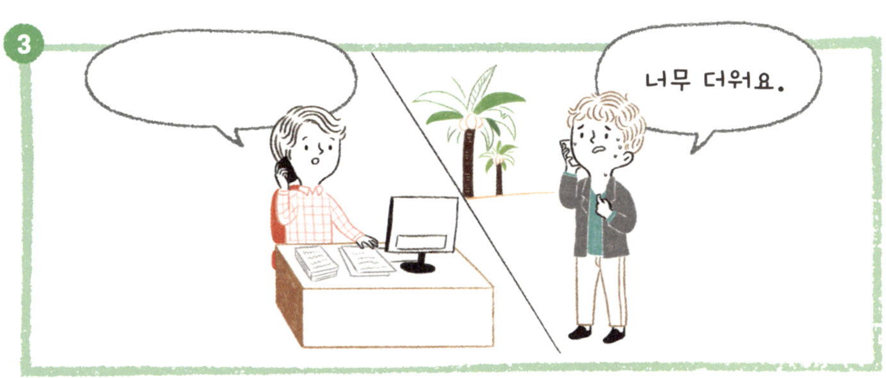


맵다 to be spicy | 가사 lyric | 참 very | 마음에 들다 to like something | 덥다 to be hot

 ## (같이) V-아요/어요

**주말에 만나요.**
Let's meet up on the weekend.

**같이 점심 먹어요.**
Let's have lunch together.

**같이 공부해요.**
Let's study together.

**주말에 만나요. / 주말에 만납시다. / 주말에 만나자.**

**V-아요/어요** is similar to "let's ~." It is used when you make a suggestion to another person. **V-아요/어요** is used between people who are still close but need to be courteous to each other. **-(으)ㅂ시다** is an even politer and more formal expression. On the other hand, **-자** is used between very close people or for those who are younger than you.

 ## N이/가 어떤가요?

**날씨가 어떤가요?**
How's the weather?

**이 옷이 어떤가요?**
How do you like this clothing?

**한국 음식이 어떤가요?**
How do you like Korean food?

**이 옷이 어떤가요? = 이 옷이 어때요?**

**N이/가 어떤가요?** is an expression used to ask a person's opinion/thoughts about something. It is also used to ask the situation of the subject in the sentence. **N이/가 어때요?** is a similar expression, but **N이/가 어떤가요?** has a softer tone.

오늘은 우리 같이 걸어요, 이 거리를
[가치]❶

밤에 들려오는 자장노래 어떤가요?
[바메]

몰랐던 그대와 단둘이 손잡고
[몰라떤]   [단두리] [손잡꼬]

알 수 없는 이 떨림과 둘이 걸어요.
[알 쑤][엄는]❷

❶ The final consonant ㅌ sounds like [ㅊ] when it comes in front of the vowel I.

**Ex** 같이 [가치]

❷ The final consonant ㅂ sounds like [ㅁ] when it comes in front of the consonant ㄴ.

**Ex** 없는 [엄는], 잡는 [잠는]

어순 **ORDER OF WORDS**

오늘은 우리 같이 걸어요, 이 거리를.
[verb]   [object]

⇒ 오늘은 우리 이 거리를 같이 걸어요.
[object]   [verb]

Generally Korean sentences have the order of subject-object-predicate.

However, this word order is often changed in song lyrics.

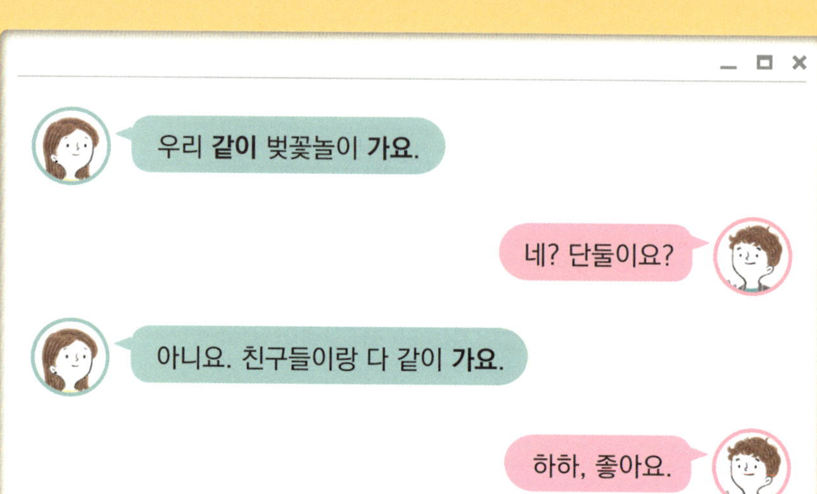


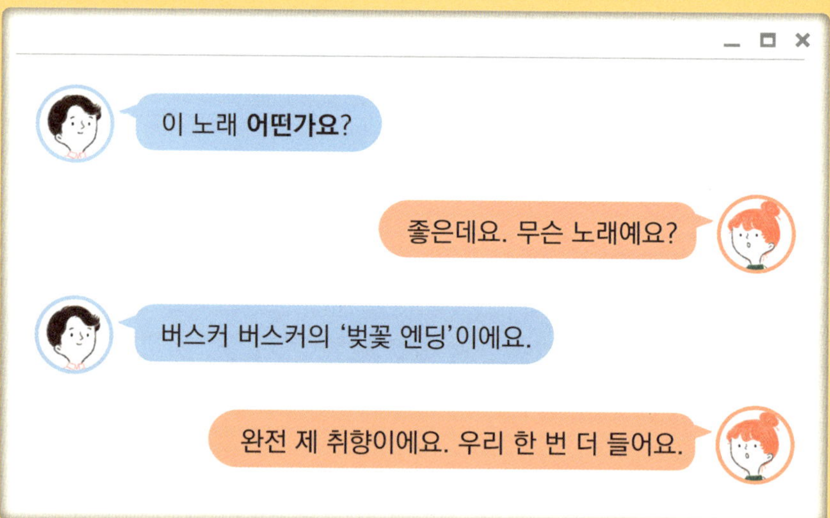


**단둘이** just the two of us | **친구** friend | **노래** song | **완전** absolutely | **취향** type, taste

# 벚꽃 엔딩

버스커 버스커

그대여 그대여 그대여 그대여 그대여[1]

오늘은 우리 같이 걸어요, 이 거리를
밤에 들려오는 자장노래 어떤가요? (oh, yeah)
몰랐던 그대와 단 둘이 손잡고
알 수 없는 이 떨림과 둘이 걸어요.

★ 봄바람 휘날리며 흩날리는 벚꽃 잎이
울려 퍼질 이 거리를 (uh, uh) 둘이 걸어요. x2

그대여 우리 이제 손 잡아요, 이 거리에
마침 들려오는 사랑 노래 어떤가요? (oh, yeah)
사랑하는 그대와 단둘이 손잡고
알 수 없는 이 거리를 둘이 걸어요.

★ 반복

바람 불면 울렁이는 기분 탓에 나도 모르게
바람 불면 저편에서 그대여 네 모습이 자꾸 겹쳐.
오 또 울렁이는 기분 탓에 나도 모르게
바람 불면 저편에서 그대여 네 모습이 자꾸 겹쳐.

사랑하는 연인들이 많군요. 알 수 없는 친구들이 많아요.
흩날리는 벚꽃 잎이 많군요. 좋아요.

★ 반복

그대여 그대여 그대여 그대여 그대여

1) The word '그대' which means 'you,' is not used in conversations while it is frequently used in the song lyrics.

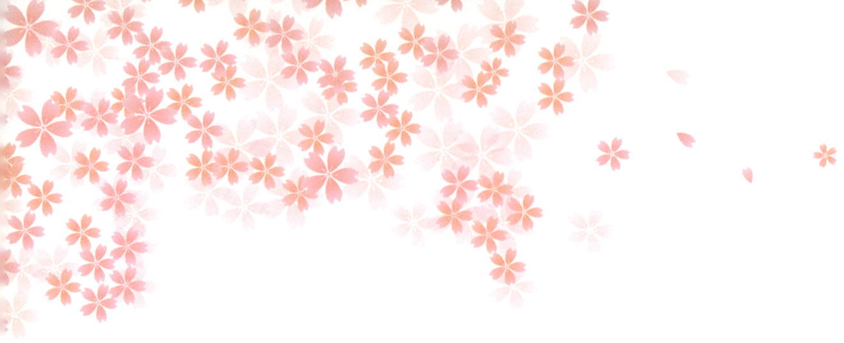

# Cherry Blossom Ending

Busker Busker

Honey, honey, honey, honey, honey

Let's walk on this street together today.
How do you like the lullaby at night? (oh, yeah)
We are just getting to know each other and holding hands together.
We are walking together nervously.

The spring breeze is full in the air.
Cherry blossom leaves are running around
In this street. (uh, uh) Let's walk together.  x2

Honey, let's hold hands together on this street;
How do you like the love song you are hearing? (oh, yeah)
Holding hands with my beloved
We are walking on this street I have never been.

★ Repeat

When the wind blows, because of my throbbing heart, I unconsciously
When the wind blows, honey, I see you here and there.
Oh, because of my throbbing heart again, I unconsciously
When the wind blows, honey, I see you here and there.

There are lots of people in love, lots of those who are hard to guess.
There are lots of cherry blossom leaves running around. Good.

★ Repeat

Honey, honey, honey, honey, honey

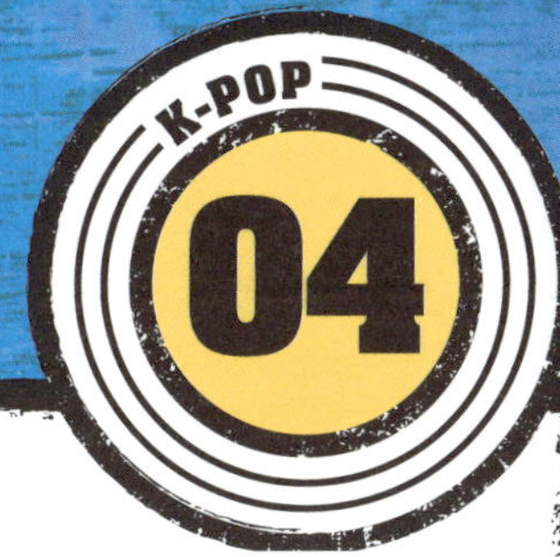


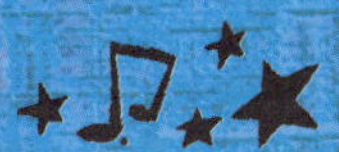


# 남자 없이 잘 살아

나는 남자 없이 잘 살아.

그러니 자신이 없으면 내 곁에 오지를 마.

나는 함부로 날 안 팔아. 왜냐면 난

I don't need a man. I don't need a man. (What?)

I don't need a man. I don't need a man. (진짜)

I don't need a man. I don't need a man. (정말)

I don't need a man. I don't need a man.

나는 남자 없이 잘 잘 살아.

## About the singer and the song

miss A is JYP's multinational girl group. It consists of the Chinese members Fei and Jia and the Korean members Min and Suzy. Their debut song <Bad Girl Good Girl> was sensational and ranked number one on several music shows. miss A established their image of being independent women through their songs. Their song < 남자 없이 잘 살아 (I'm Don't need a Man)> is about strong and independent women who are happy to live on their own.

# 나는 남자 없이 잘 살아.

I don't need a man.

## 스마트폰 없이 못 살아.
I cannot live without a smartphone.

## 너 없이 못 살아.
I cannot live without you.

## 커피 없이 일을 못해.
I cannot work without a cup of coffee.

## 베개 없이 못 자.
I cannot sleep without a pillow.

## 신분증 없이 못 들어가.
You cannot enter without your ID.

## 그 식당은 예약 없이 못 가.
You can't get a table at that restaurant without a reservation.

## 눈물 없이 못 보겠어.
I can't watch it without sobbing.

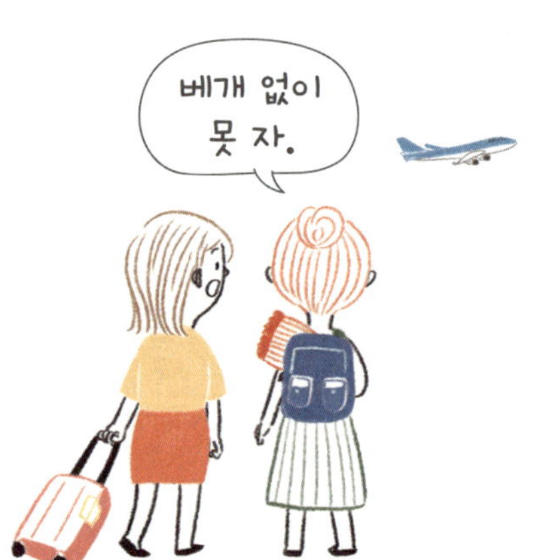

**1**

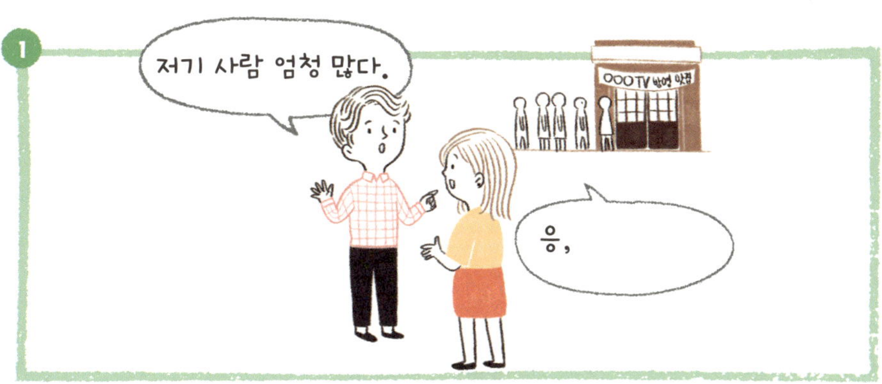


**2**

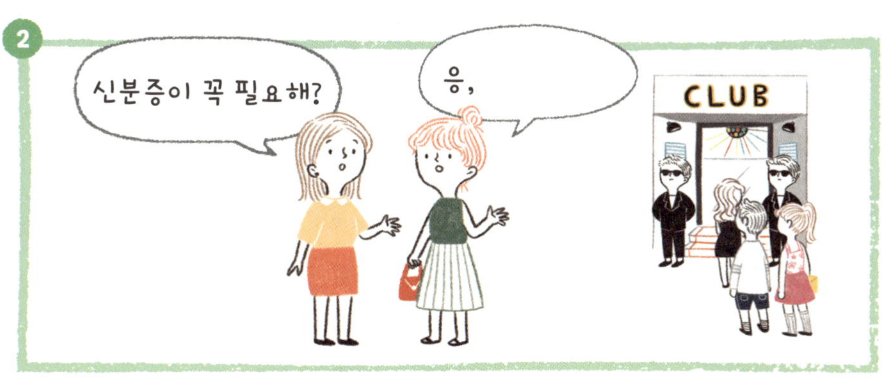


**3**

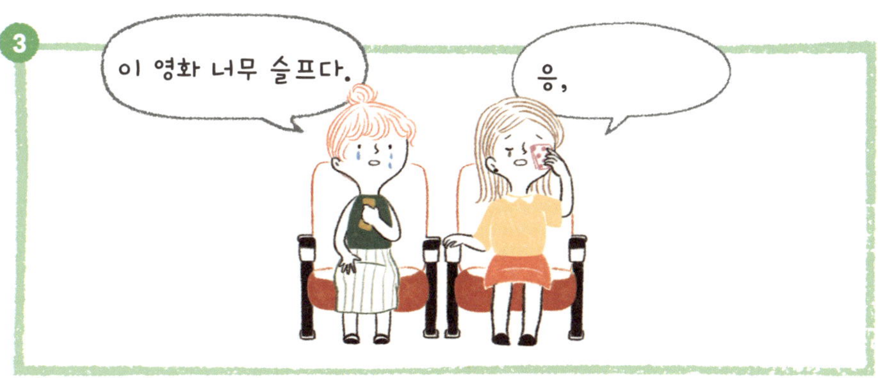


**엄청** very, lots of | **꼭** must, definitely | **필요하다** to need

# 자신이 없으면 내 곁에 오지 마.

If you do not have confidence, do not come to me.

가지 마.
Don't go.

울지 마.
Don't cry.

연락하지 마.
Don't call me.

걱정하지 마.
Don't worry.

거짓말하지 마.
Don't lie.

약속 시간에 늦지 마.
Don't be late for your appointment.

아무한테도 말하지 마.
Don't tell anyone.

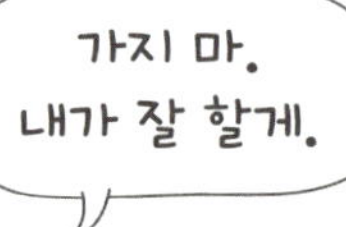

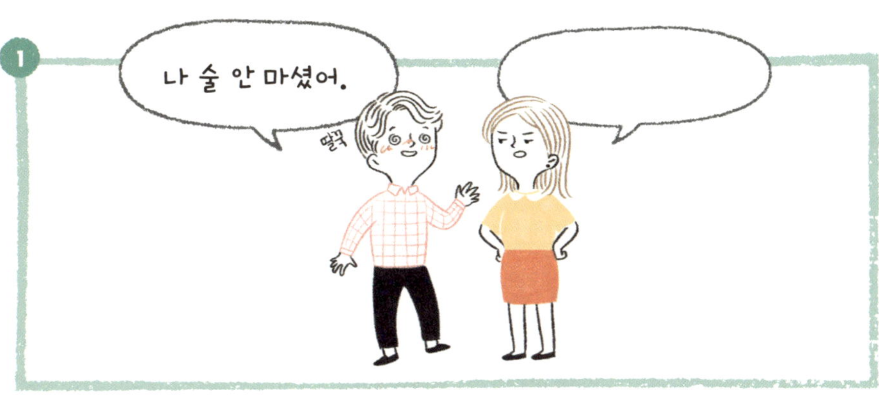


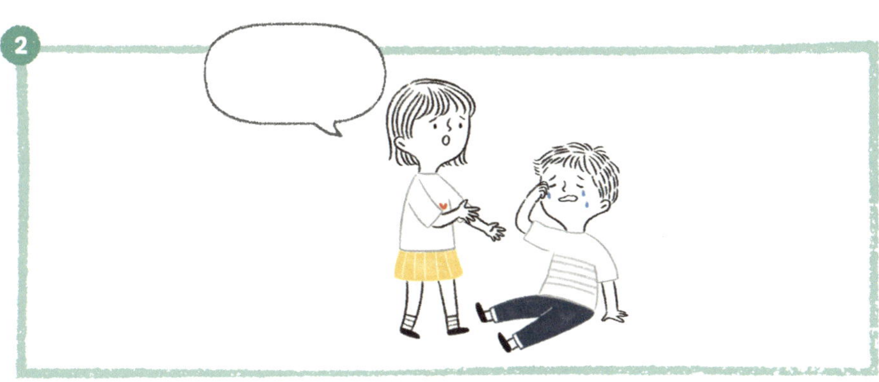

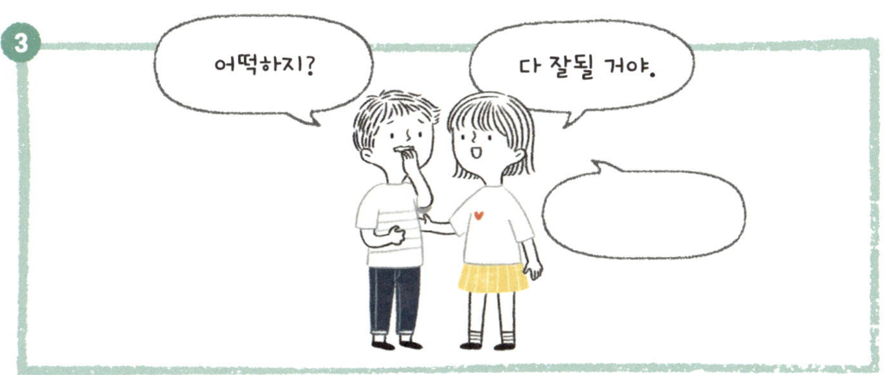


술 alcohol, liquor | 잘되다 be going to be all right

# 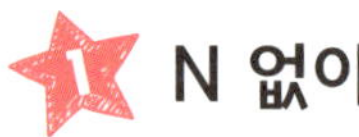 N 없이

**거기는 차 없이 못 가요.**
You can't go there without a car.

**너 없이 아무것도 할 수 없어.**
I can't do anything without you.

**한국 사람은 김치 없이는 밥을 못 먹어요.**
Koreans can't eat a meal without kimchi.

**N 없이** means that N is missing. It literally means "without." The expression is often used in the phrase **N 없이 못 V**. It means "cannot do something without somebody/something." **못 V** can also be replaced with **V–(으)ㄹ 수 없다**. We may add **는** next to **N 없이** to emphasize the phrase.

# 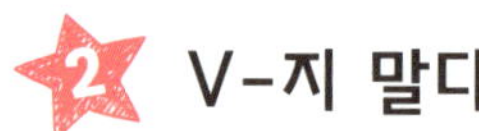 V–지 말다

**자꾸 장난치지 마.**
Stop playing around.

**그렇게 화내지 마.**
Don't be so angry.

**저한테 거짓말하지 마세요.**
Don't lie to me.

**V–지 말다** means "do not." It is used to ban certain actions. **V–지 마** is the same as **V–지 말다**, but it is used between people close to you in age or younger. **V–지 마세요** means the same thing, but it is more formal and shows respect to the other person.

나는 남자 없이 잘 살아.
[업씨] ★

그러니 자신이 없으면 내 곁에 오지를 마.
[업쓰면] ★

나는 함부로 날 안 팔아.

왜냐면 난 I don't need a man

나는 남자 없이 잘 잘 살아.
[업씨] ★

★ 없 is pronounced like [업] when you read the syllable itself. However, when a vowel comes right after 없, the vowel is affected by both the final consonants [ㅂ] and [ㅅ]. In this case, [ㅅ] sounds like [ㅆ] since it is affected by the [ㅂ] sound.

**Ex** 없으면 [업쓰면]

There is one exception: 없이 sounds like [업시] or [업씨].

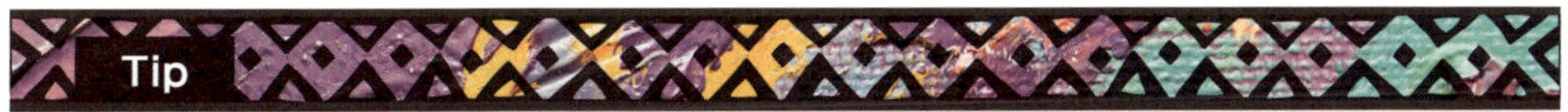

**Tip**

I don't need a man.

나는 남자가 필요 없어.

"need" means 필요하다 in Korean. We say, 필요 없다 to mean "do not need" in Korean.

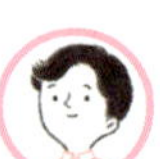


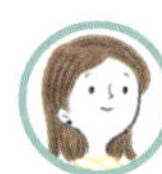


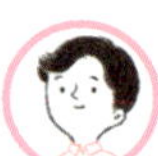


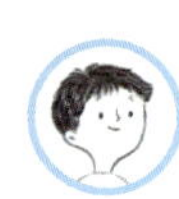


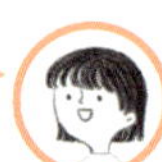


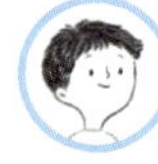


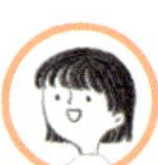


**시내** downtown | **태국** Thailand | **이따가** later | **발표** presentation | **준비** preparation
**걱정되다/걱정하다** to be worried/to worry

# 남자 없이 잘 살아

미쓰에이

This is for all the independent ladies.
Let's go.

★ 나는 남자 없이 잘 살아.
그러니 자신이 없으면 내 곁에 오지를 마.
나는 함부로 날 안 팔아.
왜냐면 난
I don't need a man. I don't need a man. (What?)
I don't need a man. I don't need a man. (진짜)
I don't need a man. I don't need a man. (정말)
I don't need a man. I don't need a man.
나는 남자 없이 잘 잘 살아.

내 돈으로 방세 다 내.
먹고 싶은 거 사 먹고 옷도 사 입고
충분하진 않지만 만족할 줄 알아.
그래서 난 나를 사랑해. (hey)

부모님의 용돈 내 돈처럼
쓰고 싶지 않아. 나이가 많아
손 벌리지 않는 게 당연한 거 아냐.
그래서 난 내가 떳떳해. (hey)

Boy don't say 내가 챙겨 줄게. 내가 아껴 줄게. No, no
Boy don't play 진지하게 올 게 아니면

★ 반복

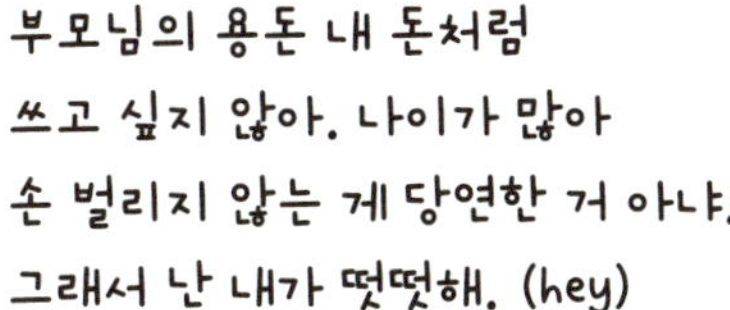

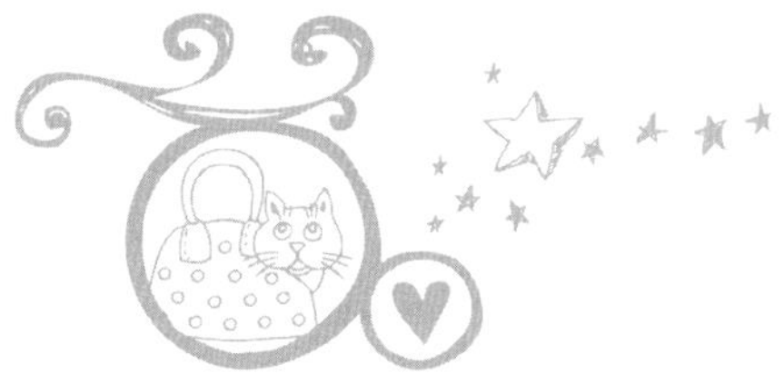

# I Don't need a Man

miss A

This is for all the independent ladies.
Let's go.

★ I don't need a man.
Don't even try if you are not sure.
I don't sell myself to anyone.
Because I,
I don't need a man. I don't need a man. (What?)
I don't need a man. I don't need a man. (Really?)
I don't need a man. I don't need a man. (Truly?)
I don't need a man. I don't need a man.

I don't need a man.
I pay the rent on my own.
I pay for what I eat and wear.
It's not enough, but I'm happy.
That's why I love myself. (hey)

I don't rely on my parents for money.
I'm a grownup.
Isn't it right not to ask for money?
That's why I am fair and square. (hey)

Boy, don't say I'll take care of you. I'm gonna take
care of you. No, no.
Boy, don't play unless you are serious.

★ Repeat

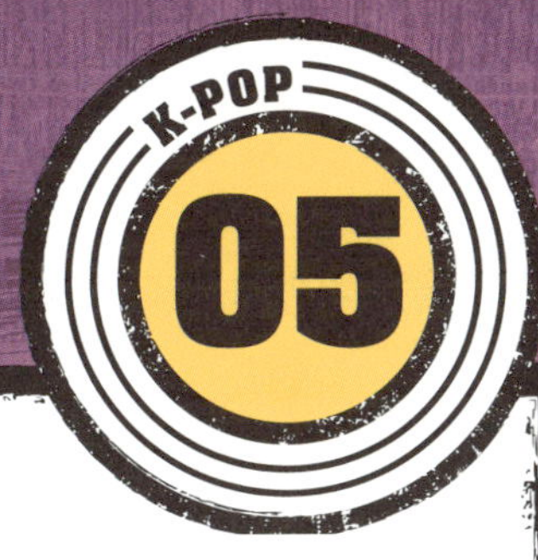




# 결혼해 줄래

내가 더 사랑할게. 내가 더 아껴 줄게.

눈물이 나고 힘이 들 때면

아플 때면 함께 아파할게.

평생을 사랑할게 평생을 지켜 줄게.

너만큼 좋은 사람 만난 걸 감사해.

매일 너만 사랑하고 싶어.

## About the singer and the song

In Korea, when a man is outstanding in every aspect of his life, we call him 엄마 친구 아들 (my mom's friend's son) or 엄친아 (umchin-ah), which is the contraction of the Korean expression. Lee Seung Gi is Korea's number one *umchin-ah*. He is a successful singer and actor and has hosted several TV shows. The song <결혼해 줄래 (Will You Marry Me?)> was released in 2009 and is loved by Koreans of all ages. You can guess by the title that it is one of the most popular wedding songs.

# 내가 더 사랑할게.

I will love you more.

나 먼저 먹을게.
I will eat first.

여기서 기다릴게.
I will wait here.

이따가 전화할게.
I will call you later.

앞으로 안 할게.
I will not do it again.

화장실 좀 갔다 올게.
I will go to the restroom and come back.

이걸로 할게요.
I will get this one.

좀 더 보고 올게요.
I will look around and come back.

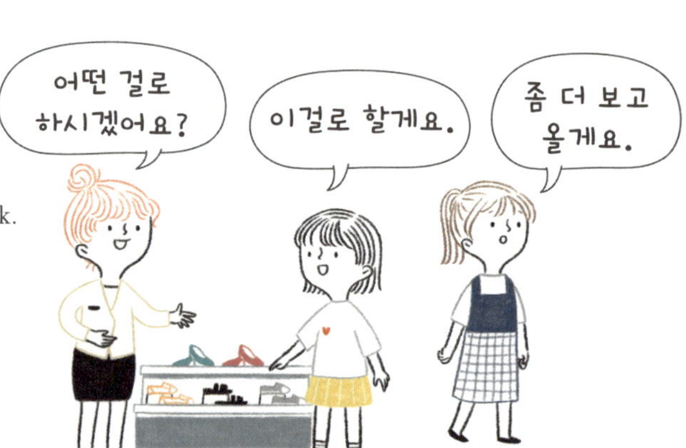

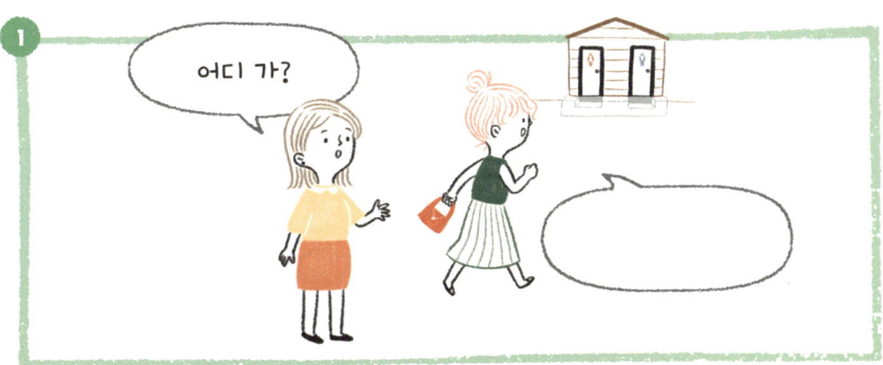


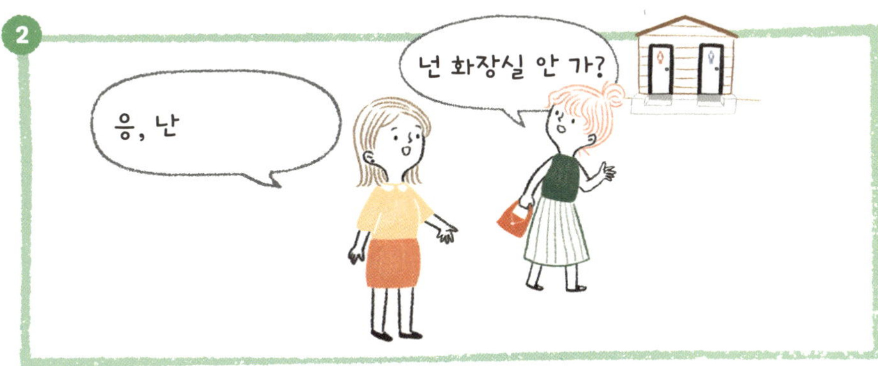


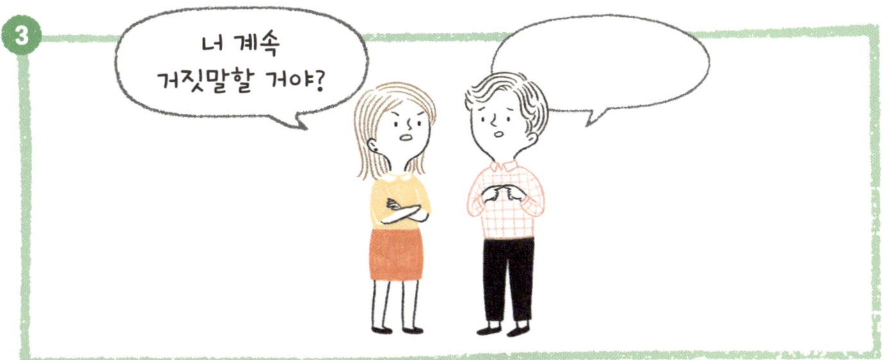


거짓말 lie

# 눈물이 나고 힘이 들 때면

When life is hard and you burst into tears

화가 나.
I'm getting upset.

짜증이 나.
I'm getting annoyed.

겁이 나.
I'm getting scared.

피가 나.
I'm bleeding.

땀이 나.
I'm sweating.

눈물이 나.
I'm bursting into tears.

열이 나.
I'm running a fever.

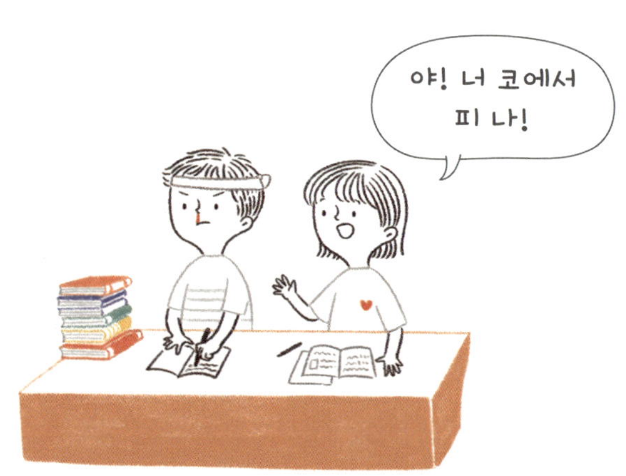

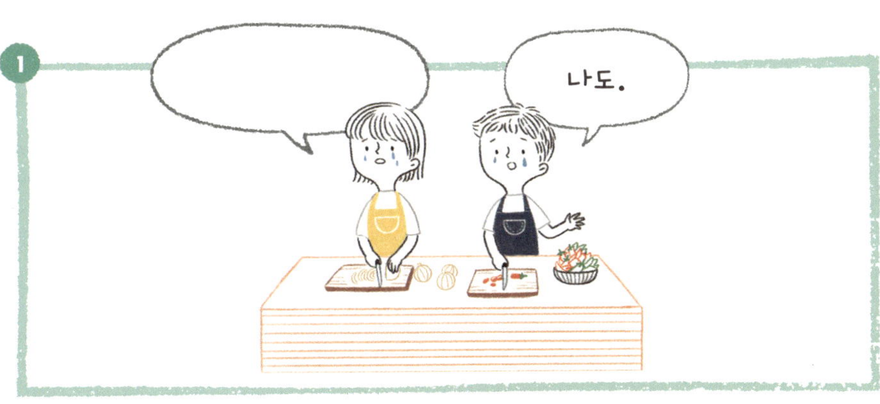


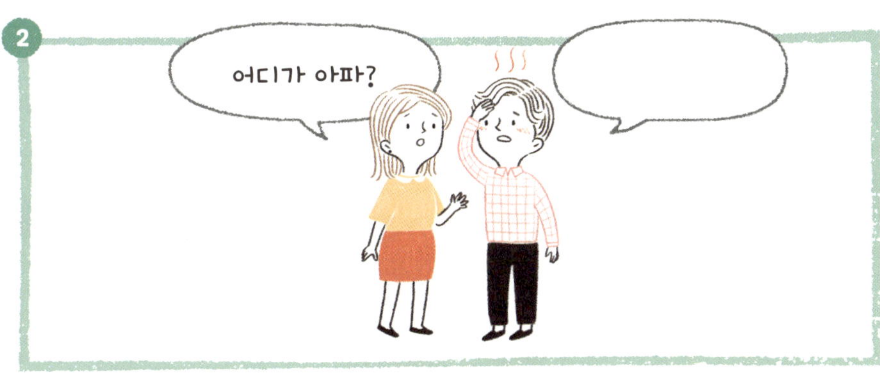


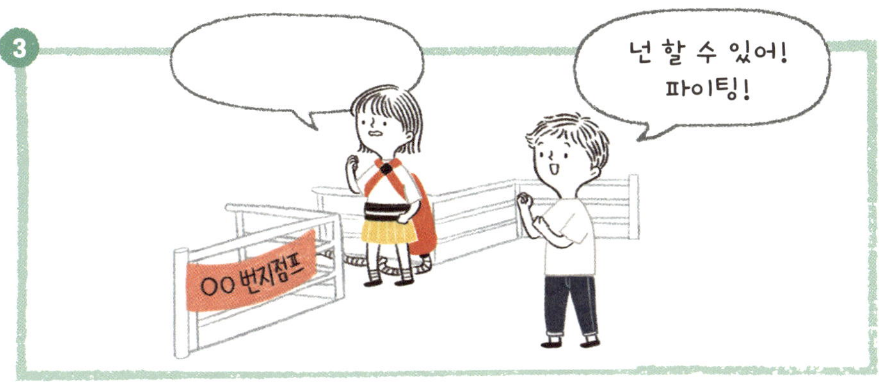


**번지점프** bungee jumping | **파이팅** Go for it!

## V-(으)ㄹ게요

**집에 가면 전화할게.**
I will call you when I get home.

**엄마, 친구 만나고 올게.**
Mom, I will go and meet a friend.

**제가 한국어 공부를 도와줄게요.**
I will help you study Korean.

**V-(으)ㄹ게요** is used to show the will of the person who is speaking. It is similar to "will" and is often used when you make a promise to someone or ask for approval.

## N이/가 나다

**자꾸 기침이 나.**
I keep coughing

**얼굴에 여드름이 났어.**
I have pimples on my face.

**이 노래는 이제 싫증이 났어.**
I am tired of this song.

**N이/가 나다** means that something which did not exist in the past has occurred. It is often used when you describe something that recently occurred to your body or emotions. In spoken Korean, you often say **N 나다** without the postposition **이/가**.

내가 더 사랑할게 내가 더 아껴 줄게
[사랑할께]❶  [줄께]❶

눈물이 나고 힘이 들 때면
[눈무리]❷

아플 때면 함께 아파할게
[아파할께]❶

평생을 사랑할게 평생을 지켜 줄게
[사랑할께]❶  [줄께]❶

너만큼 좋은 사람 만난 걸 감사해
[조은]❸

매일 너만 사랑하고 싶어

❶ When ㄱ comes right after a word that ends with the consonant ㄹ, such as –(으)ㄹ we pronounce ㄱ like [ㄲ].
**Ex** 할게 [할께], 할 거야 [할 꺼야]

❷ 눈물이 is pronounced [눈무리] just like it is spelled. Be careful not to mispronounce it by saying [눙무리].

❸ When a vowel comes right after the final consonant ㅎ it becomes a silent ㅎ.
**Ex** 좋아요 [조아요], 넣어요 [너어요], 낳은 [나은]

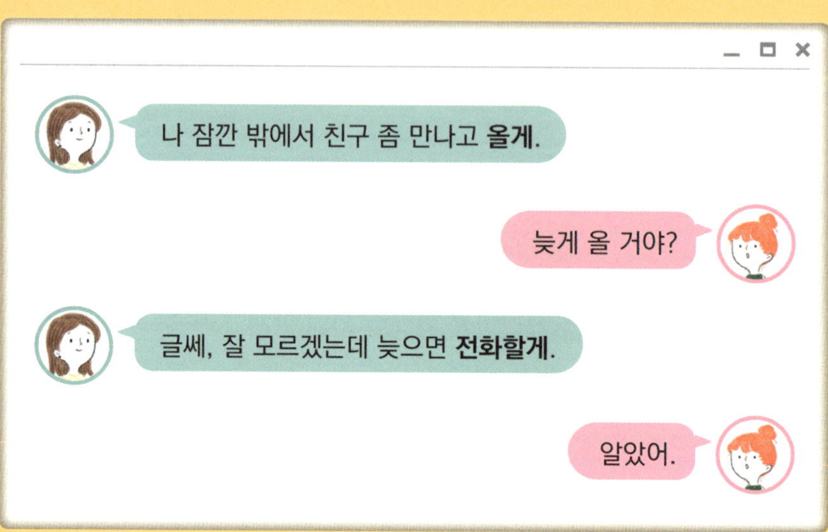


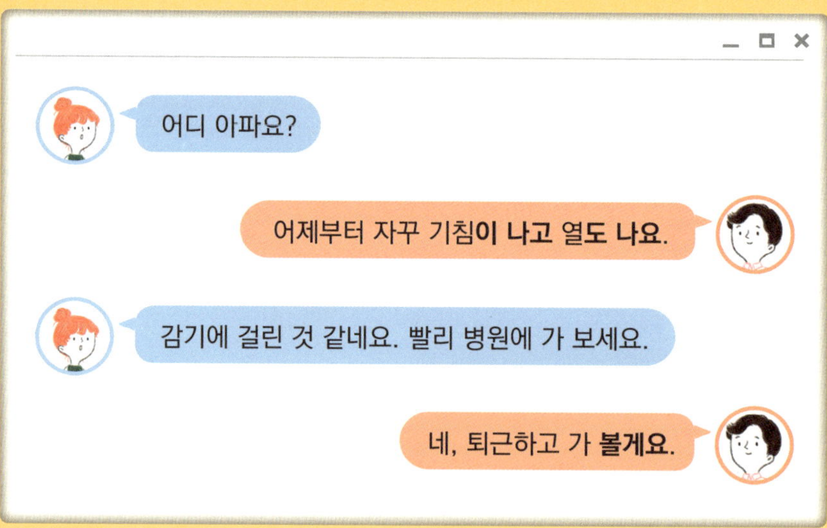


**글쎄** well | **기침이 나다** to keep coughing | **열이 나다** to run a fever | **감기에 걸리다** to catch a cold
**퇴근하다** to be off from work

# 결혼해 줄래

이승기

나랑 결혼해 줄래. 나랑 평생을 함께 살래.
우리 둘이 알콩달콩 서로 사랑하며
나 닮은 아이 하나 너 닮은 아이 하나 낳고
천 년 만 년 아프지 말고 난 살고 싶은데
솔직히 말해서 내가 널 더 좋아해.
남자와 여자 사이엔 그게 좋다고 하던데

★ 내가 더 사랑할게. 내가 더 아껴 줄게.
눈물이 나고 힘이 들 때면
아플 때면 함께 아파할게.
평생을 사랑할게 평생을 지켜 줄게.
너만큼 좋은 사람 만난 걸 감사해
매일 너만 사랑하고 싶어.

나랑 결혼해 줄래.
Marry me 매일이 행복에 겨워서 괜시리 내일이 기대되는 사람
왜 이리 왜 이리 떨리는 걸까 보고 또 봐도 내겐 제일인 사랑
검은 머리 파뿌리 될 때까지 우리들의 생이 다 끝날 때까지
손에 물은 묻혀도 눈에 눈물 절대 안 묻혀

넌 나의 반쪽 가슴 난 너의 반쪽 가슴 되어
숨을 쉬는 그 순간순간 널 사랑해 줄게.
시간이 지나서 주름이 늘어나도
꼭 지금처럼 너와 나 영원히 함께 할 거야.

★ 반복

# Will You Marry Me?

Lee Seung Gi

Will you marry me? Will you live with me forever?
We will always sweetly love each other.
We'll have a baby looking like me and one like you.
Want to be with you forever and ever.
Honestly, I love you more.
That's ideal between men and women.

★ I will love you more. I will care for you more.
When life is hard and you burst into tears,
When you are hurt, I will share your pain.
I will love you and take care of you forever.
I thank God that I met a person like you.
You are the only one I want to love each day.

Will you marry me?
Marry me. Every day is full of joy. You make me dream for tomorrow.
Why, why is my heart beating fast? The more I see you, the more I love you.
Till our hair turns gray and our lives come to an end.
I might not treat you like a princess, but I will never make you cry.

You become my other half. I become your other half.
I will love you every moment you breathe.
Even after many years with wrinkles here and there,
I will love you always and be with you forever.

★ Repeat

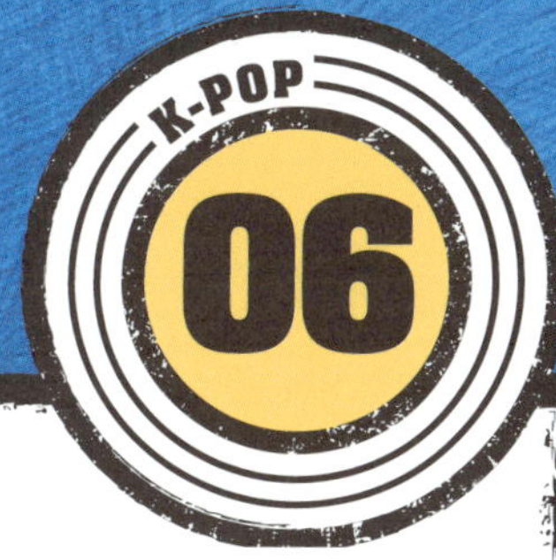



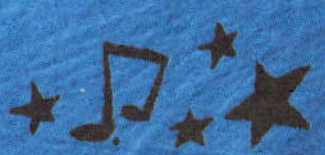

에이핑크(Apink)

# No No No

슬퍼하지 마. No no no
혼자가 아냐. No no no
언제나나나 내게 항상 빛이 돼 준 그대
내 손을 잡아요, 이제.
지금 다가와 기대.
언제나 힘이 돼 줄게.

**About the singer and the song**

Apink is a 6-member group who debuted in 2011. <No No No> is in their third album, and was their first song to be ranked number one on a public channel music show. It was also their debut song in Japan. <No No No> is a message from a girl who wants to encourage her boyfriend during a hard time. It has an uplifting beat with lovely lyrics and represents Apink well.

# 슬퍼하지 마.

Don't be sad.

힘들어하지 마.
Don't give up.

미워하지 마.
Don't hate me.

부러워하지 마.
Don't be envious.

부끄러워하지 마.
Don't be shy.

두려워하지 마.
Don't be afraid.

우울해하지 마.
Don't be depressed.

미안해하지 마.
Don't be sorry.

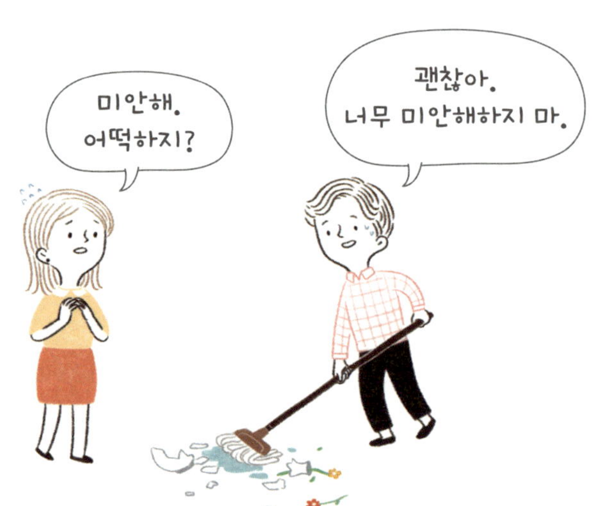

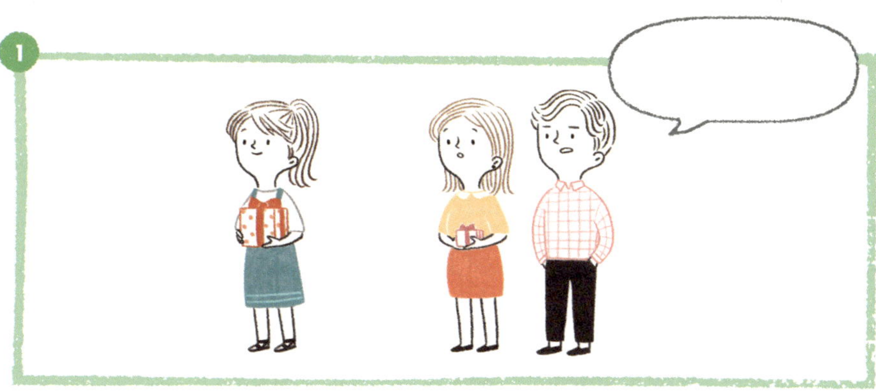

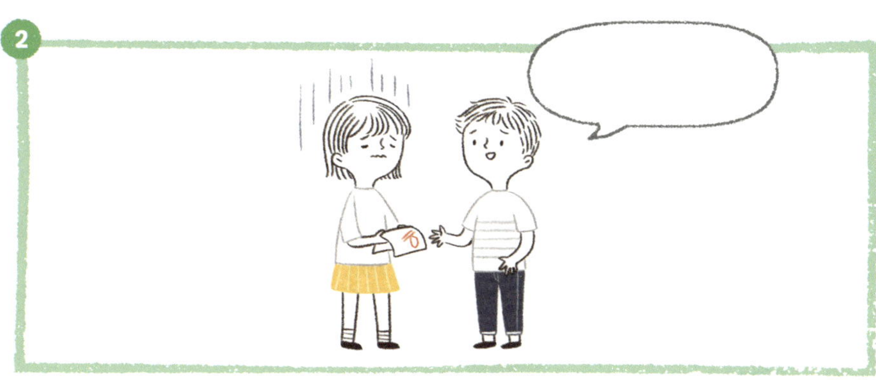

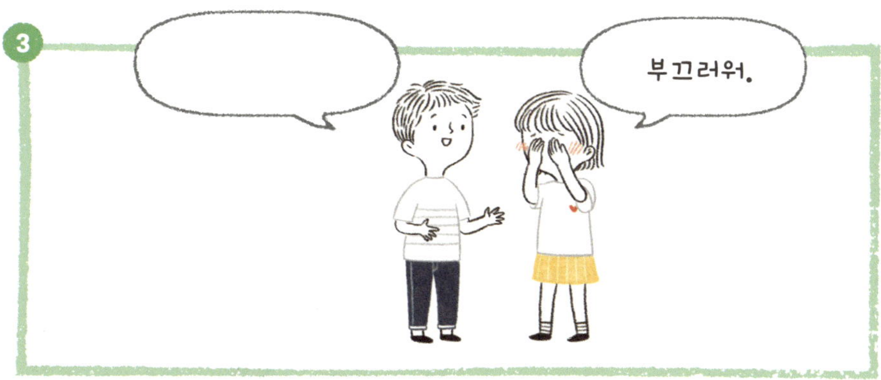
부끄러워.

# 혼자가 아냐.

You are not alone.

## 농담이 아니야.

I'm not joking.

## 거짓말이 아니야.

It's not a lie.

## 남의 일이 아니야.

It's happened to me.

## 네 잘못이 아니야.

It's not your fault.

## 별일 아니야.

It's not a big deal.

## 예전의 내가 아니야.

I'm not the person I used to be.

## 보이는 게 다가 아니야.

What you see is not everything
you can see.

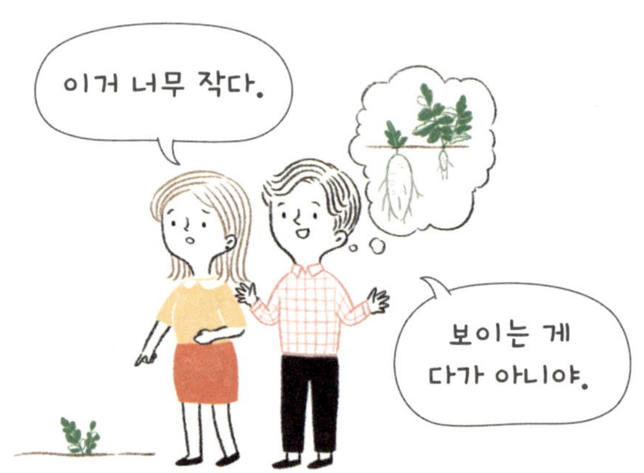

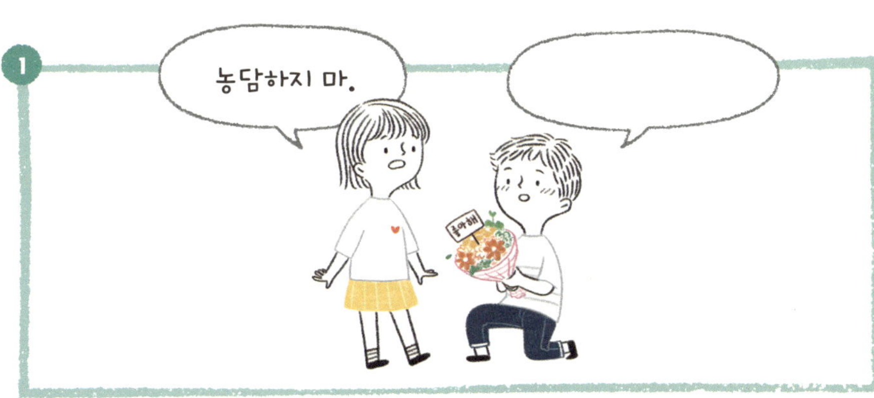


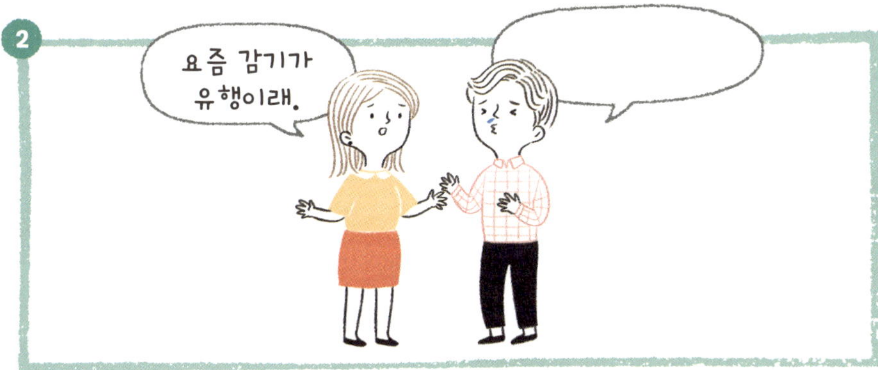


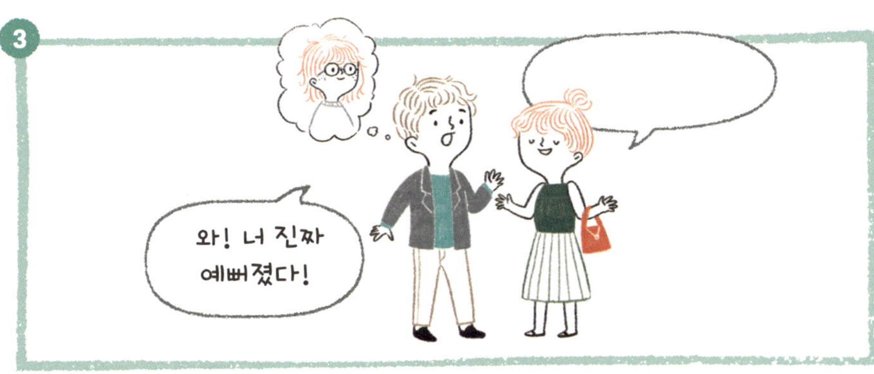


**감기가 유행이다** The flu is going around. | **예뻐지다** to become pretty; to get pretty

 ## A-아하지/어하지 말다

**아파하지 마.**
Don't be sick.

**괴로워하지 마.**
Don't anguish over things.

**슬퍼하지 마세요.**
Don't be sad.

**A-아하지/어하지 말다** is an expression used to ban something and is similar to "don't be."
**V-지 마** is another expression that is used for banning. But it needs a verb in the phrase
while **A-아하지/어하지 마** needs an adjective.

 ## (N₁은) N₂이/가 아니다

**(너는) 혼자가 아니야.**
(You are) not alone.

**(저는) 학생이 아니에요.**
(I am) not a student.

**(그건) 사실이 아니에요.**
(That is) not true.

**(N₁은/는) N₂이/가 아니다** means "N₁ is not N₂." If both the speaker and the listener know
what N₁ is, it is often not written in the sentence. **아니야** is used between friends or very
close people. **아니에요** is the honorific form of **아니야**.

슬퍼하지 마. No, no, no 혼자가 아냐. No, no, no

언제나나나 내게 항상 빛이 돼 준 그대
[비치]

내 손을 잡아요, 이제. 지금 다가와 기대.

언제나 힘이 돼 줄게.
[줄께] ★

★ –(으)ㄹ게 is pronounced like [(으)ㄹ께].
**Ex** 할게 [할께], 먹을게 [머글께]

줄임말 **CONTRACTION**

슬퍼하지 마. No, no, no 혼자가 아냐. No, no, no
= 아니야

언제나나나 내게 항상 빛이 돼 준 그대
= 되어

Many Koreans use contracted forms of words to pronounce them easier and faster.

**Ex** 아니야 → 아냐 / 아니요 → 아뇨
되어 주세요 → 돼 주세요 / 되었어요 → 됐어요

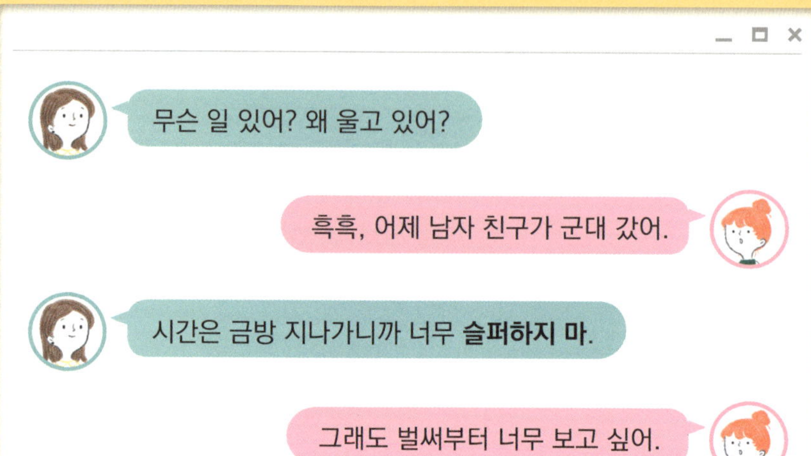


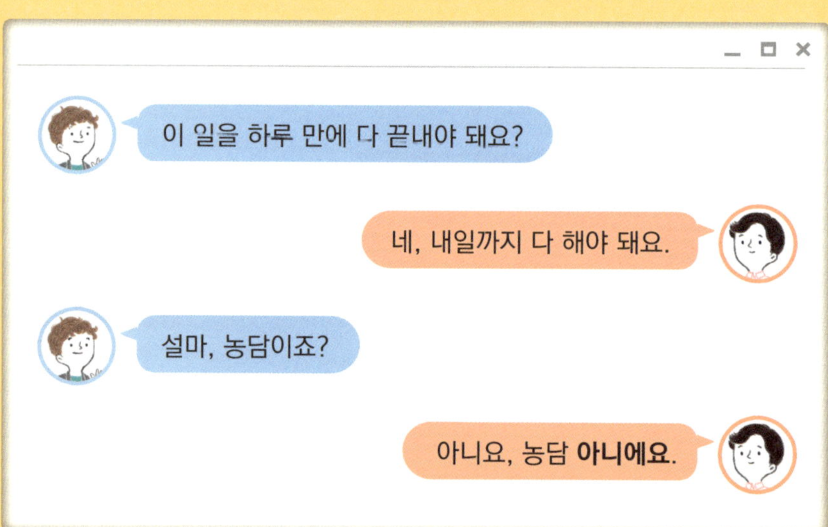


**군대*** military service or the military | **금방** soon | **지나가다** to pass | **벌써부터** already | **끝내다** to finish
**설마** no way

* Military service is mandatory for all Korean men. Therefore, the military calls upon Korean men to do their duty for a certain period of time.

# No No No

에이핑크

★ 슬퍼하지 마 No, no, no 혼자가 아냐 No, no, no
언제나나나나 내게 항상 빛이 돼 준 그대
내 손을 잡아요 이제 지금 다가와 기대.
언제나 힘이 돼 줄게.

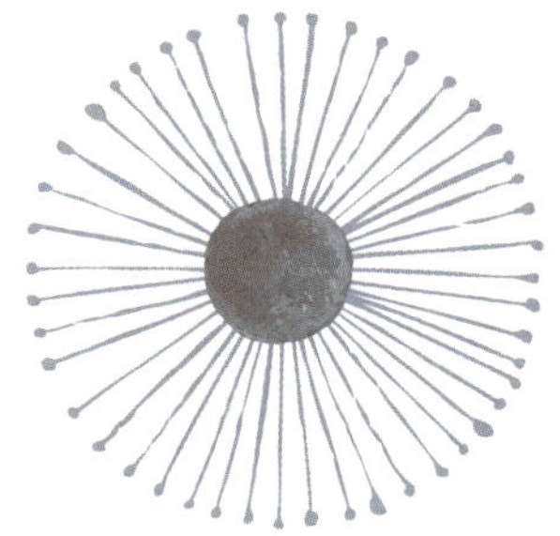

내가 힘이 들 때 내게 다가온 그대
살며시 내게로 와 입 맞춰 준 그대
마치 마법처럼 날 감싸 준
정말 이런 기분 처음이야.

가끔씩은 그대도 힘든가요?
그렇게 혼자 슬퍼하면 어떡해.
하나 둘씩 불이 꺼져 가는 공간 속에
내가 널 비춰 줄게. (Oh)

★ 반복

꿈이 많던 그땐 너무 떨리던 그때에
수많은 시련 속에 기적을 바랬고
갈수록 불어오는 바람에 흔들리는 모습
처음이야.
오랫동안 많이도 참았나요.
아무 말 않고 고개 떨구면 어떡해.
하나 둘씩 곁을 떠나 가는 세상 속에
내가 널 비춰 줄게. (Oh)

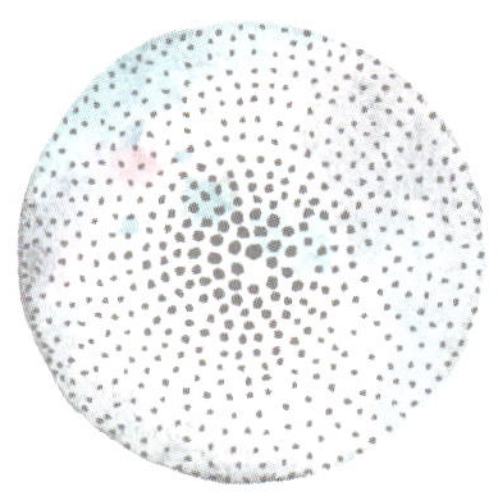

★ 반복

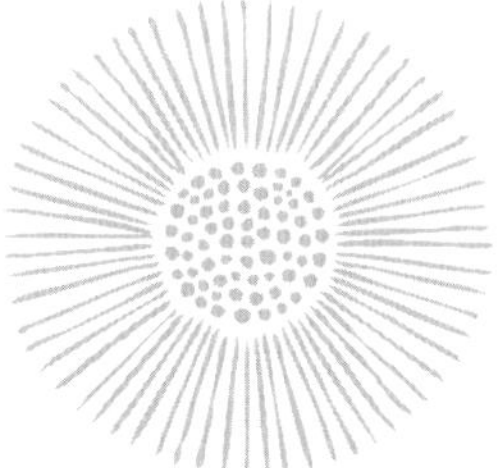

# No No No

Apink

★ Don't be sad. No, no, no. You are not alone. No, no, no.
You always lighten up my day.
Hold my hand. Come and lean on me.
I will always be on your side.

You came to me in the dark moment of my life.
You softly came and kissed me.
It was like magic around me.
I never felt this way before.

Are you having a hard time sometimes?
But don't be so sad by yourself.
When the lights go off one by one,
I will lighten up your day. (Oh)

★ Repeat

We were full of dreams and shyness.
We wished for miracles in struggles.
Never seen you swayed by the strong wind before.
Were you always being so patient?
Don't give up remaining silent.
People may leave you one by one.
I will lighten up your day. (Oh)

★ Repeat

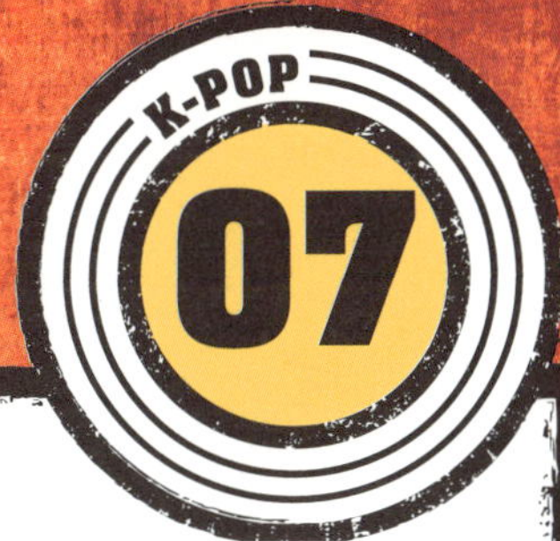


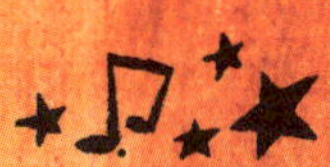


# 너뿐이야

내 눈엔 너밖에 안 보여, 너.

내 귀엔 너밖에 안 들려, 너.

내 맘엔 너밖에 안 살아.

그래서 너 없이 못 살아.

Baby girl, you're the only one for me.

난 너뿐이야, 우후 너뿐이야.

**About the singer and the song**

J.Y. Park is a singer, songwriter, producer and the CEO of JYP Entertainment. JYP Entertainment is one of the three major entertainment agencies in Korea. The Wonder Girls, 2PM, 2AM, GOT7, Twice, and other groups belong to this agency. The song <너뿐이야 (You Are the Only One)> was released in 2012. It is about a man who is comforting his girl as she is worried about their relationship.

# 내 눈엔 너밖에 안 보여.

You are the only one in my eyes.

나한테는 너밖에 없어.
You are the only one for me.

냉장고에 물밖에 없어.
There's only some water in the fridge.

지갑에 1,000원밖에 없어.
I only have 1,000 won in my wallet.

5분밖에 안 걸려.
It only takes 5 minutes.

30분밖에 안 남았어.
We only have 30 minutes left.

얼굴밖에 몰라.
I only know what she/he looks like.

한국어는 '안녕하세요'밖에 몰라요.
안녕하세요 is all I know in Korean.

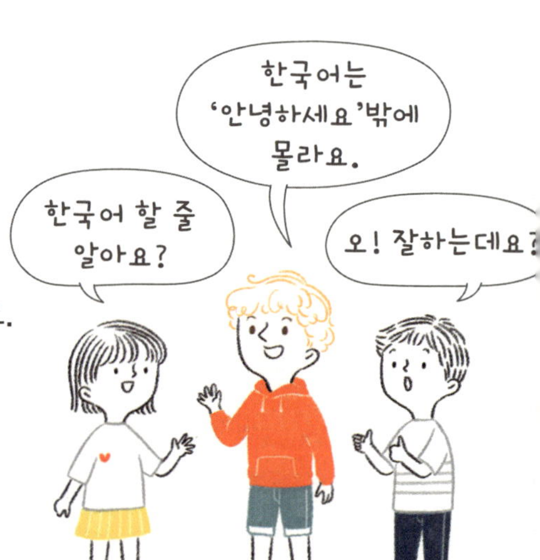

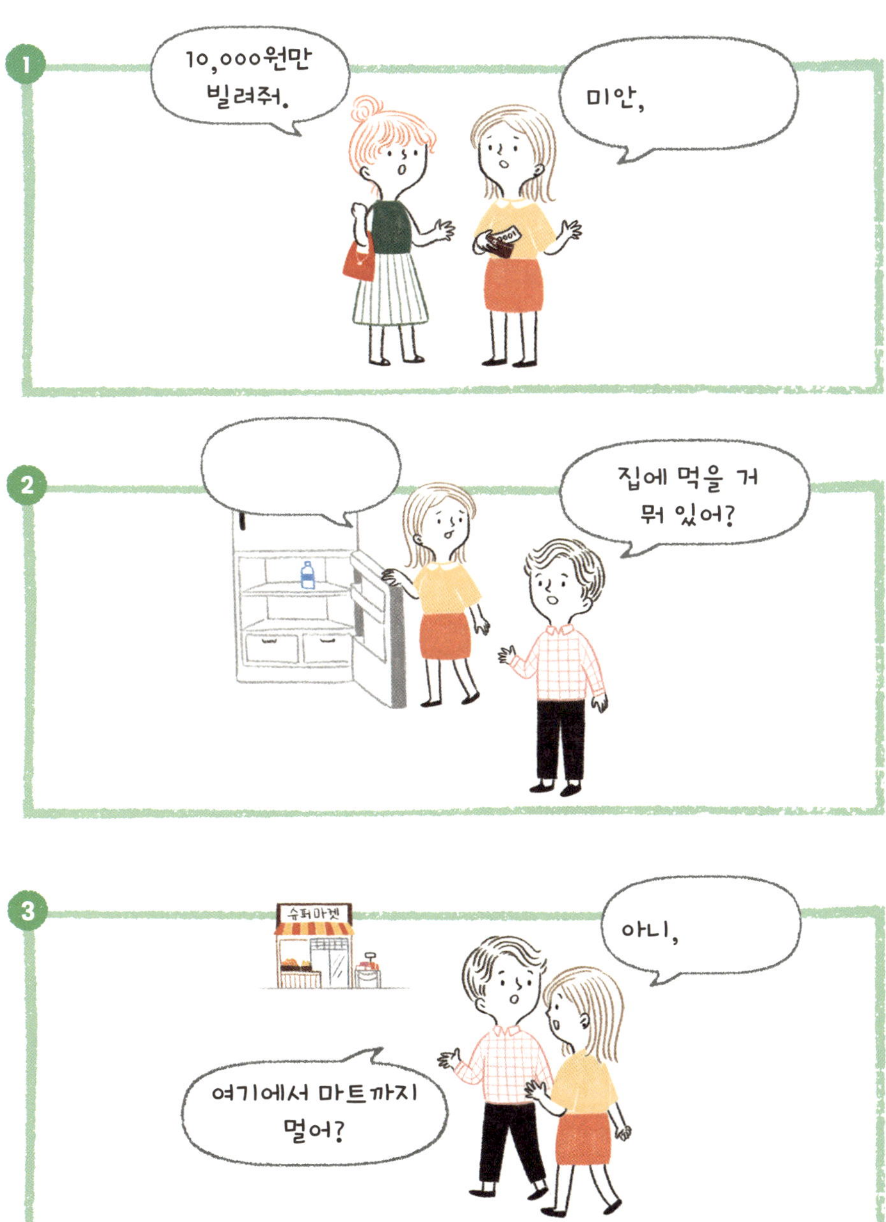


**빌려주다** to lend | **먹을 거** something to eat | **마트** market, mart | **멀다** to be far

# 난 너뿐이야.

You are the only one for me.


가진 것이 돈뿐이야.
Money is all I have.

줄 수 있는 것이 이것뿐이야.
This is the only thing I can give you.

내 걱정해 주는 사람은 너뿐이야.
You are the only one who is worried about me.

이걸 아는 사람은 오직 우리 둘뿐이야.
We are the only ones who know about this.

내가 할 수 있는 운동은 수영뿐이야.
Swimming is the only sport I can do.

나를 이해해 주는 사람은 친구뿐이야.
My friends are the only people who understand me.

힘들 때 곁에 있는 사람은 가족뿐이야.
My family members are the only ones who stay
next to me when times are hard.

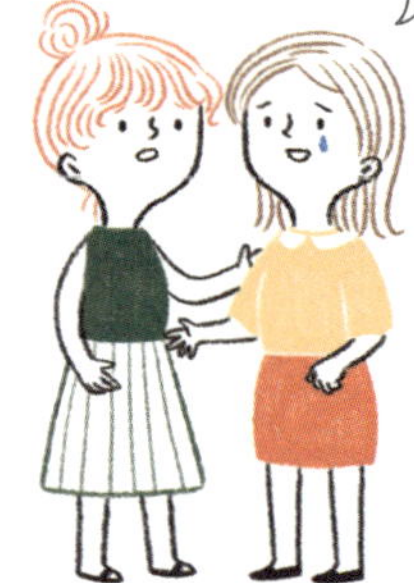

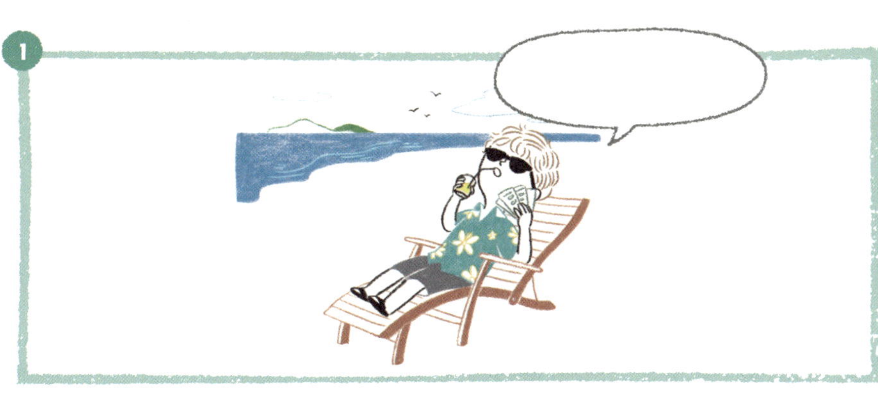

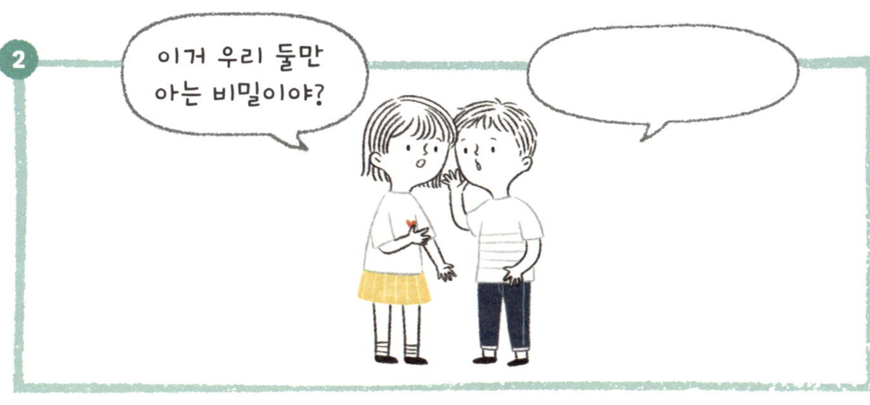



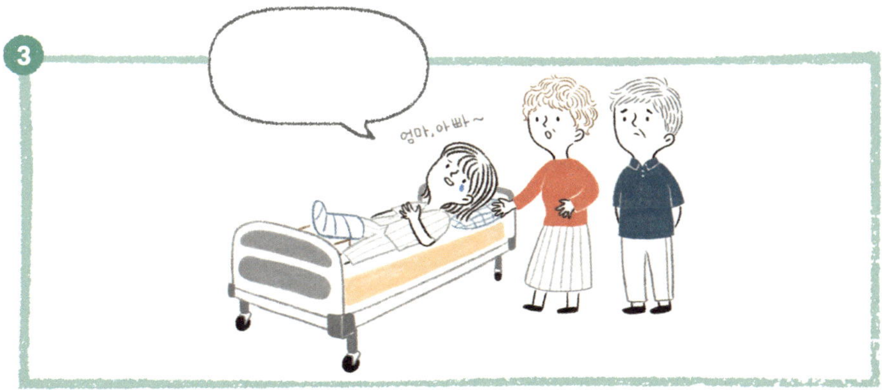



**비밀** secret

 ## N밖에

### 나한테는 너**밖에** 없어.
You are the only one for me.

### 우리 오빠는 공부**밖에** 안 해.
The only thing my brother does is study.

### 어릴 때 학교랑 집**밖에** 몰랐어.
School and home were the only places I went to when I was young.

**N밖에** is a postpositional word that limits the object in a sentence. It is similar to "only" and "just" in English, but it only comes after a noun. It is also always followed by the negative form **안, 못, 아니다, 없다** or **모르다**.

 ## N뿐이다

### 내 사랑은 오직 너**뿐이야**.
You are my only love.

### 정답은 하나**뿐이다**.
There is only one answer.

### 기회는 한 번**뿐이에요**.
There is only one chance.

### 너뿐이야. = 너밖에 없어.

**N뿐이다** is similar to **N밖에 없다** as it also limits the object in a sentence. However, **N뿐이다** does not require any negative form such as **안, 못, 아니다, 없다** or **모르다** to complete the sentence when **N밖에 없다** is followed by one of them.

내 눈엔 너밖에 안 보여, 너.
[누넨] [너바께]

내 귀엔 너밖에 안 들려, 너.
[너바께]

내 맘엔 너밖에 안 살아.
[마멘] [너바께] [사라]

그래서 너 없이 못 살아.
[업씨] [모 싸라]

난 너뿐이야, 우후 너뿐이야
[너뿌니야]★ [너뿌니야]★

★ 너뿐이야 sounds like [너뿌니야] when you read it, but if you read it fast, it sounds like [너뿌냐].



내 맘엔 너밖에 안 살아.
마음에는 (마음+에+는)

Koreans often use contractions to speak faster and easier. It is easy to find contractions in words.

**Ex** 조금 – 좀,    이야기 – 얘기,    그런데 – 근데

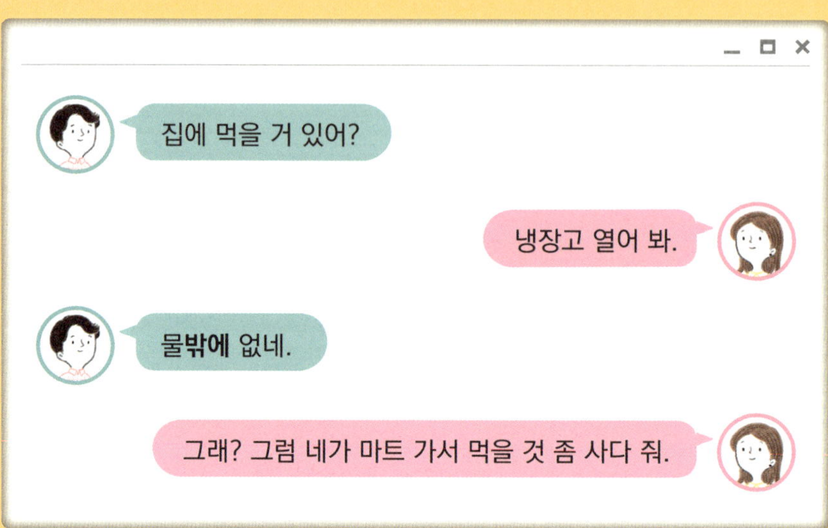


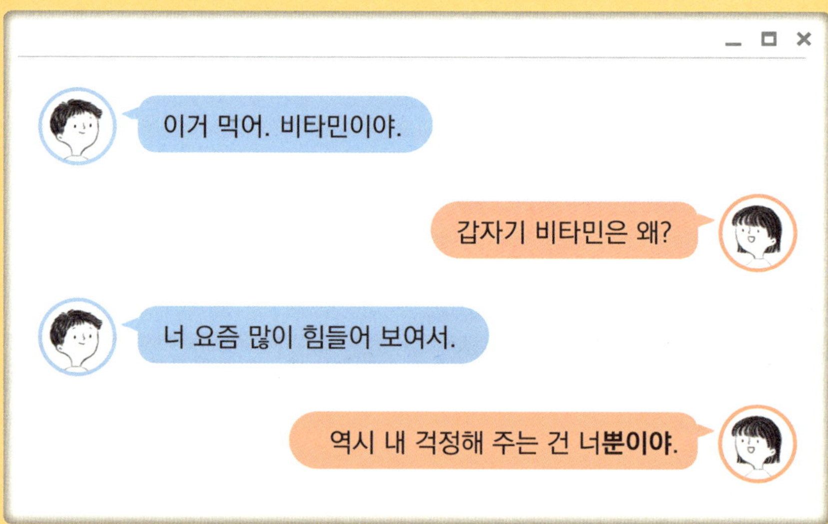


**냉장고** fridge | **사다 주다** to buy and give to ~ | **비타민** vitamin | **힘들어 보이다** to look like one is having a
hard time

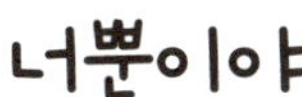

# 너뿐이야

박진영

나를 보는 네 눈을 바라보면 음
행복한데 불안해해 불안한데 행복해해.
너는 날 둘러싼 모든 게 음
언젠간 나를 흩트려 놓을까 걱정하는 거 알아.

나의 화려한 생활 주위의 화려한 여자
가까이서 보면 다 아무것도 아냐.
가까이서 봐도 아무리 가까이서 봐도
끝없이 볼 수 있는 건 정말 너뿐이야.

★ 내 눈엔 너밖에 안 보여 너, 내 귀엔 너밖에 안 들려 너
내 맘엔 너밖에 안 살아 그래서 너 없이 못 살아.
Baby girl, you're the only one for me.
난 너뿐이야 우후 너뿐이야 우후 너뿐이야 우후 너뿐이야.
너뿐이야 우후 너뿐이야 우후 너뿐이야 우후
너뿐이야.

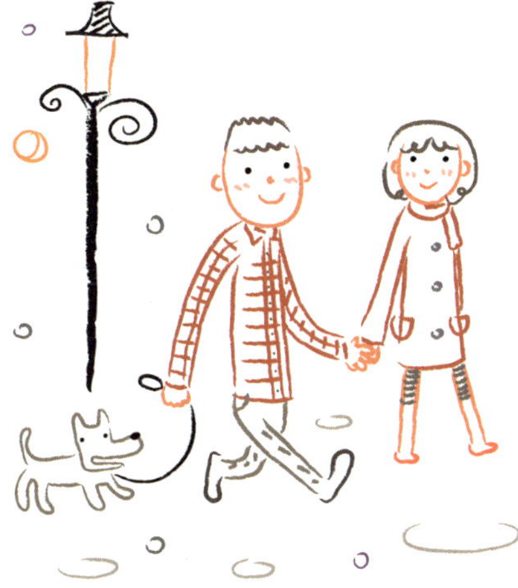

미국 일본 내가 돌아다녀 본 음
곳들마다 예쁜 여자 너무나 많고 많지만
너를 볼 때마다 느끼는 음
설레임은 찾을 수가 없어 걱정할 거 없어.

나를 보는 네 눈빛 날 만지는 손길
누구에게서도 느껴 본 적이 없어
시간이 흘러도 아무리 흘러도
변하지 않는 감정을 준 건 너뿐이야.

★ 반복

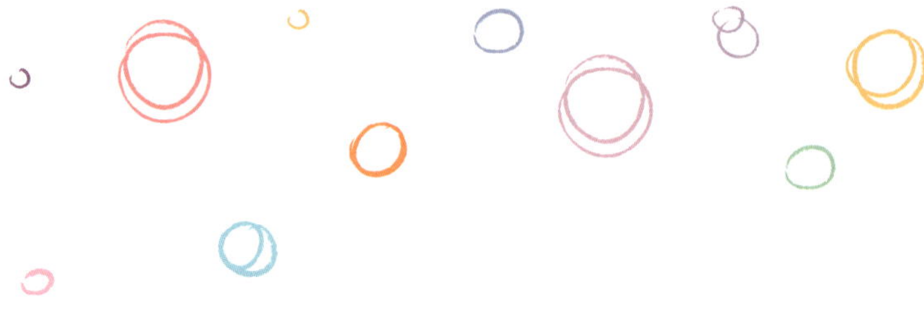

# You Are the Only One

J.Y. Park

When I see your eyes looking at me, mmm.
You look happy but nervous, nervous but happy.
You think everything around me, mmm.
Will spoil me one day. I know.

My glamorous life and fancy girls around me.
Come take a close look 'cause they're nothing.
No matter how close I get and see,
You are the only one whom I can endlessly look at.

★ You are the only one in my eyes. You are the only one I can hear.
You are the only one who live in my heart, so I can't live without you.
Baby girl, you're the only one for me.
To me, you are the only one. Woohoo. You are the only one. Woohoo.
You are the only one. Woohoo. You are the only one.
You are the only one. Woohoo. You are the only one. Woohoo. You are
the only one. Woohoo.
You are the only one.

U.S. Japan, everywhere I've been to, mmm.
There are lots of pretty girls, but
The way my heart bumps, mmm.
It's only for you. Baby, don't worry.

The way you look at me, your soft touch.
I never had them before from anyone else.
No matter how much time we spend together,
You are the only one who has loved me constantly.

★ Repeat

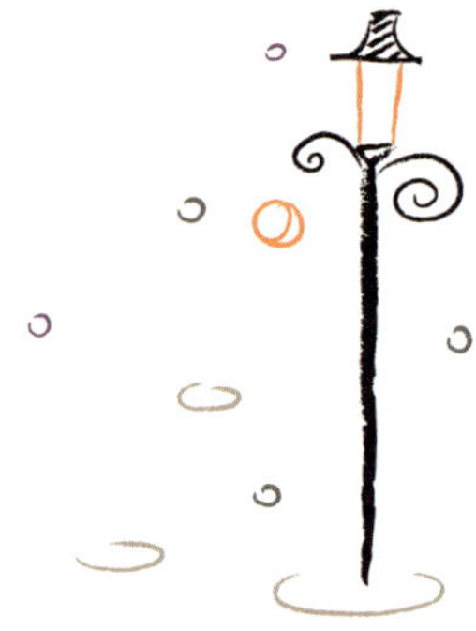

**방탄소년단(BTS)**

# 하루만

하루만 너와 내가 함께 할 수 있다면

하루만 너와 내가 손잡을 수 있다면

하루만 너와 내가 함께 할 수 있다면

하루만 너와 내가 함께 할 수 있다면

너와 하루만 있기를 바래 바래.

## About the singer and the song

BTS is a seven-member boy group. They are more popular overseas than in Korea. They make their fans' hearts throb with their upbeat rapping and powerful dancing. The song <하루만 (Just One Day)> is about a boy who longs to spend even one day with his beloved girl. The message reflects the members' genuine desire and goes well with the soft hip-hop beat.

# 하루만 너와 내가 함께할 수 있다면

I wish I could be with you for even a day.

나도 저렇게 할 수 있다면 좋겠다.
I wish I could do that as well.

매일 이렇게 먹을 수 있다면 좋겠다.
I wish I could eat like this every day.

떡볶이를 만들 수 있다면 좋겠다.
I wish I knew how to make tteokbokki (spicy rice cake).

너의 마음을 알 수 있다면 좋겠다.
I wish I knew what you think of me.

매운 음식을 잘 먹을 수 있다면 좋을 텐데.
I wish I could enjoy spicy food well.

돈 걱정 안 하고 살 수 있다면 좋을 텐데.
I wish I could live without worrying about money.

내가 도와줄 수 있다면 좋을 텐데.
I wish I could help you.

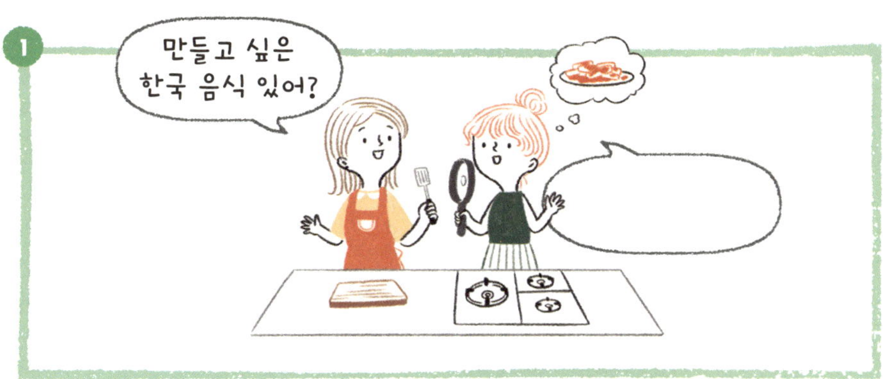


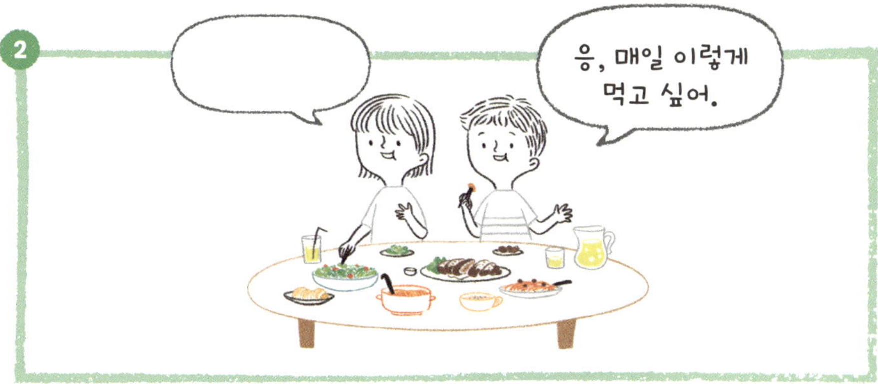


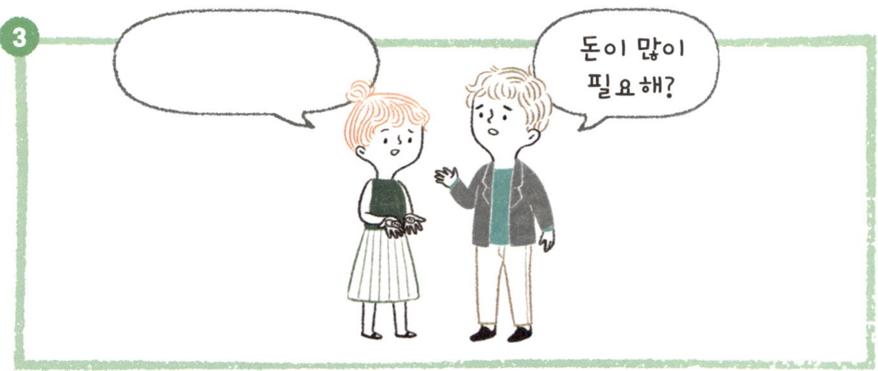


돈 money | 필요하다 to need

# 너와 하루만 있기를 바래.

I wish I could be with you for even a day.

### 행복하기를 바랍니다.

I wish you would be happy.

### 성공하기를 바랍니다.

I wish you would be successful.

### 연락 주시기를 바랍니다.

I wish you would call me.

### 알려주시기를 바랍니다.

I wish you would let me know.

### 운전 조심하시기를 바랍니다.

I hope you drive safely.

### 새해 복 많이 받으시기를 바랍니다.

I wish you a happy new year.

### 좋은 일만 가득하기를 바랍니다.

I wish everything would go well with you.

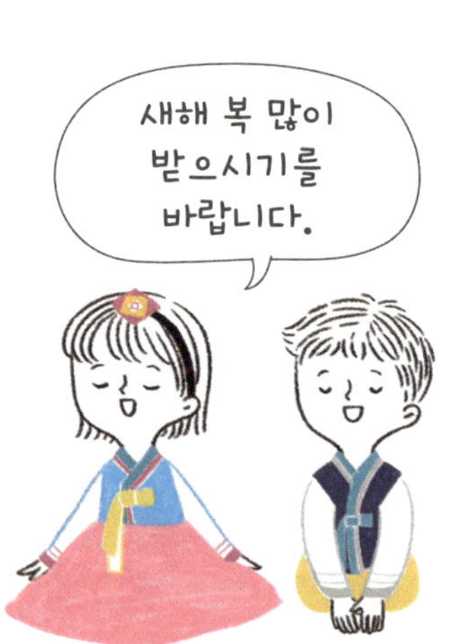

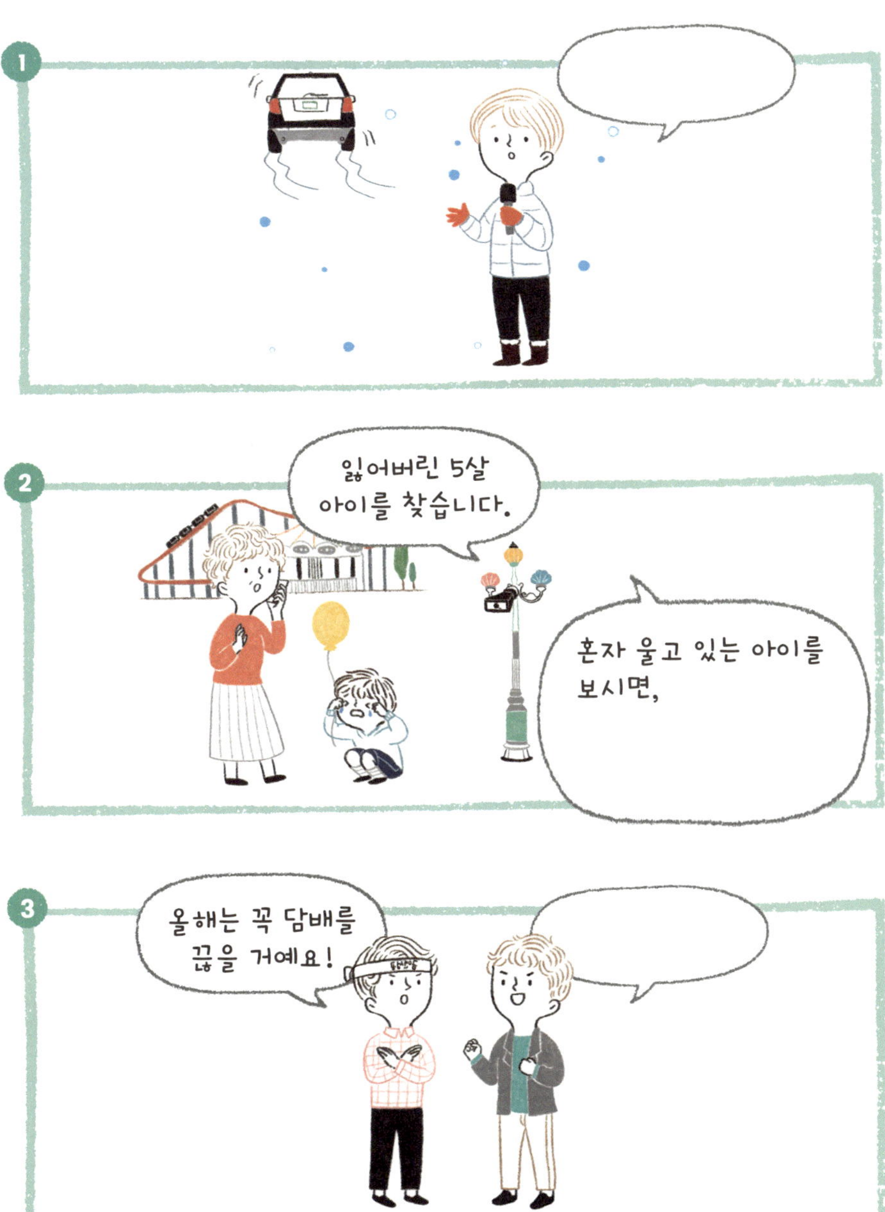



**잃어버리다** to lose | **찾다** to find | **혼자** alone | **울다** to cry | **올해** this year | **꼭** must, definitely
**담배를 끊다** to quit smoking

 **V-(으)ㄹ 수 있다면**

**한국에 한번 가 볼 수 있다면 좋겠다.**
I wish I could go to Korea once.

**BTS의 노래를 직접 들을 수 있다면 좋을 텐데.**
I wish I could hear BTS singing live.

**내가 한국어를 잘할 수 있다면 얼마나 좋을까?**
Wouldn't it be wonderful if I could be fluent in Korean?

**V-(으)ㄹ 수 있다면** is an expression used to assume the possibility of a certain situation and to express one's wish. It is usually followed by **좋겠다**, **좋을 텐데** or **얼마나 좋을까?** to complete the sentence.

 **A/V-기를 바라다**

**(나는) 네가 한국어를 잘하게 되기를 바랄게.**
I wish you could be fluent in Korean one day.

**(저는 당신이) 올해는 꼭 담배를 끊으시기를 바랍니다.**
I wish you would quit smoking this year.

**(저는 당신이) 하시는 일이 모두 잘되시기를 바랍니다.**
I wish everything would go well with you.

**V-기를 바라다** is used to express the speaker's wish. It is similar to "I wish ~," but it often involves other people's actions or an outside influence to make the wish come true. **V-기를 원하다** is synonymous with this expression.

하루만 너와 내가 함께할 수 있다면
[함께할 쑤]★

하루만 너와 내가 손잡을 수 있다면
[손자블 쑤]★

하루만 너와 내가 함께할 수 있다면
[함께할 쑤]★

너와 하루만 있기를 바래 바래
[이끼를]

★ ㅅ sounds like [ㅆ] when it comes right after a word that ends with the final consonant ㄹ such as –(으)ㄹ.

**Ex** 할 사람 [할 싸람], 할 수 있어 [할 쑤 이써]



너와 하루만 있기를 바래.

바라 ( O )

When 바라다 is combined with –아/어 the form has to be changed to 바라. However, most Koreans say 바래, not 바라 (even though 바라 is correct.) So be careful not to say 바라, because it sounds very awkward.

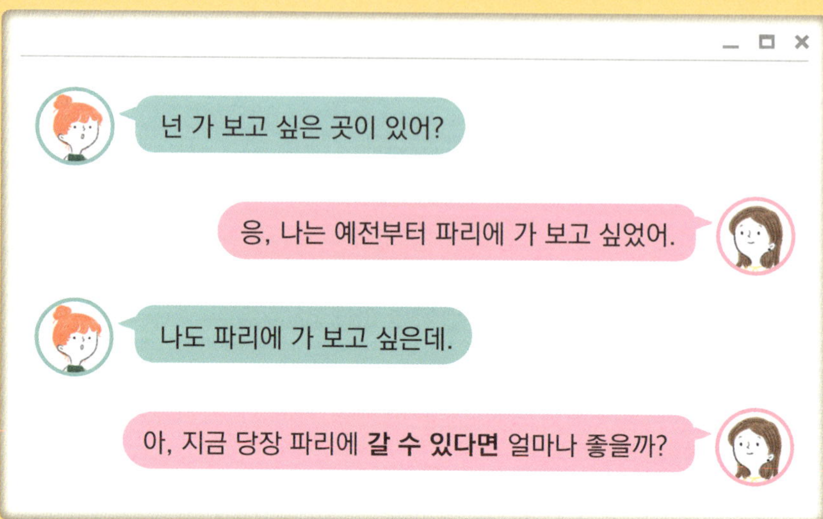


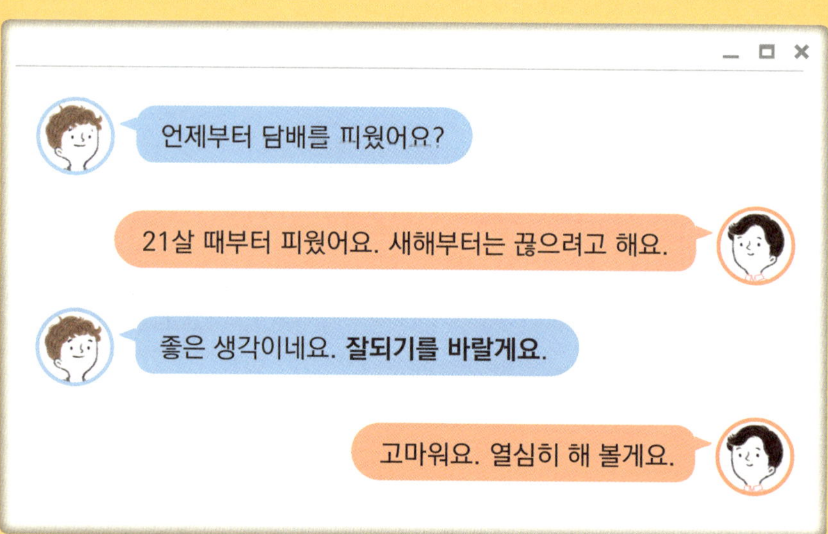


**예전부터** from old times | **파리** Paris | **당장** right away | **새해** new year | **담배를 피우다** to smoke
**잘되다** to go well

# 하루만

방탄소년단

하루만 내게 시간이 있다면
달콤한 네 향기에 취해서 곤히 난 잠들고파
빡빡한 스케줄 사이에 기회가 있다면
따스하고 깊은 눈 안에 몸 담그고파
I like that, 너의 그 길고 긴 생머리
올려 묶을 때의 아찔한 목선과 흘러내린 잔머리
서로 같이 어딜 가든 내 핸드백은 네 허리
Yo, ma honey 볼 때마다 숨이 막혀 명동 거리처럼
우리의 bgm은 숨소리
내 이름을 불러 줄 때의 네 목소리에
잠겨서 난 수영하고파 너를 좀 더 알고파
너란 미지의 숲을 깊이 모험하는 탐험가
너란 작품에 대해 감상을 해, 너란 존재가 예술이니까
이렇게 매일 난 밤새도록 상상을 해,
어차피 내게는 무의미한 꿈이니까

하루만 너와 내가 함께할 수 있다면
하루만 너와 내가 손잡을 수 있다면
하루만 너와 내가 함께할 수 있다면
하루만 (하루만)
너와 내가 함께할 수 있다면 (Do it. Do it. Do it.)
너와 하루만 있기를 바래 바래 (Do it. Do it. Do it.)
너와 단둘이 보내는 party, party (Do it. Do it. Do it.)
너와 하루만 있기를 바래 바래 (Do it. Do it. Do it.)

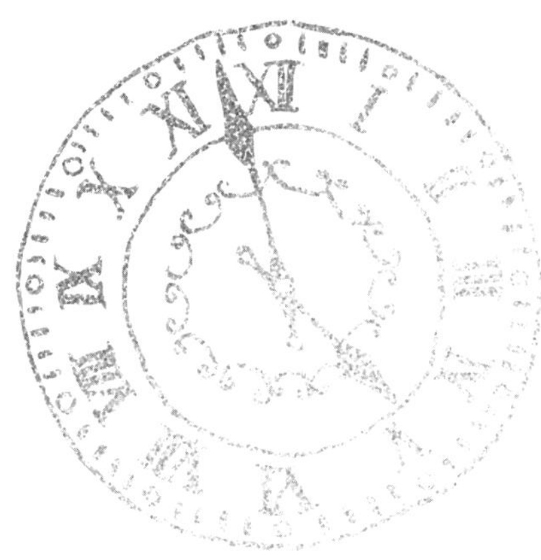

# Just One Day

BTS

Only if I had one day
I would fall asleep next to you intoxicated with your sweetness.
Only if I had some free time with my busy schedule
I would rest in your warm and deep eyes.
I like that, your soft, straight hair
Your sexy neck when your hair is tied up
Anywhere we go my arm is around your waist
Yo, ma honey make me out of breath like in the Myeongdong Street.
Our bgm is the sound of us breathing.
When you call my name, your voice is so sweet.
I want to dive into your voice and want to know you more.
You are a mystery girl. I'm an explorer.
You are an art to me, so I appreciate you.
I dream of you all night, but it's love like a firework.

Only if I had one day with you.
Only if I could hold your hands for one day.
Only if I had one day to be with you.
Just one day. (Just one day.)
Only if I could be with you. (Do it. Do it. Do it.)
I wish I had a day with you. (Do it. Do it. Do it.)
We would have our private party party (Do it. Do it. Do it.)
I wish I had a day with you. (Do it. Do it. Do it.)

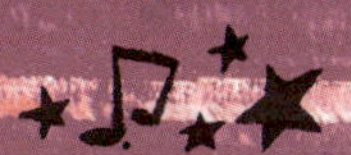


# Be My Baby

차분하려 하는데

네가 또 내 앞에만 나타나면

사랑한다고 말해 버릴 것만 같아.

(Please be my baby)

너만 생각하면 미치겠어.

네가 너무너무 갖고 싶어서 우~

(Make me your lady)

나의 사랑을 너에게 줄게.

절대 후회하지 않게 해 줄게. No

**About the singer and the song**

The Wonder Girls debuted in 2007. We can say they started Korea's girl group re-naissance. Girl group 4 Minute's Hyuna was one of their early members, but she left the group due to a health issue, and Yubin replaced her. In 2015, members Sunye and Sohee also left the group. There are now four members: Ye-eun. Sunmi. Hyelim and Yubin. The song <Be My Baby> is a sweet confession to a beloved person.

# 사랑한다고 말해 버릴 것 같아.

I think I'm going to say I love you.

## 다 말해 버릴 것 같아.
I think I'm going to say everything.

## 돈을 다 써 버릴 것 같아.
I think I'm going to spend all the money.

## 혼자서 다 먹어 버릴 것 같아.
I think I'm going to eat them all.

## 금방 포기해 버릴 것 같아.
I think I'll give up so soon.

## 그 사람이 떠나 버릴 것 같아.
I think she/he's going to leave me.

## 잃어버릴 것 같아.
I think I might lose this.

## 잊어버릴 것 같아.
I think I might forget it.

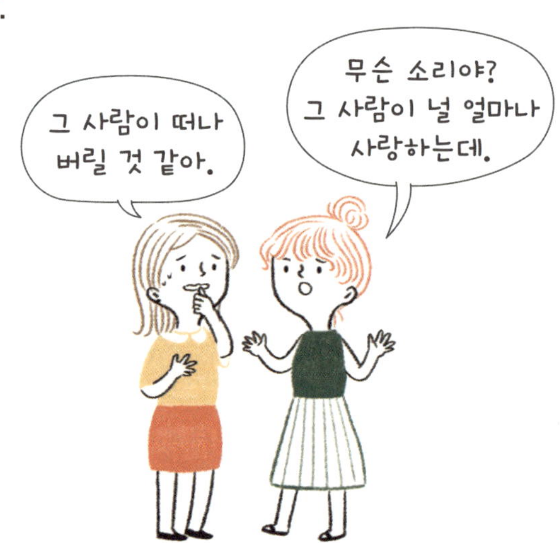

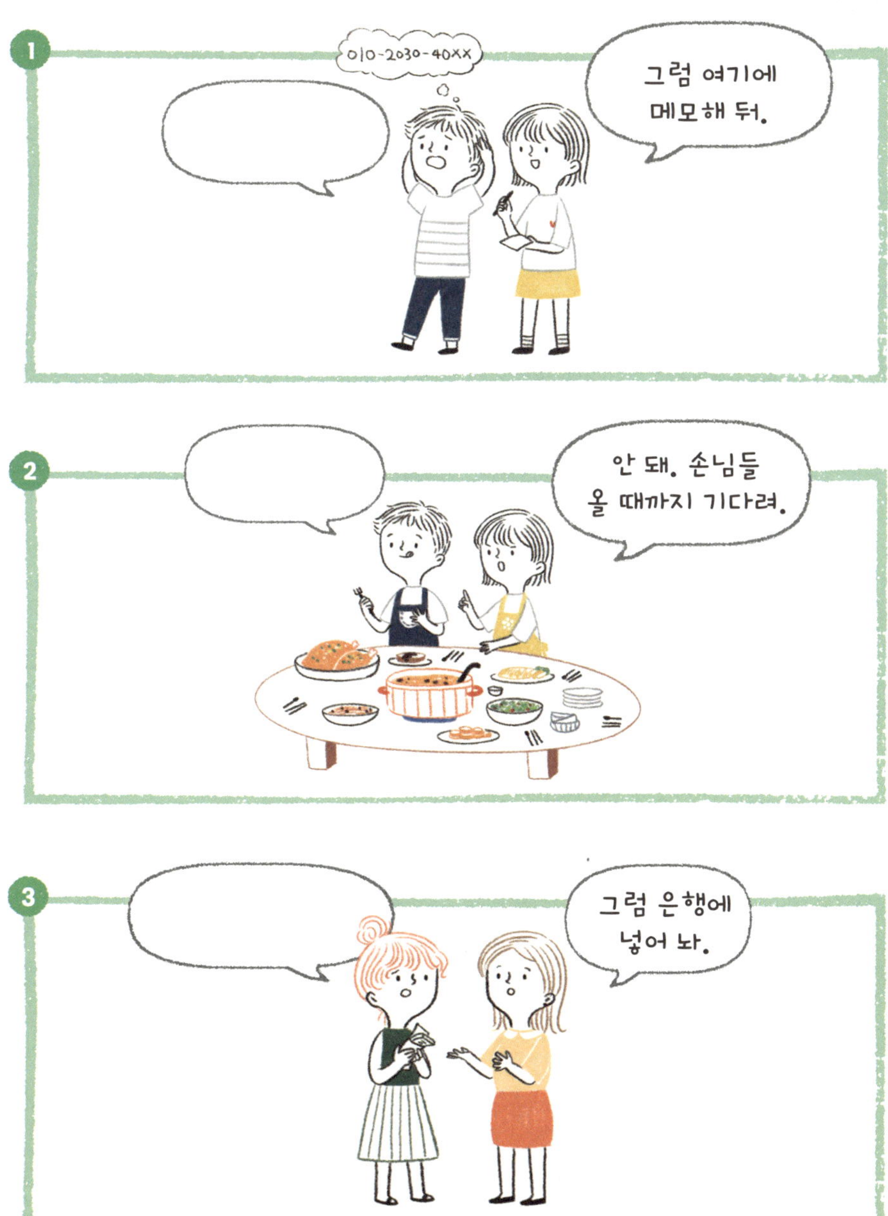


메모해 두다 to write down | 손님 guest | 은행에 (돈을) 넣어 놓다 to keep as savings (in a bank)

# 절대 후회하지 않게 해 줄게.

I won't ever let you down.

내가 도와줄게.
I will help you.

내가 빌려줄게.
I will lend it to you.

이따가 알려 줄게.
I will let you know later.

나중에 보여 줄게.
I will show you later.

아침에 깨워 줄게.
I will wake you in the morning.

사진 찍어 줄게.
I will take a photo for you.

행복하게 해 줄게.
I will make you happy.

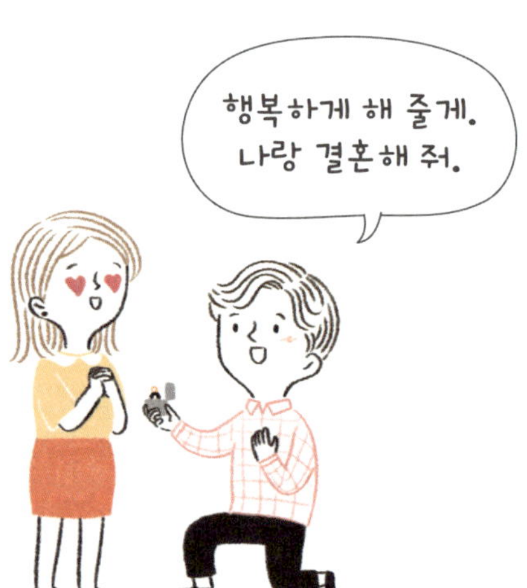

**1**

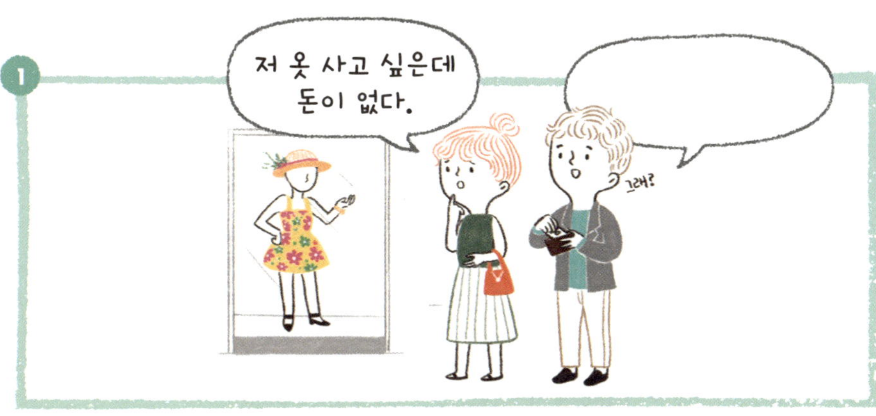


**2**

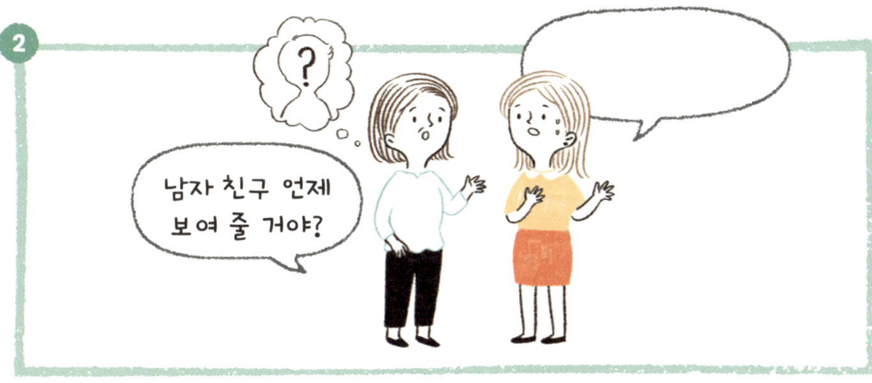


**3**

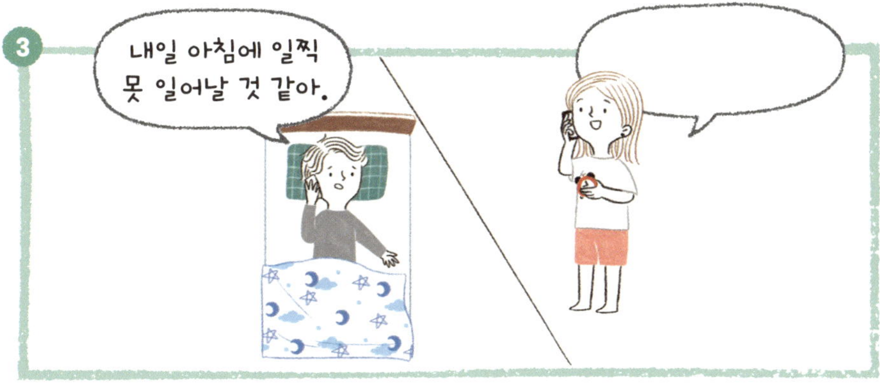


돈 money | 남자 친구 boyfriend | 일어나다 to wake up

 ## V-아/어 버릴 것 같다

**화가 나서 미쳐 버릴 것 같아.**
I'm so upset that I think I will go crazy.

**그 사람 얼굴을 보면 사실을 말해 버릴 것 같아.**
I think I will tell him everything when I see him.

**너무 피곤해서 영화 보다가 잠들어 버릴 것 같아요.**
I'm so tired that I think I will fall asleep during the movie.

**V-아/어 버릴 것 같다** is used when you are worried that something will happen or when you are about to do something which you should not do. It is a combined expression of **V-아/어 버리다** and **A/V-(으)ㄹ 것 같다**. **V-아/어 버리다** is used when something you wished would not happen occurs. **A/V-(으)ㄹ 것 같다** is similar to "I think ~," which is used to express one's assumptions.

 ## V-아/어 줄게요

**내가 이 구두 사 줄게.**
I'll get you this pair of shoes.

**너한테 노래 한 곡 불러 줄게.**
I'll sing a song for you.

**내가 한국어 책을 빌려줄게요.**
I'll lend you my Korean book.

**V-아/어 줄게요** is used when you make a promise to a person for that person's sake. It is similar to "I will ~" in English. The subject of this phrase is always "I."

차분하려 하는데 네가 또 내 앞에만 나타나면
[차부나려]  [니가]

사랑한다고 말해 버릴 것만 같아
[마래버릴 껀만]❶

너만 생각하면 미치겠어
[생가카면]

네가 너무너무 갖고 싶어서 우
[니가]  [가꼬]

나의 사랑을 너에게 줄게
[나에]  [줄께]

절대 후회하지 않게 해 줄게 No
[절때]❷  [안케]  [줄께]

❶ The final consonant ㅅ sounds like [ㄷ] when it is used in the word 것. But when ㄴ or ㅁ comes right after 것, the final consonant ㅅ sounds like [ㄴ] because [ㄷ] is nasalized.

　**Ex** 것만 [걷][만] → [건만]

❷ When ㄷ, ㅅ, and ㅈ come right after the final consonant ㄹ, they are tensed and usually pronounced like [ㄸ], [ㅆ], and [ㅉ] in a noun.

　**Ex** 일등 [일뜽], 일상 [일쌍], 일주일 [일쭈일]

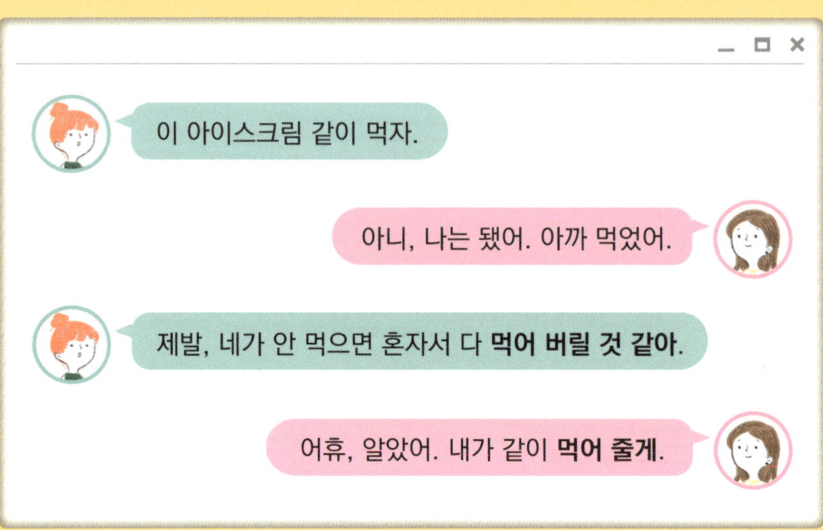


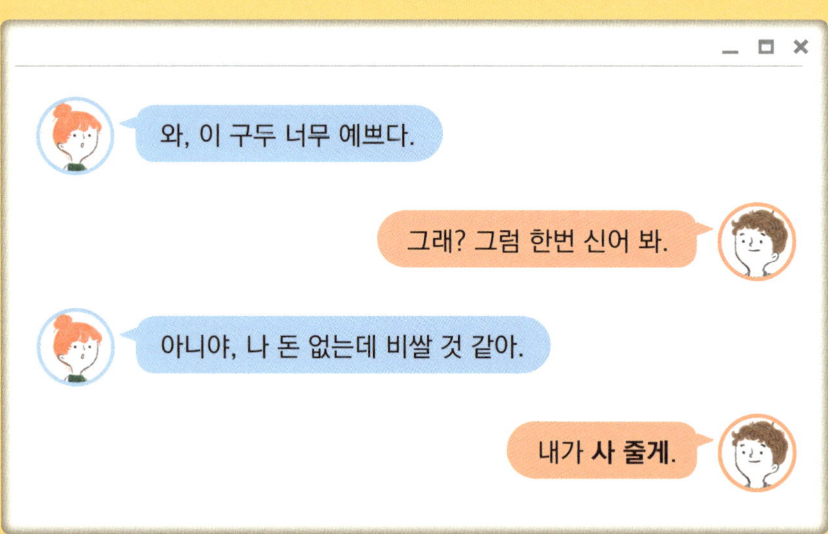


**아이스크림** ice cream | **혼자서** alone | **신다** to wear (shoes) | **비싸다** to be expensive

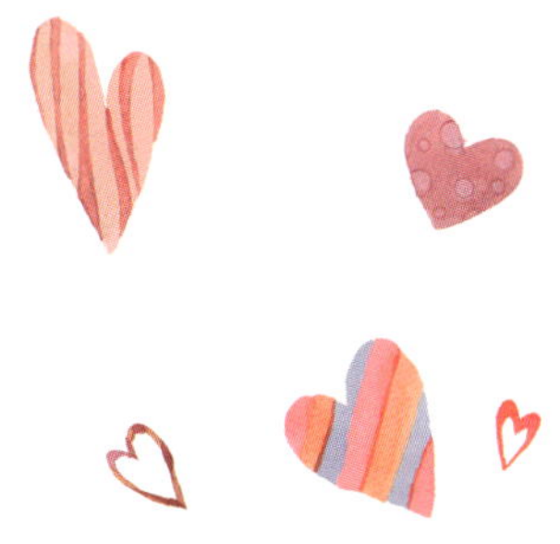

# Be My Baby

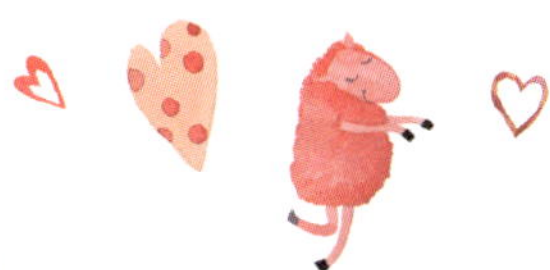

원더걸스

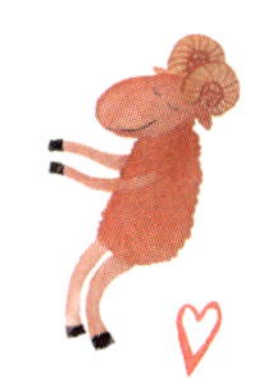

Watching 계속 바라보며 난
Waiting 네가 다가오기만을 바래.
어서 내게 와 날 데려가 제발
Dreaming 네 맘도 나 같기를
Praying 가슴 졸이며 난 기도해.
저 하늘에 이렇게 두 손을 모아서

이런 적이 없는데 내 가슴이 두근두근 두근대고
몇 번 본 적 없는데 네 모습이 자꾸 꿈에 나와

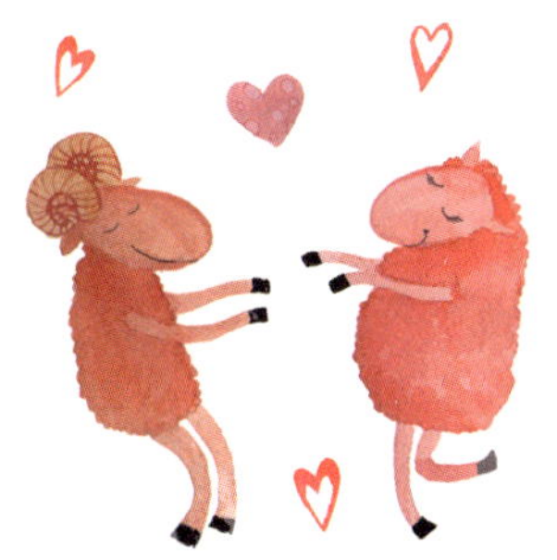

★차분하려 하는데 네가 또 내 앞에만 나타나면
사랑한다고 말해버릴 것만 같아.

Please be my baby. Please be my baby.
너만 생각하면 미치겠어.
네가 너무너무 갖고 싶어서 우
Make me your lady. Make me your lady.
나의 사랑을 너에게 줄게.
절대 후회하지 않게 해 줄게. No

Crazy 내가 미쳤는지 왜
Lately 하루 종일 난 뭘 하든지
너의 사진이 머릿속에 박혔어.
Perfect 모든 게 완벽해.
Terrific 겉과 속 모두 다 어쩜 너는
모자라는 게 하나도 없는 건지

★ 반복

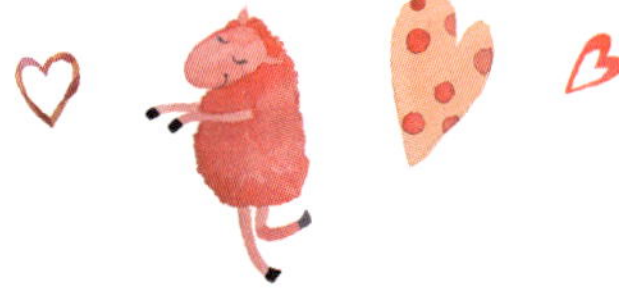

# Be My Baby

Wonder Girls

Watching As I'm watching you
Waiting I'm waiting for you to come closer
Come and get me, please
Dreaming Dreaming you would feel the same way
Praying Praying with desperate heart
Folding my hands and asking God

Never happened before, My heart bumps so fast
Haven't met you so much but so often you are in my dreams

★ I try to calm down but whenever I see you
I think I'm going to say "I love you"

Please be my baby, Please be my baby
I go crazy whenever I think about you
Cause I want you so bad Wooh
Make me your lady, Make me your lady
I will give my love to you
I won't ever let you down No

Crazy Think I got crazy
Lately I think of you all day long
All I think of is you
Perfect Everything about you is perfect
Terrific in and out, in every way
To me, you are flawless

★ Repeat

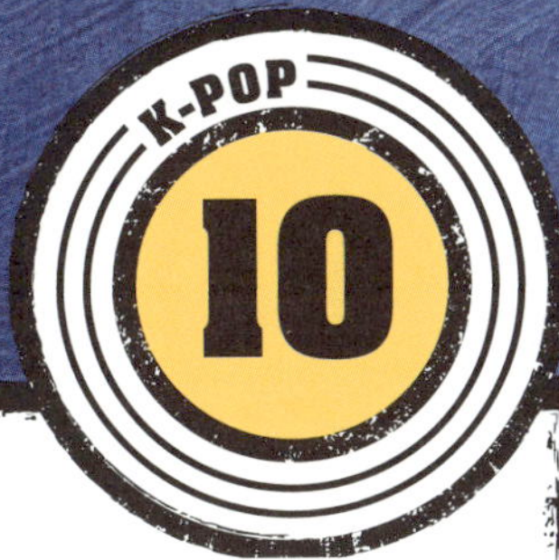



# 노래가 늘었어

노래가 늘었어, 너와 헤어지고 나서

음악에 미쳐 살았더니 모든 노래 가사가

내 얘기 같았어. 죽도록 불렀어.

조금씩 조금씩 차차 눈물이 말라 갔어.

**About the singer and the song**

Ailee made a debut in 2012 with her single album <Heaven>. She won the second place in a singing competition on NBC TV's <Maury Show>. One of her performances was uploaded on Youtube and reached 10 million views. Since then, her nickname became 'The 10 million Girl'. The song <노래가 늘었어 (My Singing got Better)> is about a woman who gets over with her breakup by singing.

# 너와 헤어지고 나서 노래가 늘었어.

My singing got better after I broke up with you.

먹고 나서 후회해.
I always feel regret after eating.

운동하고 나서 배가 고파.
I get hungry after working out.

커피를 끊고 나서 잠이 늘었어.
I need more sleep after I quit drinking coffee.

남자 친구와 헤어지고 나서 너무 힘들어.
It's really hard after breaking up with my boyfriend.

시험 보고 나서 우울해졌어.
I'm really depressed after the test.

비가 오고 나서 날씨가 추워졌어.
It has become really cold after the rain.

화장품을 바꾸고 나서 피부가 좋아졌어.
My skin has become so much better after using
the cosmetic product.

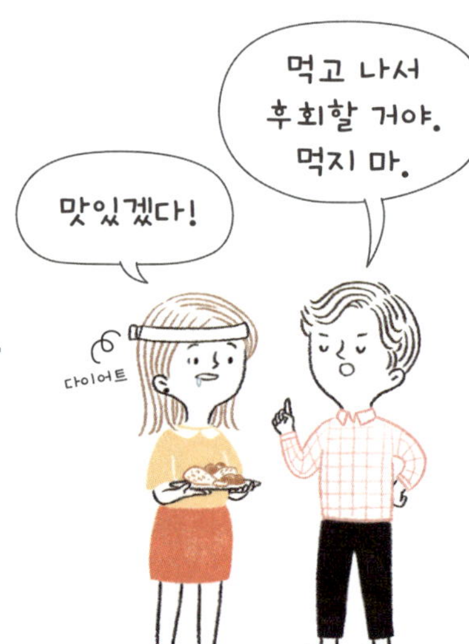

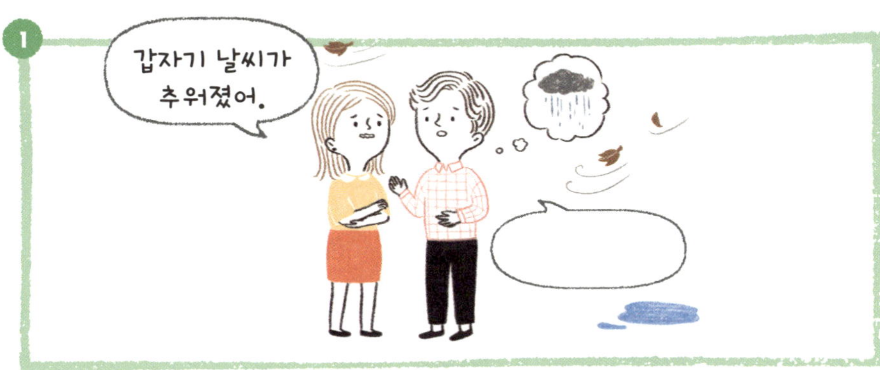


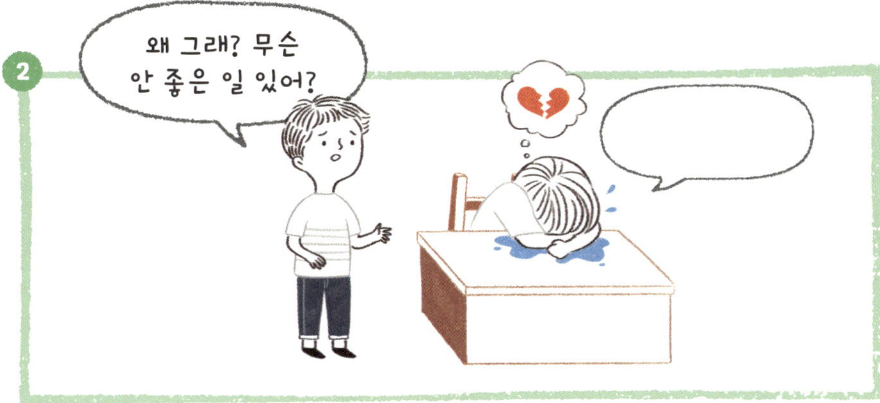


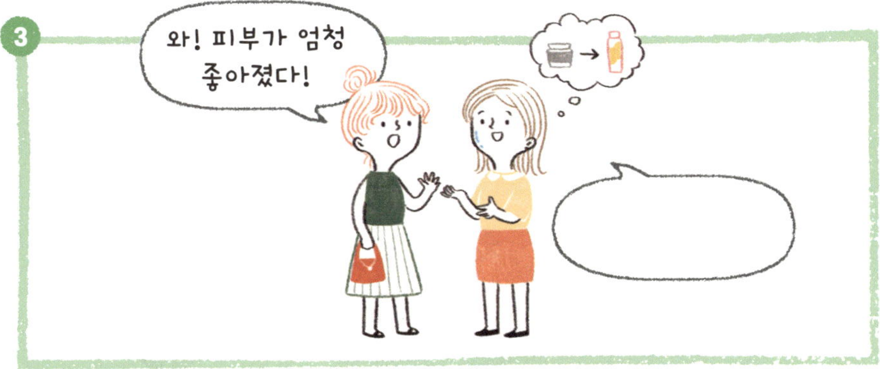


**갑자기** all of a sudden | **엄청** so

# 모든 노래 가사가 내 얘기 같았어.

All the lyrics in the songs were like my story.

## 하루가 1분 같았어.
Today passed very quickly.

## 오늘 하루가 지옥 같았어.
It was like a hell today.

## 오늘 하루가 꿈 같았어.
I felt like I was dreaming today.

## 학교가 감옥 같아.
Our school is like a prison.

## 너 오늘 연예인 같아.
You look like a celebrity today.

## 너 우리 엄마 같아.
You are like my mom.

## 나 정말 바보 같아.
I feel like a jerk.

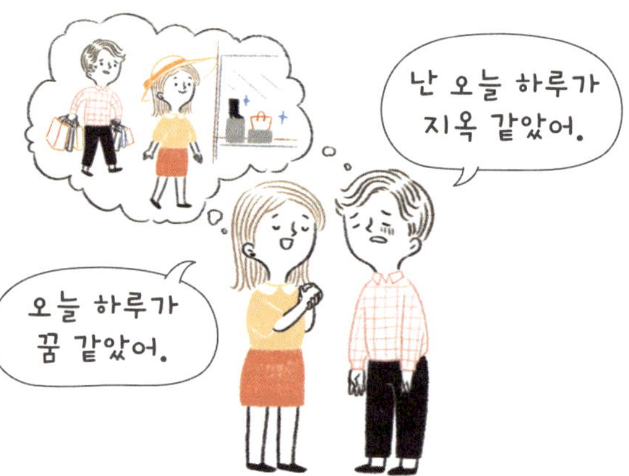

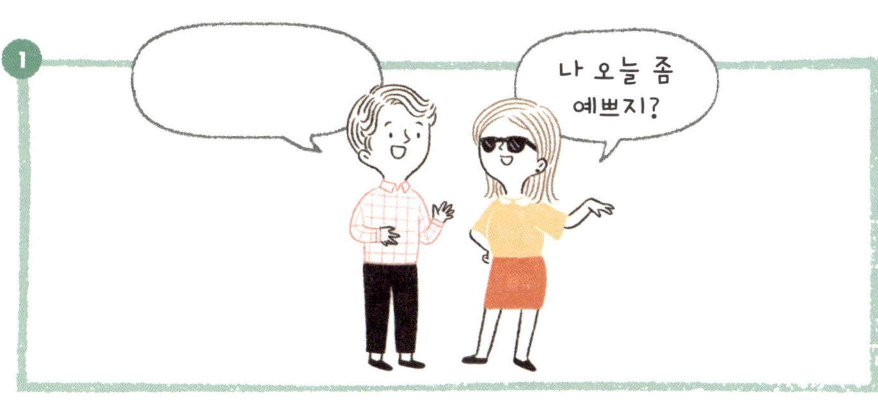


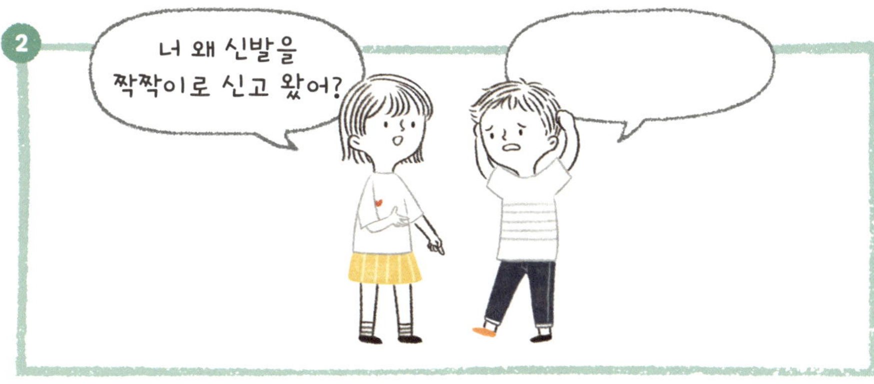


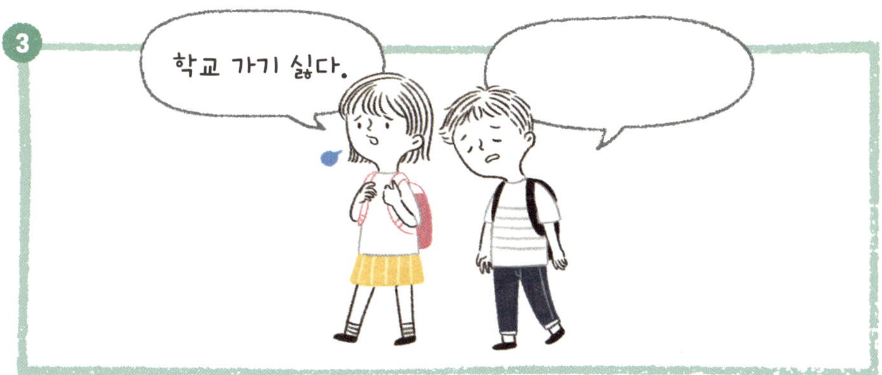


신발 shoes | 짝짝이 unmatched; mismatched | 신다 to wear shoes

 ## V-고 나서 A/V

**다이어트를 하고 나서 건강해졌어요.**
I got healthier after I went on a diet.

**한국어를 배우고 나서 자신감이 생겼어요.**
I've gained confidence after learning Korean.

**남자 친구와 헤어지고 나서 많이 외로웠어요.**
I felt so lonely after breaking up with my boyfriend.

**V-고 나서** is used when you talk about a consequence of a certain action or an incident. It is similar to "after + gerund phrase" in English. There is no big difference in meaning with or without **나서**, but **나서** clarifies the order of the action.

 ## N 같다

**이 노래 가사가 꼭 내 얘기 같아.**
The lyrics of this song are just like my story.

**우리 아버지는 친구 같으세요.**
My dad is just like my friend.

**오늘은 목요일인데 마치 금요일 같아.**
It's Thursday today, but I feel like it is Friday.

**N 같다** is used when you want to say that two different things are similar. It's an expression similar in meaning to "like ~." **N 같다** is often used with the expressions 꼭 and 마치.

노래가 늘었어 너와 헤어지고 나서
[느러써]

음악에 미쳐 살았더니 모든 노래 가사가
[미처] *[사라떠니]

내 얘기 같았어 죽도록 불렀어
[가타써]  [죽또록]

조금씩 조금씩 차차 눈물이 말라 갔어
[눈무리]

★ 차, 처, 초, 추 and 챠, 쳐, 쵸, 츄 are combinations of 8 different vowels and ㅊ.
However, the latter four syllables sound the same as the former ones.
(차 = 챠 [차], 처 = 쳐 [처], 초 = 쵸 [초], 추 = 츄 [추])



노래가 늘었어 너와 헤어지고 나서

⇒ 너와 헤어지고 나서 노래가 늘었어.

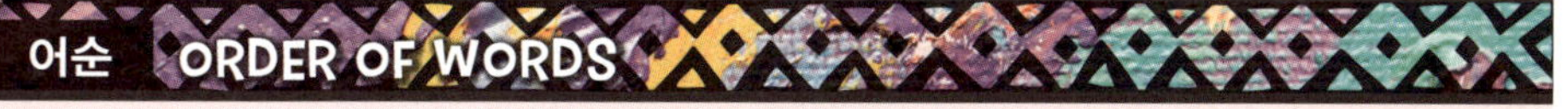

❶                    ❷

-고 나서 comes after ① which involves a certain action.

-고 나서 is followed by ② that tells the changes of the preceding action. It can

be also followed by an action that is consequent to the preceding action.

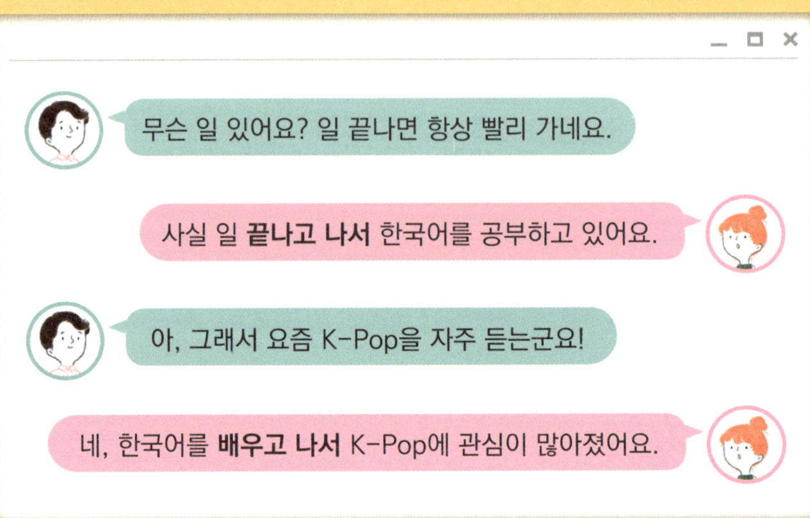


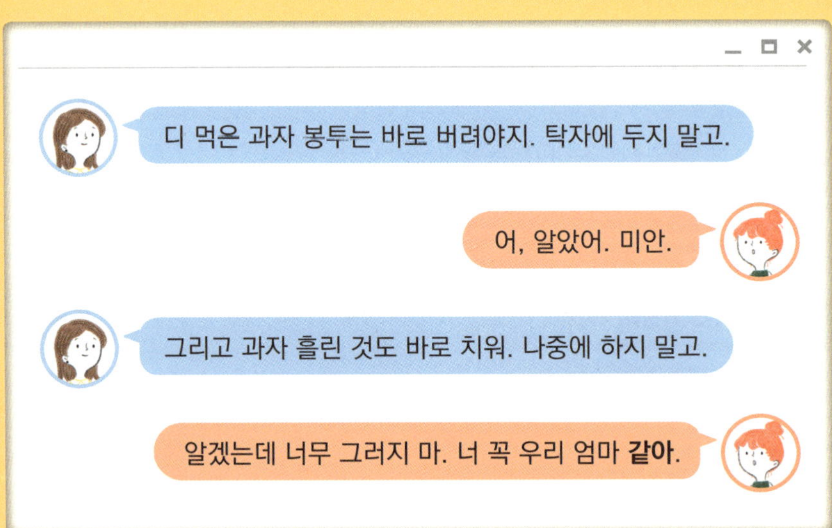


~에 관심이 많아지다 to get more interested in ~ | 과자 cookie, snack | 봉투 pack, bag | 버리다 to throw away
탁자 table | 두다 to leave | 흘리다 to spill; to drop | 치우다 to clean up

# 노래가 늘었어

에일리

정신이 나갔었지 너의 자상함에
너의 달콤함에 너의 거짓말에
꿈이 변했었지 유명한 가수보다
좋은 아내가 되려 했지 정말
정말 바보 같았어 정말 바보 같았어.

★ 노래가 늘었어 너와 헤어지고 나서
음악에 미쳐 살았더니 모든 노래 가사가
내 얘기 같았어 죽도록 불렀어.
조금씩 조금씩 차차 눈물이 말라 갔어.

눈앞이 캄캄했지 어찌나 힘든지
욕도 많이 했지 속도 다 버렸지.

이젠 다 끝났어 난 너 하나를 잃고
더 큰 희망을 얻은 거야.
정말 정말 잘된 일이야 정말 잘된 일이야.

★ 반복

언젠가 너에게 연락이 오겠지.
그 땐 남자답게 축하해 주길 바래.

네 덕분이니까 고맙다는 인사
나도 멋지게 준비해 둘게.

★ 반복

차차 눈물이 말라 갔어.
차차 그렇게 널 잊었어.

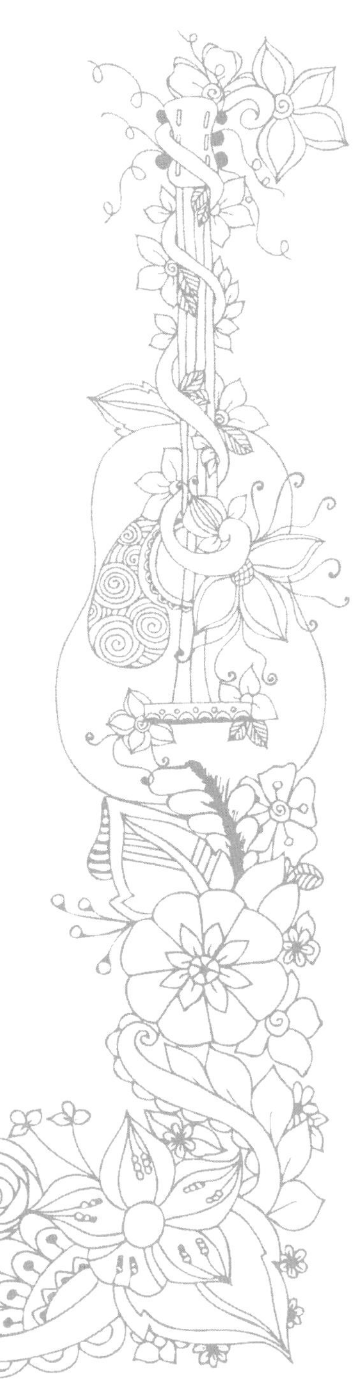

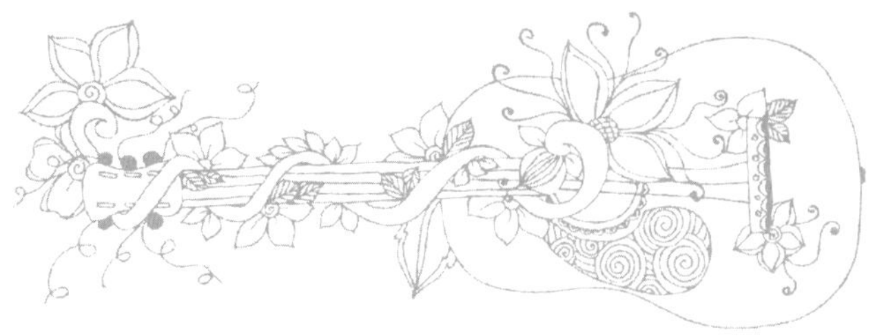

# My Singing Got Better

Ailee

I was out of my mind because of your gentleness.
Your sweetness and your lies.
I gave up my dream to be a great singer.
And tried to become a good wife. I was
Such a fool, such a fool.

★ My singing got better after breaking up with you.
 I got crazily into music and all the lyrics in the songs
 Sounded like my story. I sang them to death.
 And my tears dried out as time passed by.

Life became hopeless and full of pain.
Cursing and drinking, I wore myself out.

It's all over now. I lost you in my life.
But found greater hope ahead.
Truly, truly, it's so much blessing, so much blessing.

 ★ Repeat

Some day you will probably call me.
That day, hope you bless me like a man.

And I will say, "Thank you,"
since my singing got better after our breakup.

 ★ Repeat

My tears dried out as time passed by.
You have faded away as time passed by.

# 남자가 사랑할 때

남자가 사랑할 때엔 꼭 항상

곁에 머물면서 늘 해 주고 싶은 게 참 많아.

사랑에 빠질 땐 내 삶의 모든 걸 다 주고서

단 하나 그 맘만 바래, 사랑에 빠질 땐

**About the singer and the song**

INFINITE made their debut in 2010 as a seven-member boy group. Their songs such as <내꺼하자> are well known for reversing 1980~2000's rhythms into a modern style. Their rhythmic dancing is also very popular. The song <남자가 사랑할 때 (Man in Love)> describes how a man reacts when he's in love. It's an addictive song with an uplifting melody.

# 남자가 사랑할 때

When a man is in love

치킨 먹을 때 맥주를 마셔요.
I drink beer when I eat (fried) chicken.

집에 있을 때 반바지를 입고 있어요.
I wear shorts when I'm at home.

어릴 때 운동을 안 좋아했어요.
I didn't like to work out when I was young.

첫눈이 올 때 고백할 거예요.
I'm going to confess my love on the first day it snows.

여행 갈 때 선글라스를 가지고 갈 거예요.
I'm going to bring my sunglasses when I travel.

우울할 때 단 음식을 먹어요.
I eat sweets when I get depressed.

목이 아플 때 따뜻한 물을 많이 드세요.
Drink a lot of warm water when
you have a sore throat.

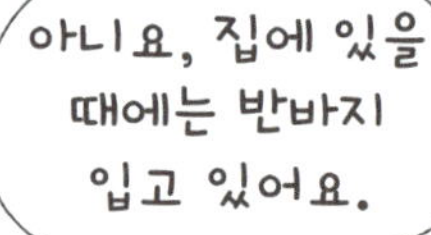


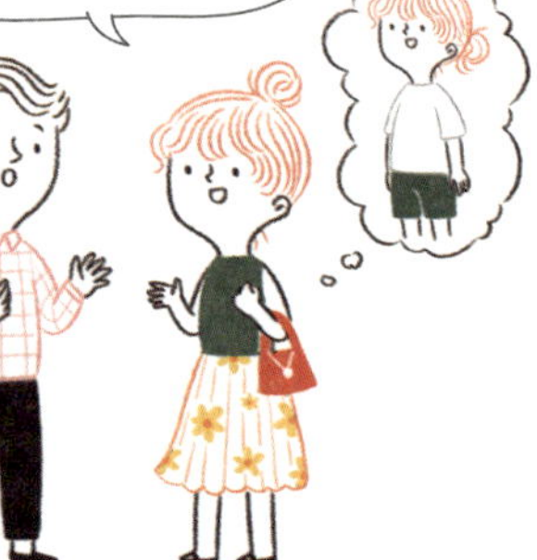

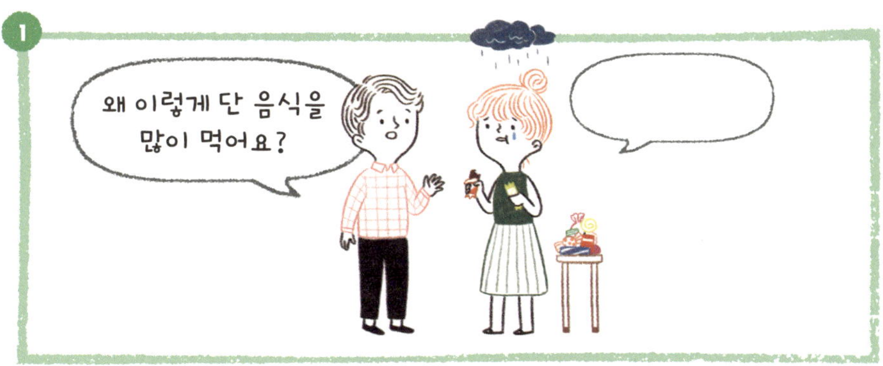
왜 이렇게 단 음식을
많이 먹어요?

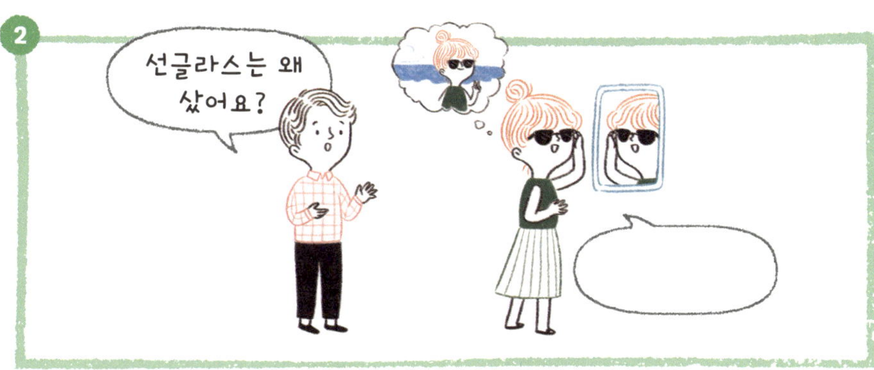
선글라스는 왜
샀어요?

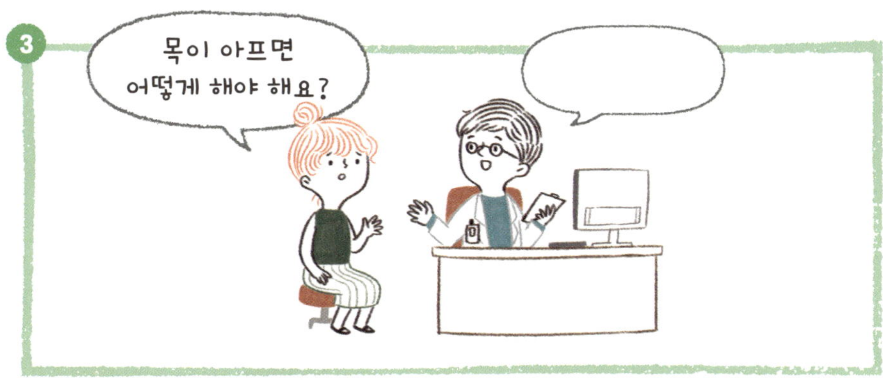
목이 아프면
어떻게 해야 해요?

# 늘 해 주고 싶은 게 참 많아.

I always want to do many things for you.


꼭 하고 싶은 게 있어요.
There's something I really want to do.


갖고 싶은 게 있어요.
There's something I want to have.


물어보고 싶은 게 있어요.
There's something I want to ask.


보여 주고 싶은 게 있어요.
There's something I want to show.


사고 싶은 게 없어요.
There's nothing I want to buy.


먹고 싶은 게 없어요.
There's nothing I want to eat.


하고 싶은 게 아무것도 없어요.
There's nothing I want to do.

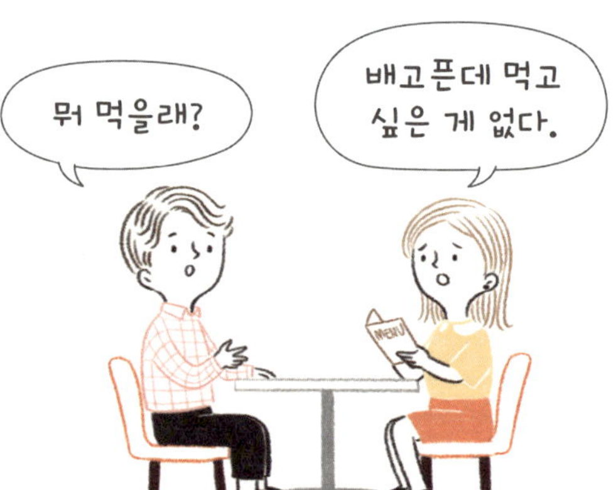

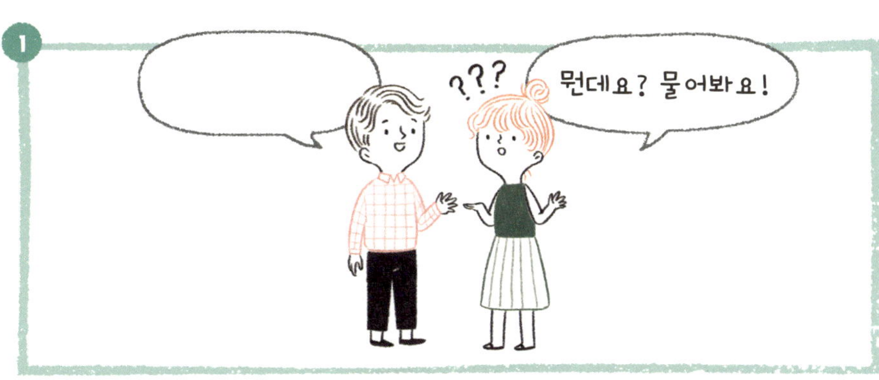

???
뭔데요? 물어봐요!


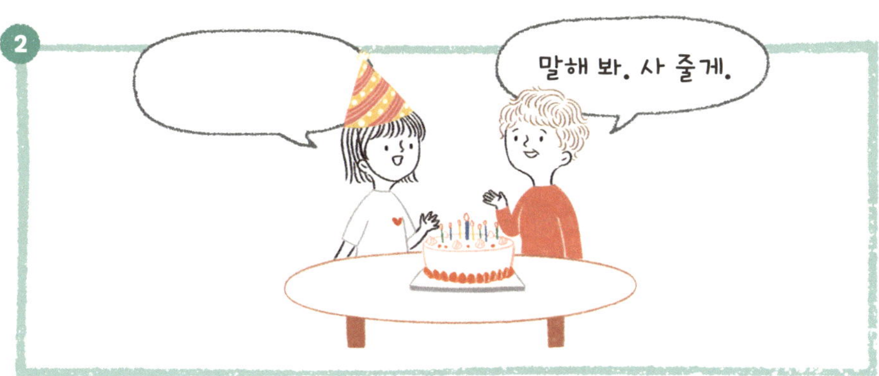

말해 봐. 사 줄게.


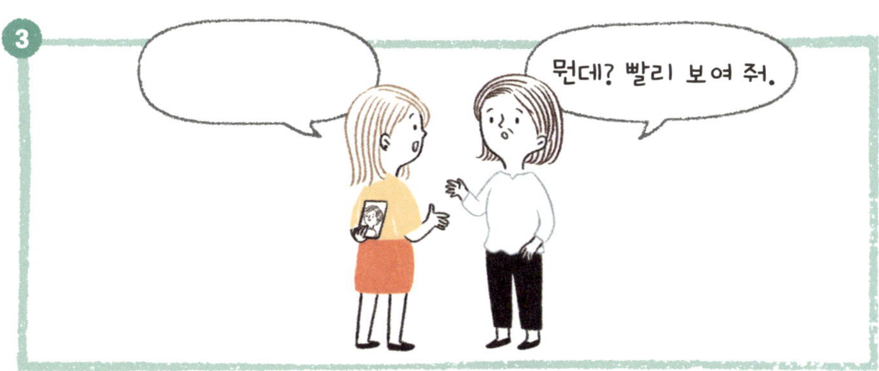

뭔데? 빨리 보여 줘.

## 1  A/V-(으)ㄹ 때

**집에 갈 때 지하철을 타요.**
I take the subway when I go back home.

**고향 음식을 먹을 때 부모님 생각이 납니다.**
I think of my parents when I eat Korean food.

**제가 말을 할 때에는 조용히 해 주세요.**
Please don't talk (lit. be quiet) when I'm speaking.

**A/V-(으)ㄹ 때** is used to describe a moment or to indicate a certain case when an action occurs. It is similar to "when" or "in case of." 에는 can come right after **A/V-(으)ㄹ 때** to emphasize the moment of the an action or the action itself.

## 2  V-고 싶은 게 있다/없다/많다

**너한테 꼭 받고 싶은 게 있어.**
There's something I really want you to get me.

**백화점 세일 때는 사고 싶은 게 많아요.**
There are so many things I want to buy at department stores when they're on sale.

**다른 사람에게는 말하고 싶지 않은 게 있습니다.**
There's something I don't want to tell other people.

**가고 싶은 곳이 있다. / 만나고 싶은 사람이 있다.**
There's somewhere I want to go. / There's someone I want to meet.

**V-고 싶은 게 있다** means that there is something you want to do. When it's a place, you use **V-고 싶은 곳**. When it's a person, you use **V-고 싶은 사람**. When it's something you want to say, you can say **V-고 싶은 말** instead of **V-고 싶은 게**.

남자가 사랑할 때엔 꼭 항상
[꼬 캉상]

곁에 머물면서 늘 해 주고 싶은 게 참 많아
[겨테]　　　　　　　　　　　　　　　[마나]

사랑에 빠질 때엔 내 삶의 모든 걸 다 주고서
[땐] ❶　　[살메] ❷

단 하나 그 맘만 바래 / 사랑에 빠질 때엔
[다 나나] ❸　　　　　　　　　　　　[땐]

❶ When you say 때엔 quickly, it sounds like [땐] because ㅐ and ㅔ sound the same.

❷ When you read 삶 as one syllable, it sounds like [삼]. However, when a vowel comes right after it, you pronounce both the final consonant ㄹ and ㅁ.

　　**Ex** 삶이 [살미], 삶은 [살믄]

❸ When you read 단 하나, it literally sounds like [단 하나]. However, when you read or say it quickly, [ㅎ] sound becomes weaker, and it sounds like [다 나나].



남자가 사랑할 때엔
때에는 (때+에+는)

는 assists the word it is combined with. When 는 comes after a syllable that does not have consonant placed underneath, then 는 can be contracted as ㄴ. For example, 에는 can be contracted as 엔.

**Ex** 1시에는 – 1시엔 / 오후에는 – 오후엔 / 일요일에는 – 일요일엔

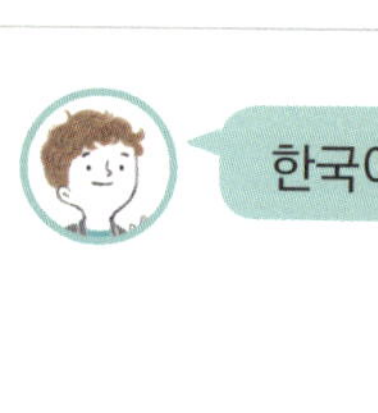
한국어로 '치맥'이 무슨 뜻이에요?

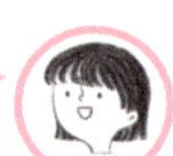
'치킨과 맥주'의 줄임말이에요.

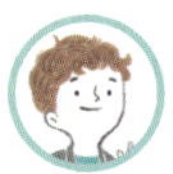
치킨과 맥주가 무슨 관계인데요?

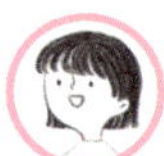
한국에서 치킨을 **먹을 때** 맥주를 함께 마시거든요.

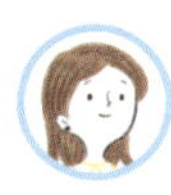
다음 주에 내 생일이야.

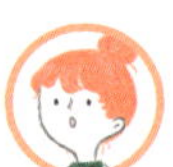
축하해! 혹시 생일 때 **받고 싶은 게 있어**?

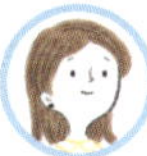
받고 싶은 거? 글쎄 지금은 생각이 안 나는데?

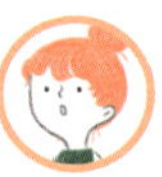
그래? 그럼 생각나면 얘기해 줘. 내가 사 줄게.

---

**치킨** (fried) chicken | **맥주** beer | **줄임말** contracted word | **관계** relevance | **생일** birthday
**생각이 나다** to come up with

# 남자가 사랑할 때

인피니트

관심 없던 사랑 노랠 흥얼거리고
세상 멜로 드라마는 모두 내 얘기 같고
전에 없던 멋을 내며 외모에 신경 쓰고
커피의 쓴 맛을 알아가.

시간은 참 빠르게 가 마음만 조급해져 가고
내 곁에 너를 상상해 혼자만의 영화 찍어.

★ 남자가 사랑할 때엔 꼭 항상
곁에 머물면서 늘 해 주고 싶은 게 참 많아.
사랑에 빠질 땐 내 삶의 모든 걸 다 주고서
단 하나 그 맘만 바래 사랑에 빠질 땐

남자가 사랑할 때엔 남자가 사랑할 때엔

점점 붉어지는 볼에 천천히 떨어지는 내 고개
너만을 바라본 채 I'm On My Way
미친 듯 달려온 내 고백
남자가 사랑할 땐 하나를 위해 열을 잃어도
후회로 끝나지 않게
오늘이 끝인 것처럼 줘 All I Have.

철없는 어린애처럼 괜시리[1] 웃음이 나고
남들과 다른 나라고 스스로 컨트롤을 하지.

1) The standard form of
괜시리 is 괜스레.

★ 반복

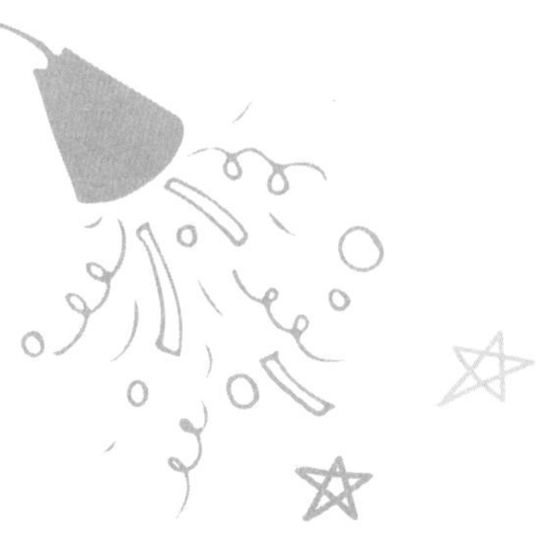

# Man in Love

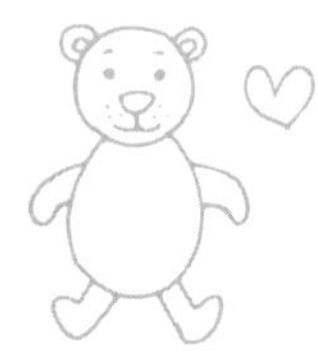

INFINITE

I'm humming the love songs that I used to think silly.
All the love stories sound like my own story.
I care about my style and worry about my look.
I am getting to know the bitterness of the coffee flavor.
(lit. I get to know how bitter the coffee is.)

Time flies, and my heart gets impatient.
I imagine you next to me and create a movie of my own.

★ When a man's in love, he always
Wants to be with the girl and give all he can give.
When I'm in love, I give all I have,
And all I want is love when I'm in love.

When a man's in love. When a man's in love.

My face is slowly blushing. My head is slowly sinking .
You're the only one I look at. I'm on my way.
I madly ran to you with a confession.
When a man's in love, he doesn't mind losing ten to win one.
He would give all he has as if it was his last day.
He doesn't want to regret not giving.
All I have.

I keep laughing just like a little boy.
And I tell myself, "I'm a different guy."

★ Repeat

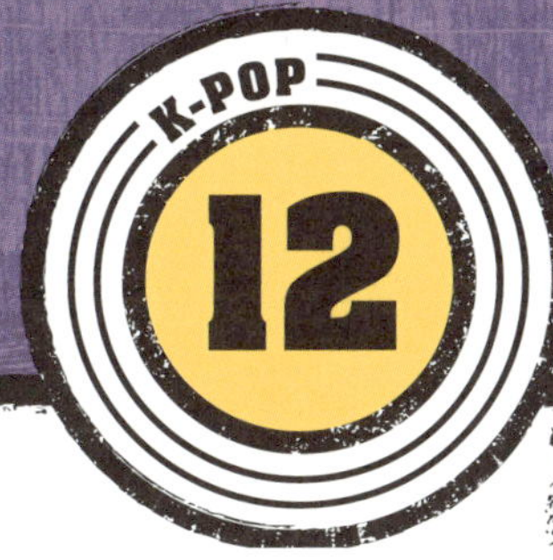


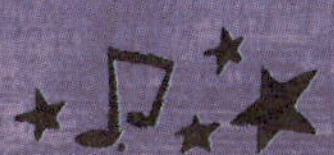

**러블리즈 (Lovelyz)**

# Ah-Choo

Ah-Choo 널 보면 재채기가 나올 것 같아.
너만 보면 해 주고픈 얘기가 참 많아.
나의 입술이 너무 간지러워 참기가 힘들어.
Ah-Choo 내 맘에 꽃가루가 떠다니나 봐.
널 위해서 해 주고픈 일들이 참 많아.
나의 마음이 내 사랑이 더 이상은
삼키기 힘들어.

## About the singer and the song

Lovelyz is an eight-member girl group with a girly pop image. Their song <Ah-Choo> was released in 2015 and was noticed by many people. <Ah-Choo> is the sound people make when they sneeze. Just like it is hard to control your sneezing, the song says that it is hard to control your feelings toward the person you love. It describes the shy love of a girl well.

# 내 맘에 꽃가루가 떠다니나 봐.

I think there is a flower blossoming in my heart.

자나 봐.
I think she/he is sleeping.

싸우나 봐.
I think they are in a fight.

일이 늦게 끝나나 봐.
I think she/he works late these days.

요즘 열심히 공부하나 봐.
It looks like you are studying hard these days.

길이 많이 막히나 봐.
I think the traffic is heavy.

직접 만들어 오나 봐.
I guess she/he is making it herself/himself.

싸게 파나 봐.
I think they are selling it for a lower price.

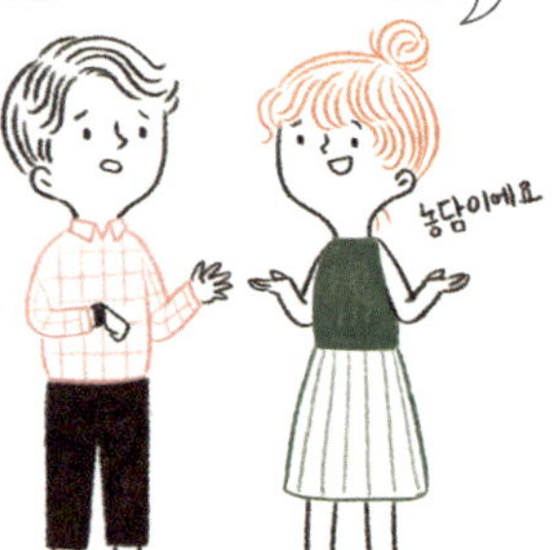

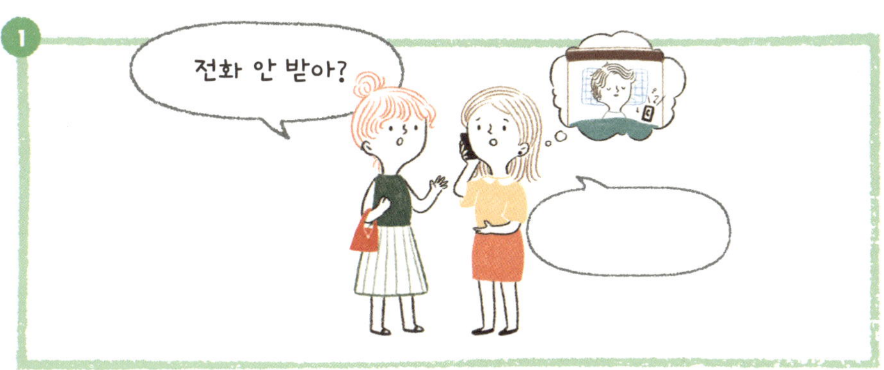


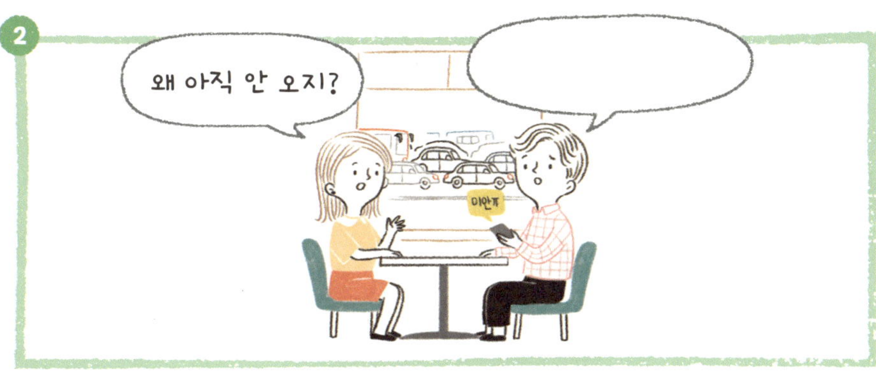


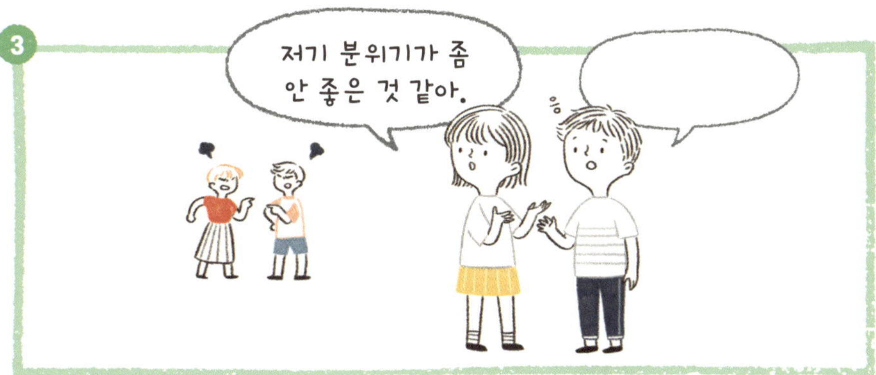


**아직** yet | **분위기** atmosphere

# 참기가 힘들어.

It is hard to stand.

취직하기가 힘들어.
It is hard to get a job.

혼자 하기가 힘들어.
It is hard to do by myself.

아침에 일찍 일어나기가 힘들어.
It is hard to get up early in the morning.

좋은 집을 구하기가 힘들어.
It is hard to get a nice house.

바빠서 얼굴 보기가 힘들어.
It is hard to catch up with her/him
because I'm so busy.

시끄러워서 집중하기가 힘들어.
It is so noisy that it is hard to concentrate.

다리가 아파서 오래 서 있기가 힘들어.
It is hard to stand for a long period of time
because my legs hurt.

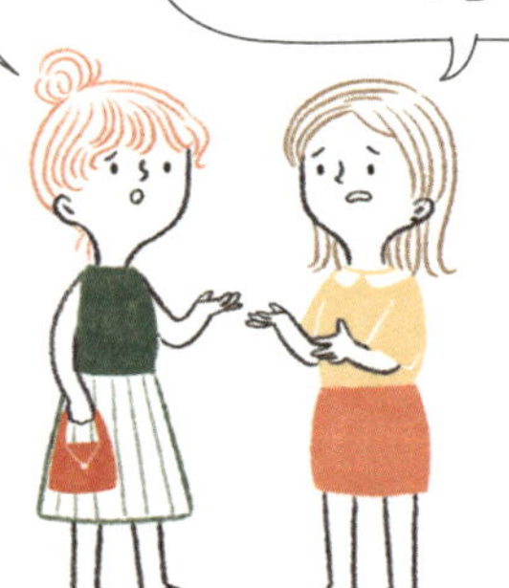

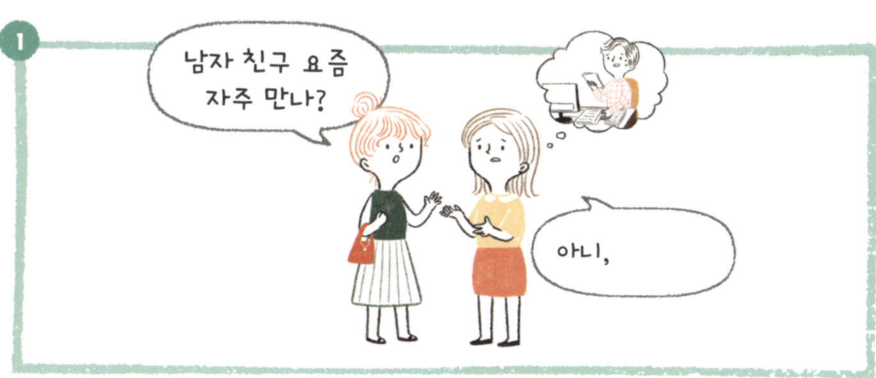

남자 친구 요즘 자주 만나?
아니,


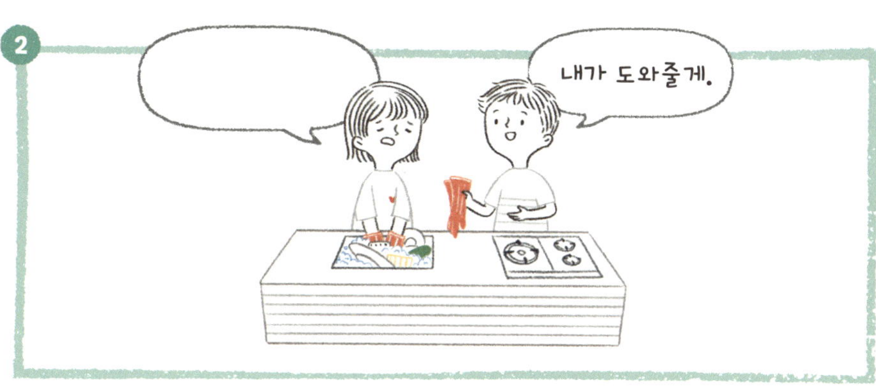

내가 도와줄게.


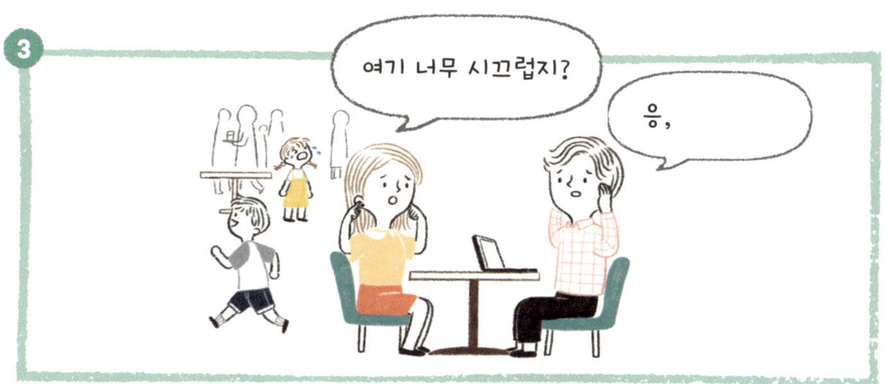

여기 너무 시끄럽지?
응,

 ## V-나 보다

밖에 비가 **오나 봐요**. 사람들이 우산을 쓰고 가요.
I think it's raining outside. People are carrying umbrellas.

친구가 지금 **자나 봐요**. 전화를 안 받아요.
I think my friend is sleeping. She/He is not answering the phone.

둘이 **싸웠나 봐요**. 서로 말을 안 해요.
I think they were in a fight. They are not talking to each other.

**V-나 보다** is used when you make an assumption about someone's behavior or a situation by observing a current situation. When you make an assumption about a past incident, you use **V-았/었나 보다**. **V-는 것 같다** is a similar expression but when you use **V-나 보다**, a supportive idea is required for the assumption you are making.

 ## V-기(가) 힘들다

저 지금 전화 **받기가 힘들어요**.
It's hard to answer the phone right now.

미안, 오늘은 **만나기 힘들어**.
Sorry. It's hard to meet up today.

너무 더워서 밖에서 **운동하기가 힘들어요**.
It's too hot to exercise outdoors.

**오늘은 만나기 힘들어요. = 오늘은 만나기 어려워요.**

**V-기 힘들다** means that something is hard to be done. It is similar to "it's hard to ~." In the expression, 힘들다 can be replaced with 어렵다.

Ah-Choo 널 보면 재채기가 나올 것 같아.
[나올 꺼 까타]

너만 보면 해 주고픈 얘기가 참 많아.
[마나]

나의 입술이 너무 간지러워 참기가 힘들어.
[나에]　　　　　　　　[참끼]가]★

Ah-Choo 내 맘에 꽃가루가 떠다니나 봐.
[꼬까루가]

널 위해서 해 주고픈 일들이 참 많아.
[마나]

나의 마음이 내 사랑이 더 이상은 삼키기 힘들어.
[나에]

★ The lax consonants ㄱ, ㄷ, ㅅ, and ㅈ make tensed sounds like [ㄲ, ㄸ, ㅆ, ㅉ] when they come after the nasal final consonants ㅁ and ㄴ that are placed under the stem of a word.

**Ex** 참고 있다 [참꼬 이따], 참다 [참따], 찾습니다 [참씀니다], 참지 마 [참찌 마]



너만 보면 해 주고픈 얘기가 참 많아.
주고 싶은

V-고프다 is a contracted form of V-고 싶다, and it means that you want to do something. V-고 싶다 is more often used in conversations, and V-고프다 is often used in poems and lyrics.

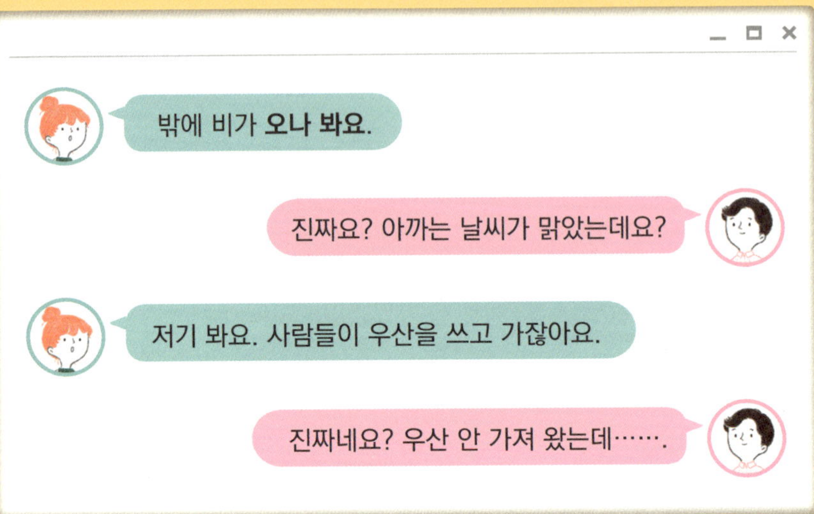


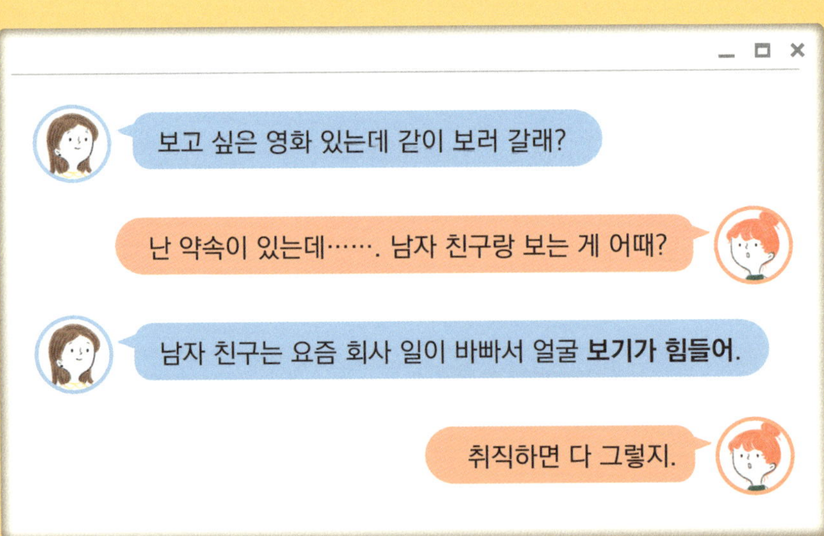


아까 a while ago | 날씨가 맑다 The weather is sunny. | 우산 umbrella | 가져오다 to bring | 회사 일 work
취직하다 to get a job

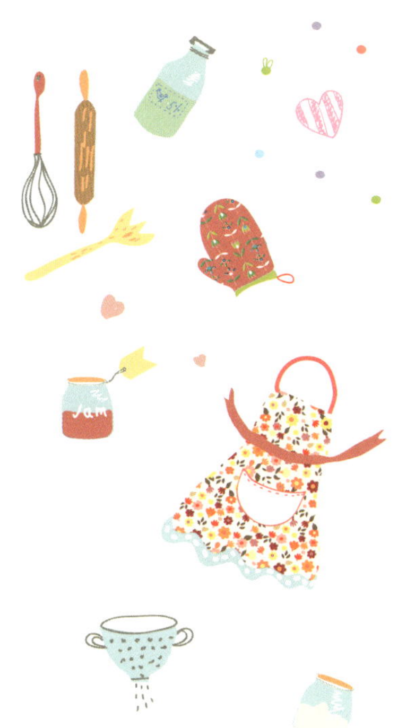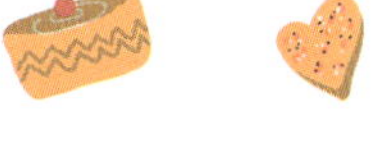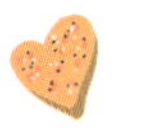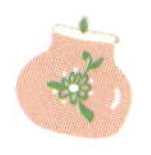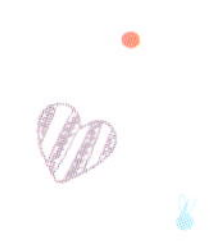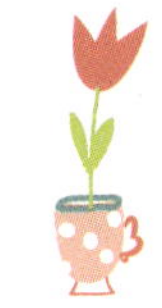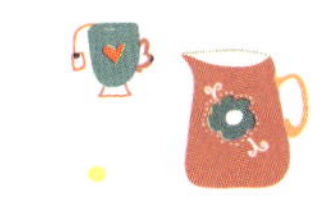

# Ah-Choo

러블리즈

맛있는 걸 해 주고 싶은
그런 사람이 난 생겼어.
아직 요리는 잘 못하지만
나 연습하고 있어요.
나 그댈 위해 몰래 감춰 놓은
애교도 있는 걸
매일 지루하지 않게
웃게 해 줄 텐데.
너는 내 맘 모르지.

★ Ah-Choo 널 보면 재채기가 나올 것 같아.
너만 보면 해 주고픈 얘기가 참 많아.
나의 입술이 너무 간지러워 참기가 힘들어.
Ah-Choo 내 맘에 꽃가루가 떠다니나봐.
널 위해서 해 주고픈 일들이 참 많아.
나의 마음이 내 사랑이 더 이상은 삼키기 힘들어.

다정하게 깨우고 싶은
그런 사람이 난 생겼어.
아침잠이 좀 많긴 해도
잘 일어날 수 있어요.
그 사람이 막 지쳐 보일 때면
내가 더 슬픈 걸
혹시 내가 필요할 땐 거기 있어 줄게.
너는 내 맘 모르지.

★ 반복

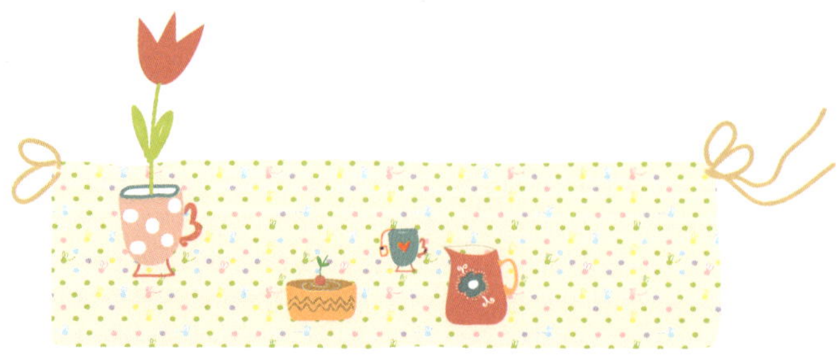

# Ah-Choo

Lovelyz

I found someone
I would like to make nice food for.
I'm not good at cooking yet,
but I'm practicing.
I also have some sweetness
that you don't know yet.
I would make you smile every day.
You would never get bored.
You don't know my heart, do you?

★ Ah-Choo, I feel like to sneeze when I see you.
There's so much to share with you when I see you.
My lips are tickling. It's hard to stand.
Ah-Choo, I think there's a flower blossoming in my heart.
There are so many things I want to do for you.
My heart and love have become too big to hide now.

I found someone
I would like to wake up warmly.
I am not a morning person,
but I can wake up for you.
When I see him down,
It saddens me even more.
I will be there for you whenever you need me.
You don't know my heart, do you?

★ Repeat

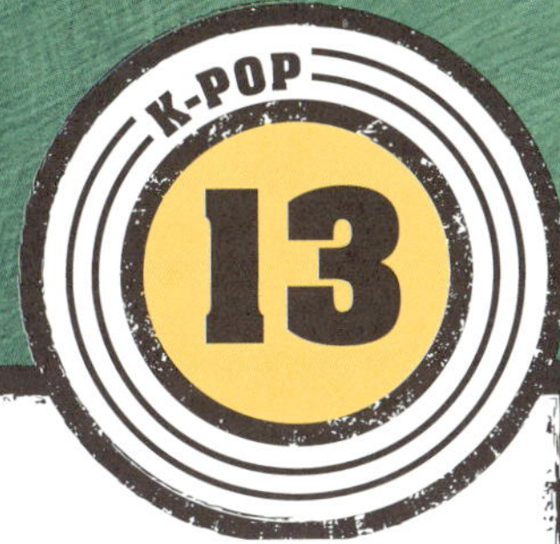

**FT아일랜드(FT Island)**

# 사랑 사랑 사랑

안녕, 내 사랑 사랑 사랑

잘 가요, 내 사랑 사랑 사랑

차오르는 나의 눈물이 온몸을 적셔도

이제는 goodbye, goodbye, goodbye

나를 떠나 부디 행복해.

한 걸음 한 걸음 네가 멀어진다.

## About the singer and the song

FT Island debuted in 2007 as a five-member boy group. They are different from other boy groups in that they perform musical instruments on stage while other groups mainly dance. The main vocalist Lee Hong Gi's powerful singing and the other members' marvelous performances are widely loved. The song <사랑 사랑 사랑 (Love Love Love)> was released in 2010. It is about a man who is trying to let go of his beloved after a  breakup.

# 나의 눈물이 온 몸을 적셔도

Even though I'm soaked with a flood of tears

피곤해도 씻고 자.
Wash up before you go to sleep even if you are tired.

바빠도 밥은 먹고 나가.
Eat before you leave even if you are busy.

비가 와도 축구하러 갈 거야.
I'm going to play soccer even if it rains.

힘들어도 포기 안 할 거야.
I'm not going to give up even if it's hard.

배고파도 밤에 음식 먹으면 안 돼.
Don't eat at night even if you are hungry.

무슨 일이 있어도 끝까지 할 거야.
I will do it till the end no matter
how challenging it is.

재미없어도 끝까지 들어 주세요.
Please listen until I'm done even if it's not fun.

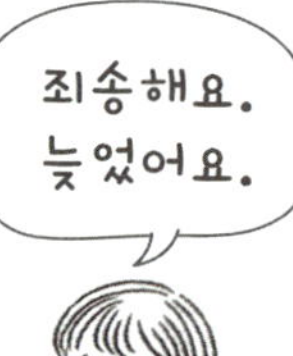


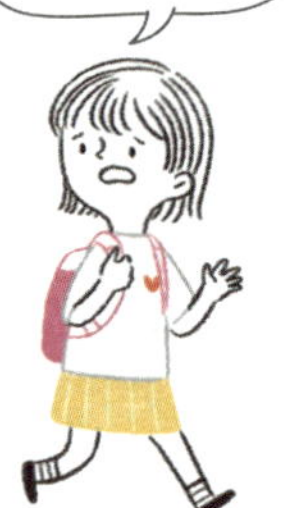


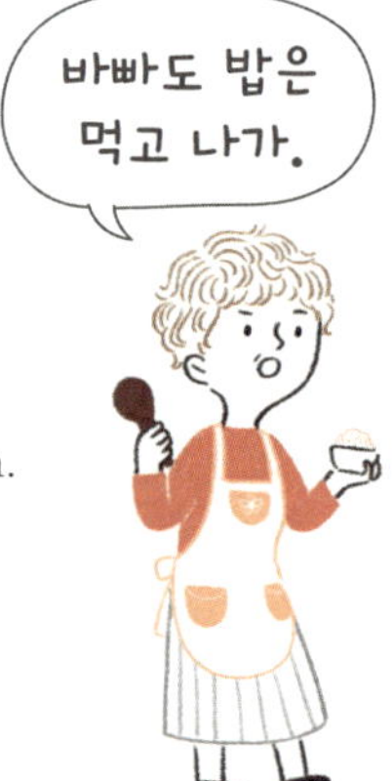

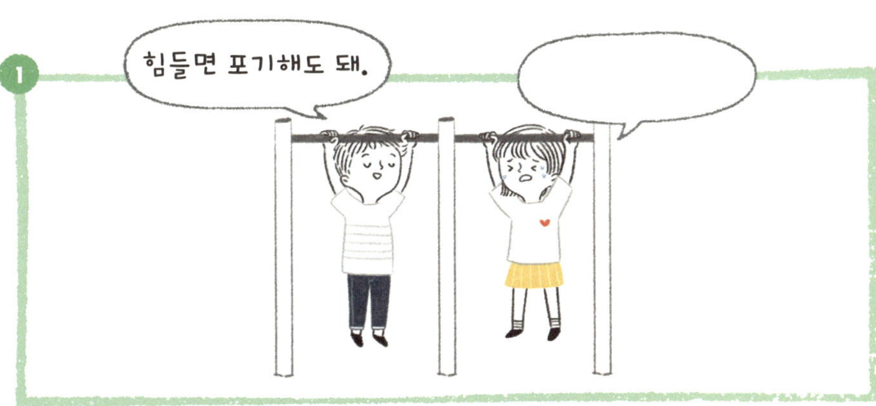
힘들면 포기해도 돼.

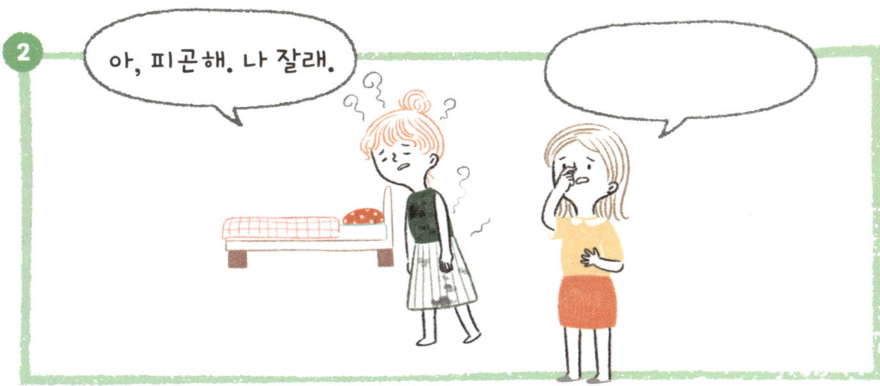
아, 피곤해. 나 잘래.

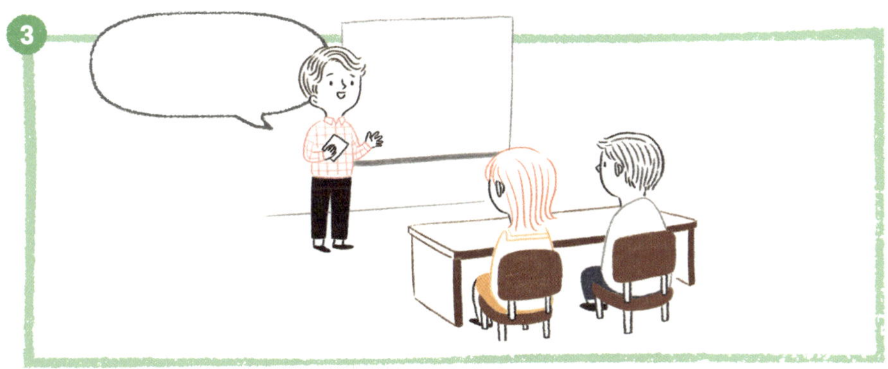

# 한 걸음 한 걸음 네가 멀어진다.

One step, two steps, you're getting farther.

네가 좋아졌어.
I'm starting to like you.

기분이 나빠졌어.
I got upset.

날씨가 추워졌어.
It became cold.

스마트폰이 이상해졌어.
My smartphone got weird.

인터넷이 느려졌어.
The Internet got so slow.

지갑이 없어졌어.
I lost my wallet.

친구가 몰라보게 예뻐졌어.
My friend got so pretty.

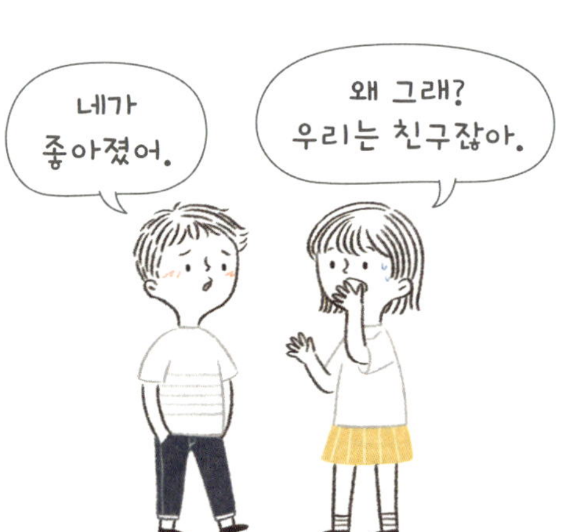

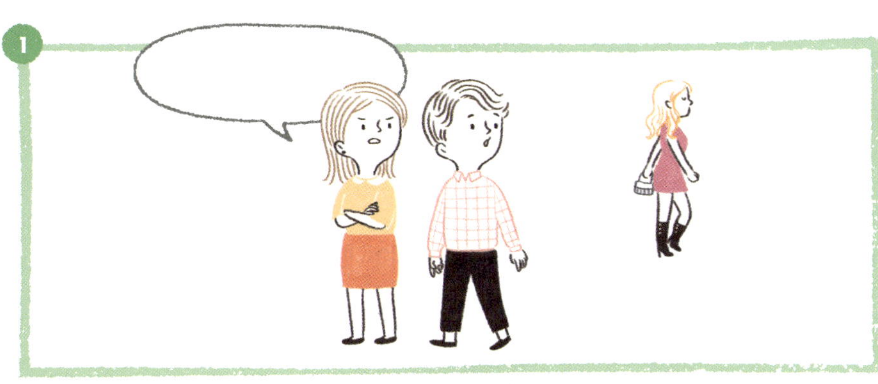

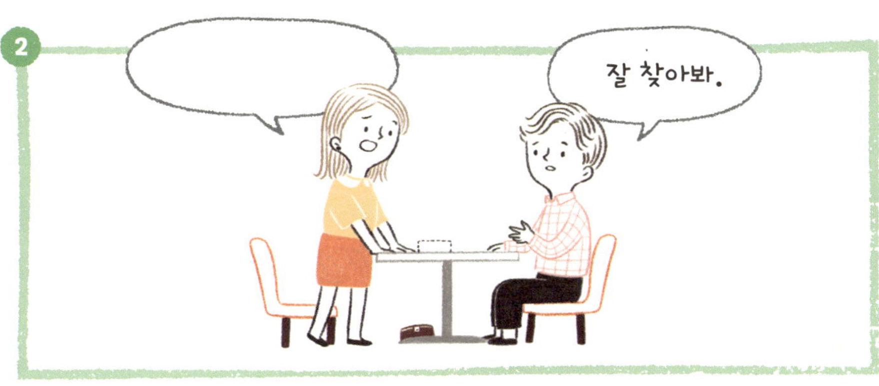


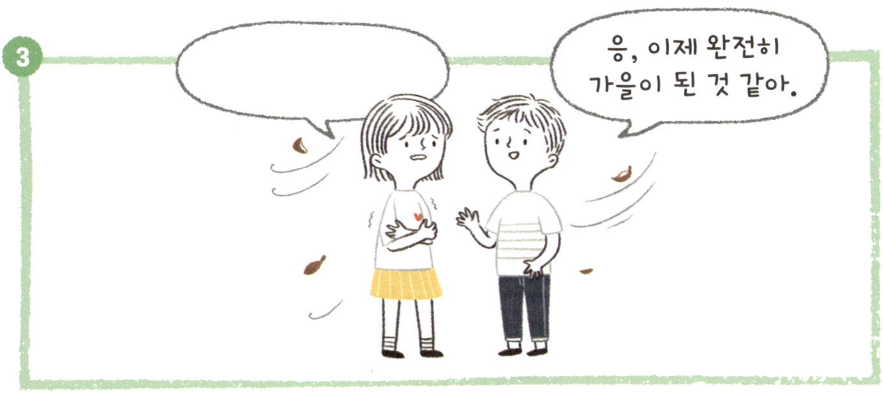


**찾다** to look for | **이제** now | **완전히** truly, completely, perfectly | **가을** fall

## A/V-아도/어도

### 조금 **힘들어도** 참으세요.
Be a little more patient even if it's hard.

### 제 동생은 **아파도** 병원에 안 가요.
My brother doesn't go to see the doctor even when he's sick.

### 이 부분은 **공부해도** 잘 모르겠어요.
I don't understand this part even though I'm studying hard.

**A/V-아도/어도** is used when the consequence of an action or somebody's behavior turns out to be different from the way you expected it to be. It's similar to "even if" or "even though."

## A-아지다/어지다

### 취직하고 **바빠졌어요**.
I got busy after getting my job.

### 운동하고 나서 **날씬해졌어요**.
I got slim after I started to work out.

### 나이가 들어서 눈이 **나빠졌어요**.
My eyesight got bad as I got older.

**A-아지다/어지다** is used to indicate a change in a situation. It is similar to "get + adjective" or "become + adjective." The phrase is often used with the past tense **A-아졌어요/어졌어요** to tell the change in an object.

안녕 내 사랑 사랑 사랑
[사랑] ❶

잘 가요 내 사랑 사랑 사랑

차오르는 나의 눈물이 온몸을 적셔도
[나에] [눈무리] ❷

이제는 good bye good bye good bye

나를 떠나 부디 행복해
[행보캐]

한 걸음 한 걸음 네가 멀어진다
[니] 가 ❸

❶ 사랑 is literally pronounced like [사랑]. Be careful not to mispronounce it like [싸랑].

❷ 눈물이 is literally pronounced like [눈무리]. Be careful not to mispronounce it like [눙무리].

❸ 네(you) and 내(my) sound the same, so people often pronounce 네(you) like [니] to keep it from being mistaken for 내(my).



안녕. (Bye.) / 잘 가. (Bye.) / 다음에 또 봐. (See you again.)
연락할게. (I'll call you later.)

The above expressions are those you use when you say, "Goodbye." These are casual expressions to use between friends or close people who are younger.

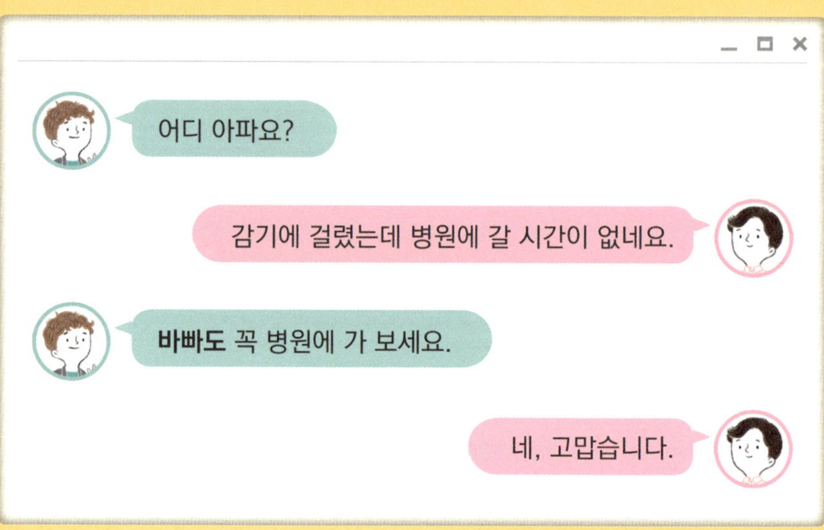


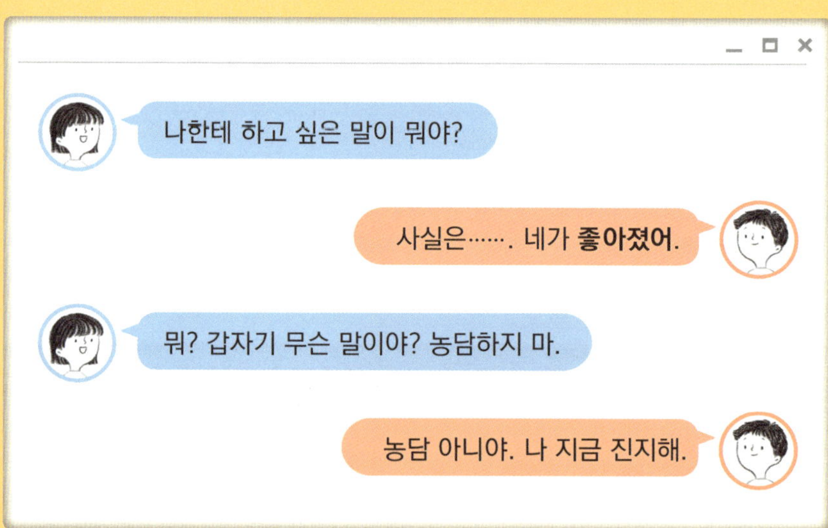


**감기에 걸리다** to catch a cold | **병원** hospital | **갑자기** all of a sudden | **농담하다** to joke | **진지하다** to be serious

# 사랑 사랑 사랑

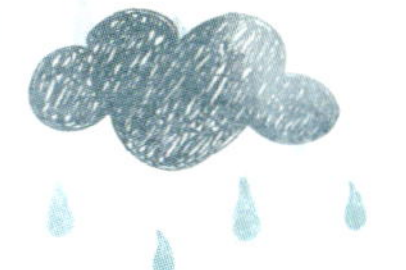
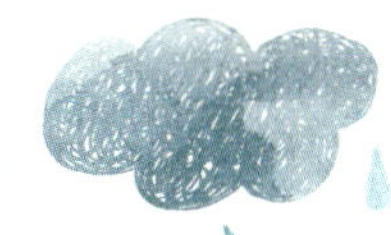

FT아일랜드

심장이 멈춘다 내 숨이 멎는다 네가 떠난다.
가슴이 시리게 너만 사랑했다 행복했었다.
네 남자로 태어나서 한없이 사랑했었다.
그걸로 됐다 눈물 꾹 참아보련다.
빗물이 온몸을 적신다.
또 애써 고개를 들어 하늘을 바라본다.
내 눈에 들어간 비가
너를 생각하며 참고 또 참아왔던
눈물을 대신해 준다.

★ 미치도록 사랑해서 너무나 행복했었다.
사랑한 추억을 내게 준 너를 보낸다.
안녕 내 사랑 사랑 사랑
잘 가요 내 사랑 사랑 사랑
차오르는 나의 눈물이 온몸을 적셔도
이제는 good bye good bye good bye
나를 떠나 부디 행복해.
한 걸음 한 걸음 네가 멀어진다.

말없이 술잔을 채운다.
힘겹게 손에 들며 한숨을 뱉어 본다.
한 잔을 마셔 본다.
너를 생각하며 참고 또 참아왔던
눈물을 함께 삼킨다.

★ 반복

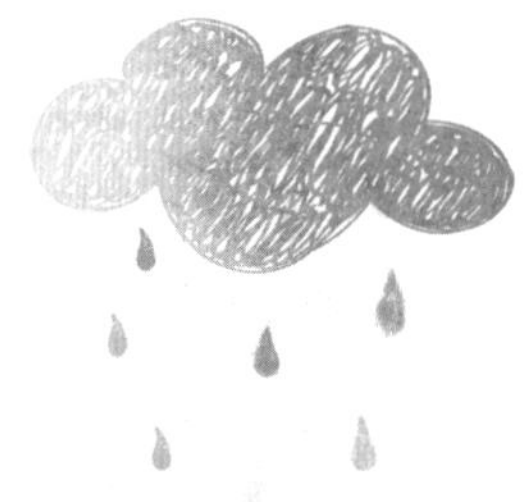

# Love Love Love

FT Island

My heart stops. My breathing dies. You are leaving.
I was painfully in love with you. I was happy.
I was born to be your man and gave all I could give.
That's enough to me. I'm not going to cry.
Raindrops fall all over me.
I try to look up at the sky again.
The raindrops fell in my eyes.
Became my tears and comfort my heart.
Tears that I've been holding back.

★ I was crazily in love and was so happy.
You gave me memories of love, and I'll let you go.
Goodbye, my love, love, love.
Adieu, my love, love, love.
Even though I'm soaked with a flood of tears,
Now, goodbye, goodbye, goodbye.
Please be happy after you leave me.
One step, two steps, you're getting farther.

Quietly, I fill the glass with alcohol.
I barely grab it and sigh.
I slowly drink it
and drink my tears as well.
My tears that I've been holding back.

★ Repeat

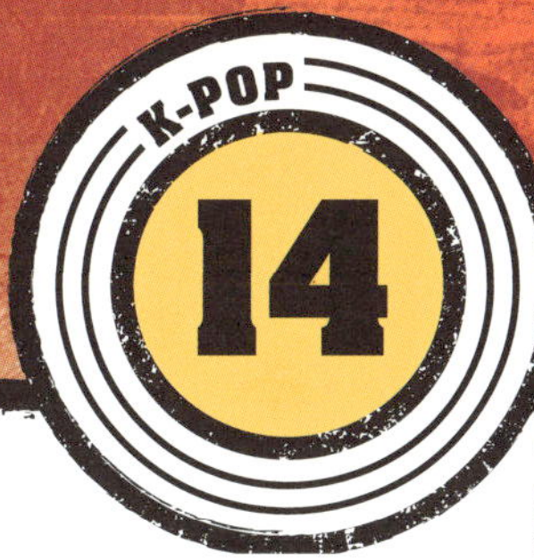




# 너의 모든 순간

물끄러미 너를 들여다보곤 해.

그것 말고는 아무것도 할 수 없어서

너의 모든 순간 그게 나였으면 좋겠다.

생각만 해도 가슴이 차올라

나는 온통 너로

## About the singer and the song

Ballads are among the most popular types of music in Korea. Sung Si Kyung has a solid position in this genre and is called "the prince of ballads" in Korea. <너의 모든 순간 (Every Moment of You)> is on the soundtrack of the Korean drama <별에서 온 그대 (My Love from the star)>, which was a huge hit in Asia. You can enjoy Sung Si Kyung's soft voice and get a taste of Korean ballads by listening to the song.

# 생각만 해도 가슴이 차올라.

I'm overwhelmed just by thinking of you.

생각만 해도 떨려.
I'm so nervous when I even think of it.

생각만 해도 기분이 좋아.
It's so good when I even think of it.

생각만 해도 짜증 나.
I get so annoyed when I even think of it.

생각만 해도 무서워.
I get scared when I even think of it.

생각만 해도 끔찍해.
It's awful to even think of it.

생각만 해도 눈물이 나.
I burst into tears even when I just think of it.

생각만 해도 화가 나.
I get upset even when I think of it.

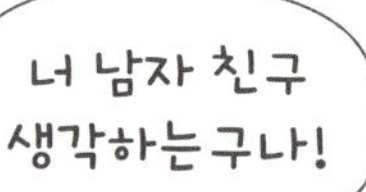


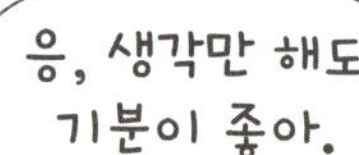


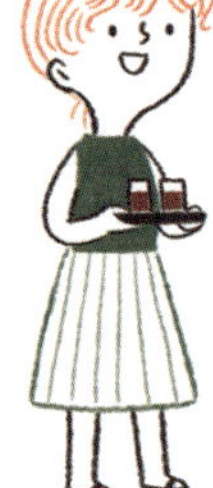
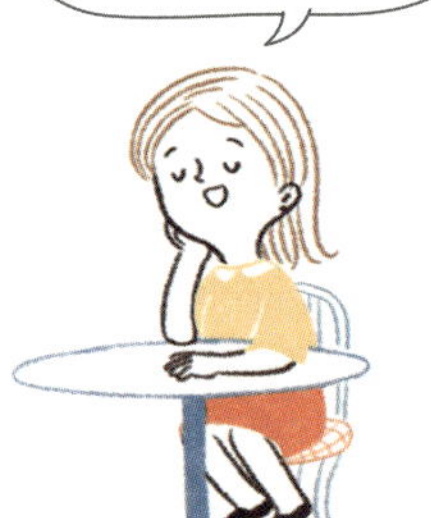

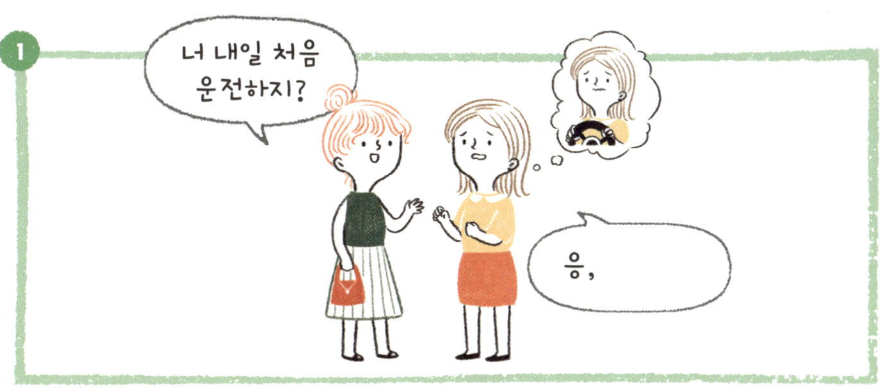


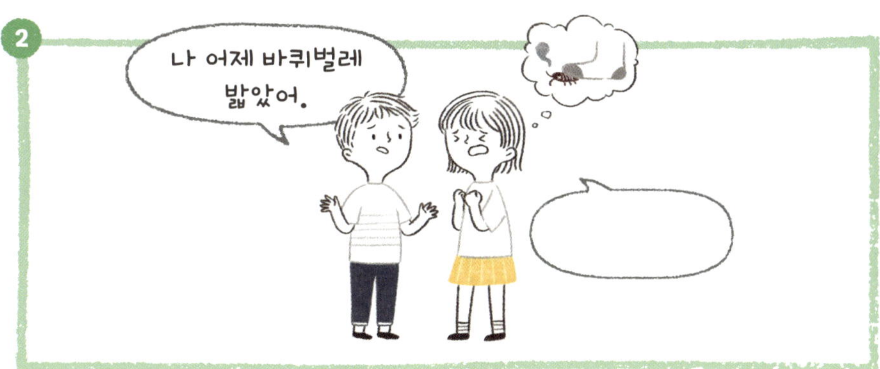


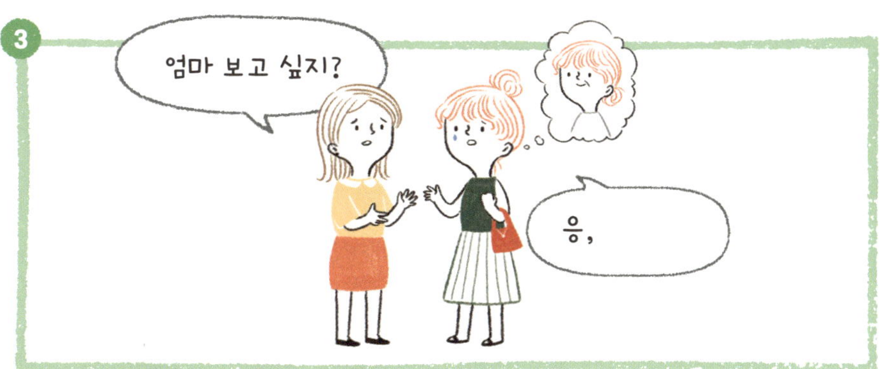


**처음** for the first time | **운전하다** to drive | **바퀴벌레** cockroach | **밟다** to step on

# 물끄러미 너를 들여다보곤 해.

Sometimes I gaze at you.

이런 생각을 하곤 해.
Sometimes I think this way.

가끔 상상하곤 해.
Sometimes I imagine it.

이런 실수를 자주 하곤 해.
I often make such mistakes.

집에 음식이 없으면 시켜 먹곤 해.
I order food when there's no food at home.

요즘도 가끔 연락하곤 해.
We still keep in touch sometimes.

주말에는 늦잠을 자곤 해.
I usually wake up late on the weekend.

일할 때 음악을 듣곤 해.
I listen to music when I work.

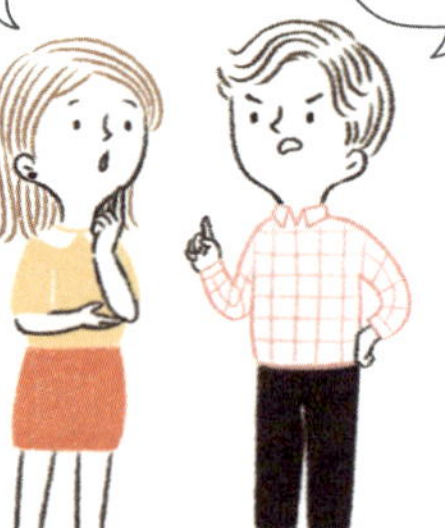

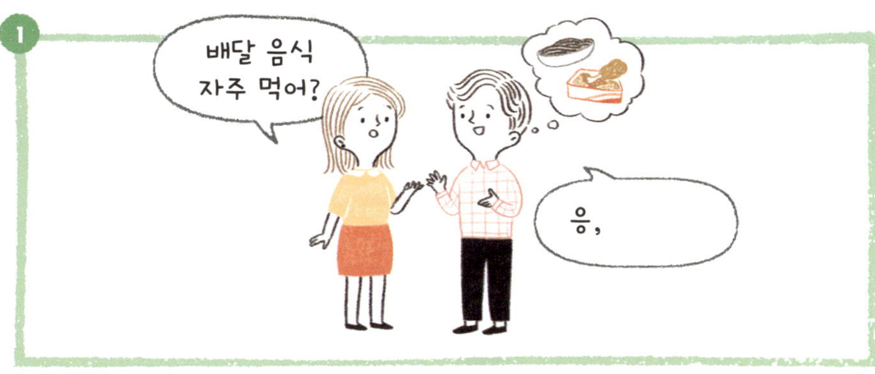


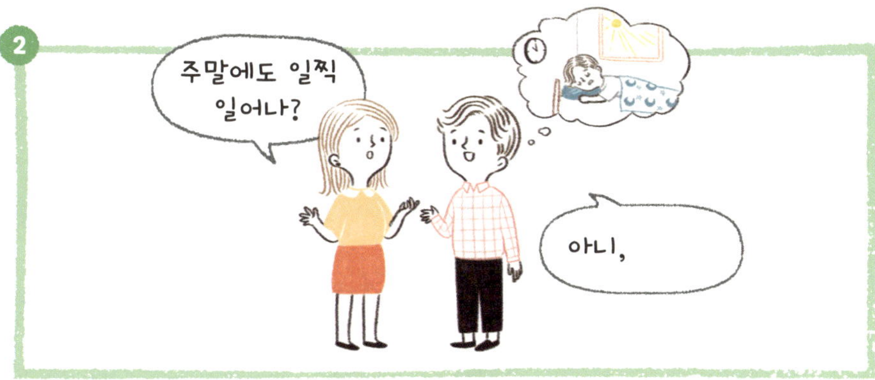


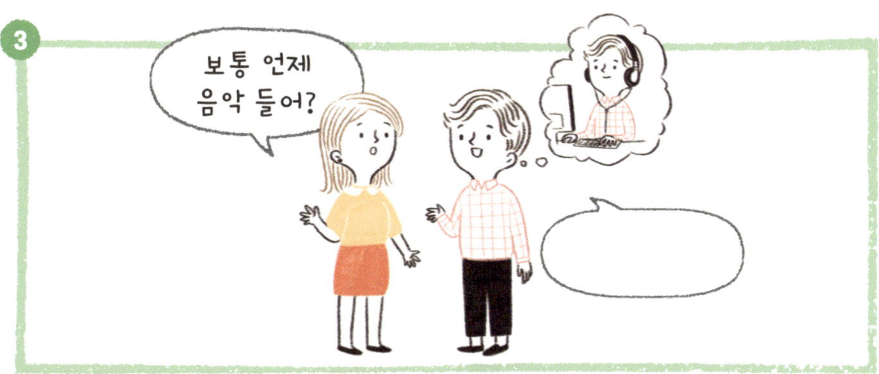


**배달 음식** delivery food | **자주** often | **일어나다** to wake up

# 그게 나였으면 좋겠다.

I wish that (person) were me.

부자였으면 좋겠다.
I wish I were rich.

내 남자 친구였으면 좋겠다.
I wish you were my boyfriend.

몸이 10개였으면 좋겠다.
I wish there were more hours in a day.
(lit. I wish I had 10 bodies.)

진짜였으면 좋겠다.
I wish it were true.

이게 꿈이었으면 좋겠다.
I wish this was a dream.

오늘이 금요일이었으면 좋겠다.
I wish it was Friday today.

여기가 우리 집이었으면 좋겠다.
I wish this was our home.

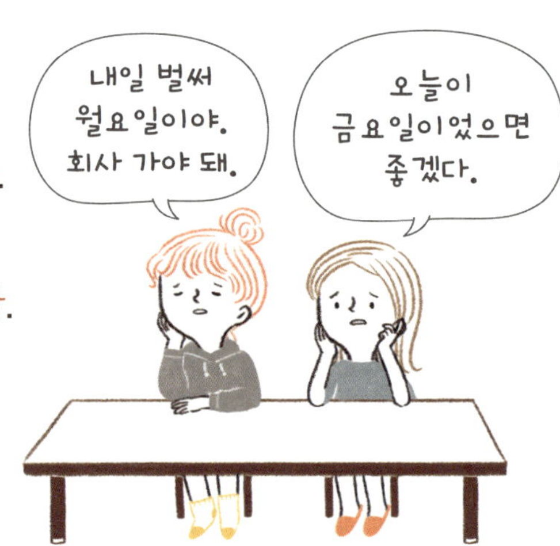

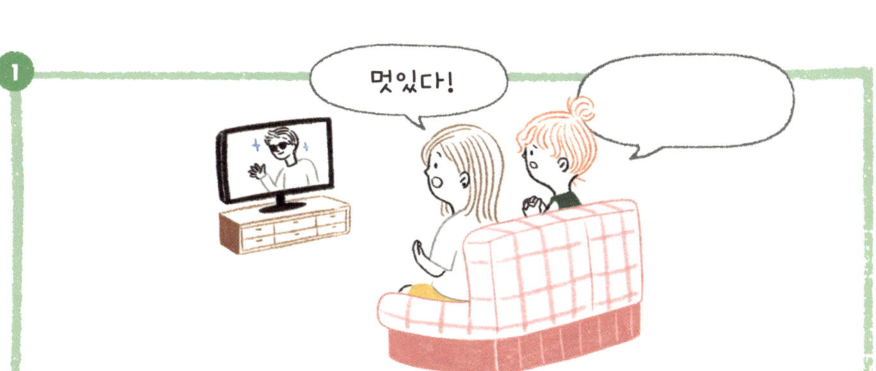
멋있다!

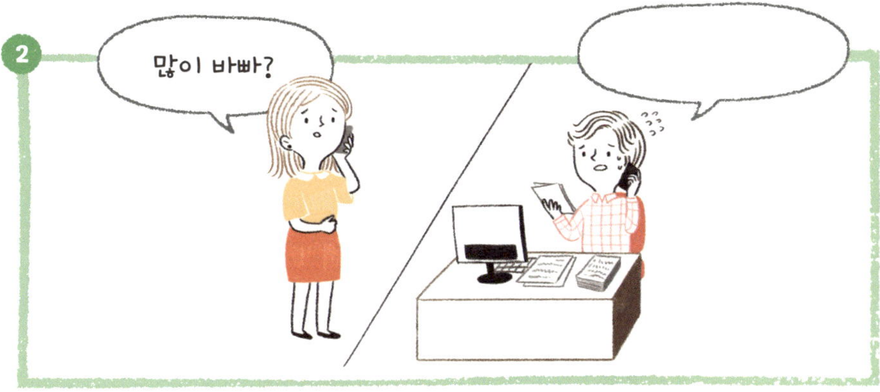
많이 바빠?

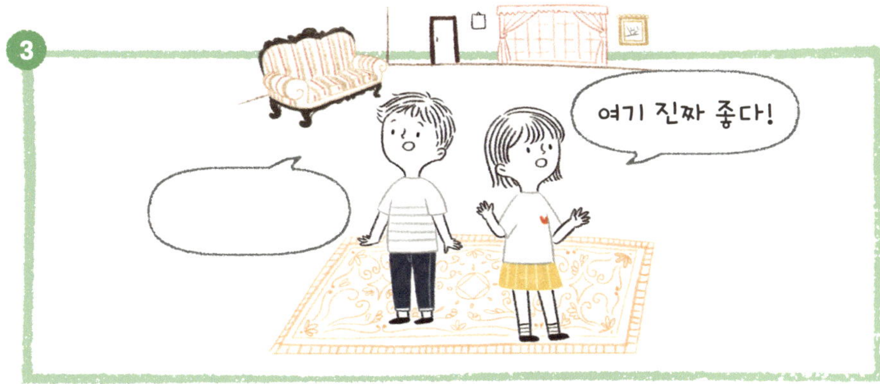
여기 진짜 좋다!

 ## 생각만 해도 + A

**이번 휴가는 바다로 갈 거야. 생각만 해도 좋아.**
I'm going to go to the beach this vacation. I feel good when I even think of it.

**다음 달에 K-Pop 콘서트가 있어. 생각만 해도 떨려.**
There's a K-Pop concert next month. I'm so excited to even think of it.

**생각만 해도** is used when you feel as if you've done something that you haven't really done. It's similar to "just to think of ~."

 ## V-곤 하다

**어릴 때 가족들과 영화를 보러 가곤 했어요.**
I used to watch movies with my family.

**지금도 가족들이 함께 모여 TV로 영화를 보곤 해요.**
We still watch movies on TV together.

**V-곤 하다** is used to describe an action that has been done by the speaker repetitively for a certain period of time. The verb **하다**'s tense tells whether the action described in the phrase happened habitually in the past or is still done in the present.

 ## N이었으면/였으면 좋겠다

**(나는) 오늘이 일요일이었으면 좋겠다.**
(I) wish it was Sunday today.

**(나는) 네가 내 여자 친구였으면 좋겠다.**
(I) wish you were my girlfriend.

**N이었으면/였으면 좋겠다** is used to express the speaker's hope or wish. It is similar to "I wish." The subject of this phrase is always "I" but in spoken Korean, we often say it without "I."

물끄러미 너를 들여다보곤 해.
[드려다보고내]

그것 말고는 아무것도 할 수 없어서
[그건말고는]❶ [아무거또] [할 쑤]❷ [업써서]

너의 모든 순간 그게 나였으면 좋겠다.
[너에] [조 케따]

생각만 해도 가슴이 차올라 나는 온통 너로
[생강만]

❶ When ㄴ or ㅁ comes after a word that has the final consonant [ㄱ], [ㄷ], or [ㅂ], these final consonants become nasalized, and they sound like [ㅇ]([ŋ]), [ㄴ], and [ㅁ].

> **Ex** [ㄱ] → [ㅇ]: 생각 나 [생강 나], [ㄷ] → [ㄴ]: 받는 사람 [반는 사람],
> [ㅂ] → [ㅁ]: 밥 먹어 [밤 머거]

❷ When ㅅ comes after the word that ends with –(으)ㄹ, it sounds like [ㅆ].

> **Ex** 할 수 있다 [할 쑤 이따], 먹을 사람 [머글 싸람]

---

어순 **ORDER OF WORDS**

생각만 해도 가슴이 차올라 나는 온통 너로
verb    subject

⇒ 나는 생각만 해도 온통 너로 가슴이 차올라.
subject                        verb

The order of words in Korean is more flexible than in many other languages. Word order is even more flexible in song lyrics. There is a simple rule in spoken Korean: the subject usually comes at the beginning of the sentence while the verb or adjective comes at the end.

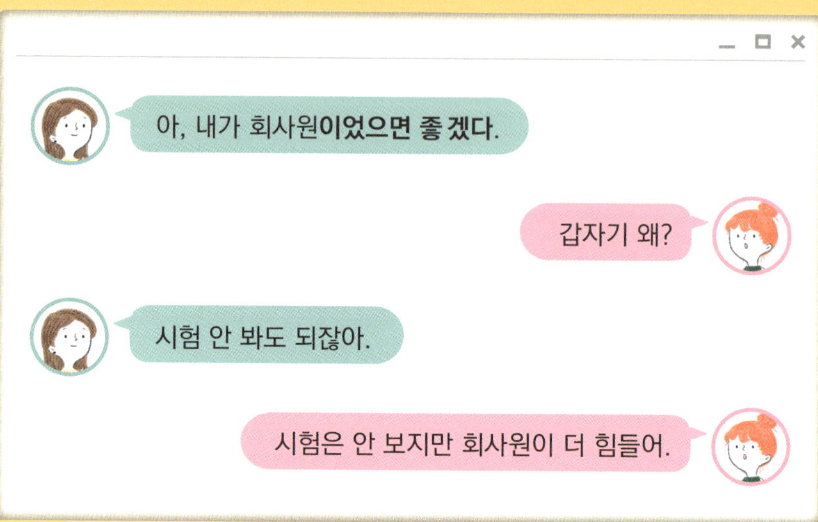


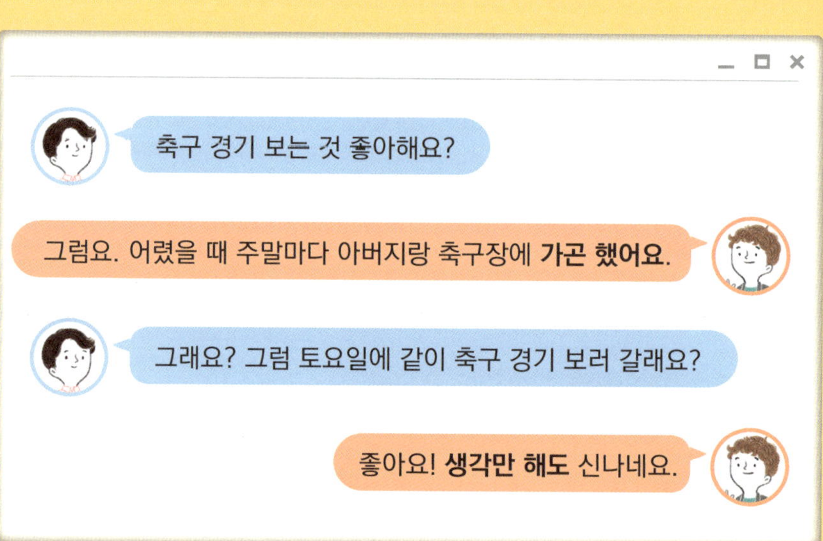


**회사원** office worker | **시험** (take) test | **축구** soccer | **경기** match | **어렸을 때** when one was young
**신나다** to be excited

# 너의 모든 순간

성시경

이윽고 내가 한눈에 너를 알아봤을 때
모든 건 분명 달라지고 있었어.
내 세상은 널 알기 전과 후로 나뉘어

네가 숨 쉬면 따스한 바람이 불어와.
네가 웃으면 눈부신 햇살이 비춰.

거기 있어 줘서 그게 너라서
가끔 내 어깨에 가만히 기대 주어서
나는 있잖아 정말 빈틈없이 행복해.
너를 따라서 시간은 흐르고 멈춰.

물끄러미 너를 들여다보곤 해.
그것 말고는 아무것도 할 수 없어서
너의 모든 순간 그게 나였으면 좋겠다.
생각만 해도 가슴이 차올라 나는 온통 너로

# Every Moment of You

Sung Si Kyung

When I recognized you at last,
Everything was clearly changing.
My life has changed since I met you.

Your breath is like a warm breeze.
Your smile is like the sun's rays.

Because you are the one who's there for me.
Because you lean on my shoulder sometimes.
You know, I'm perfectly happy.
My time goes and stops as I follow you.

Sometimes I gaze at you
Because that's all I can possibly do.
Every moment of you, I wish you would think of me.
I'm overwhelmed just thinking of you.

# Hands Up

울려 퍼지는 음악에 맞춰

Everyone put your hands up and get your drinks up.

온 세상이 함께 미쳐

Everyone put your hands up and get your drinks up.
Now, put your hands Up. Put your hands up.
Put put put put.

볼륨을 높여, 스피커 터지도록

그리고 모두 함께 미쳐, 정신 빠지도록

온몸을 흔들어 봐 봐, 아무 생각 안 나도록

**About the singer and the song**

2PM debuted in 2008 with their song <10점 만점에 10점 (10 out of 10)>. Their acrobatic dancing and manly image have given them the nickname "savage idol group." The group pursues lively songs that would lighten the mood at 2:00 in the afternoon. The song <Hands Up> is a funky club music track that encourages you to shake your body along with the song.

# 볼륨을 높여 스피커 터지도록

Increase the volume so that the speaker nearly explodes.

죽도록 아팠어.
I was deathly ill.

죽도록 일만 했어.
I worked so hard I nearly died.

죽도록 운동했어.
I exercised so hard I nearly died.

배가 터지도록 먹었어.
I ate so much that my stomach nearly exploded.

코피가 터지도록 공부만 했어.
I studied so hard that my nose bled.

머리가 터지도록 고민하고 있어.
I am trying to think so hard that my
brain is about to explode.

네가 미치도록 보고 싶어.
I miss you so much that I am going crazy.

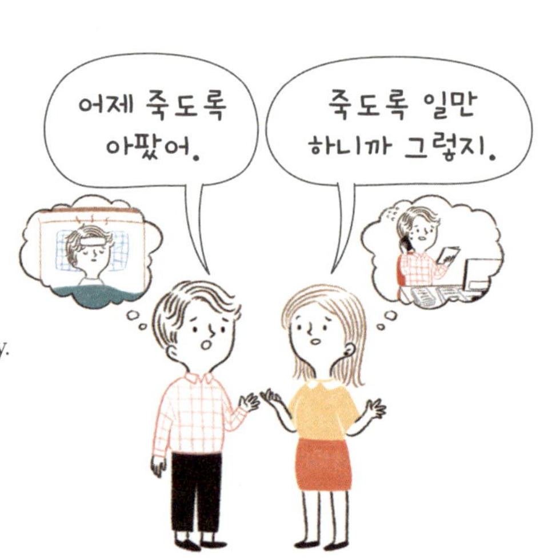

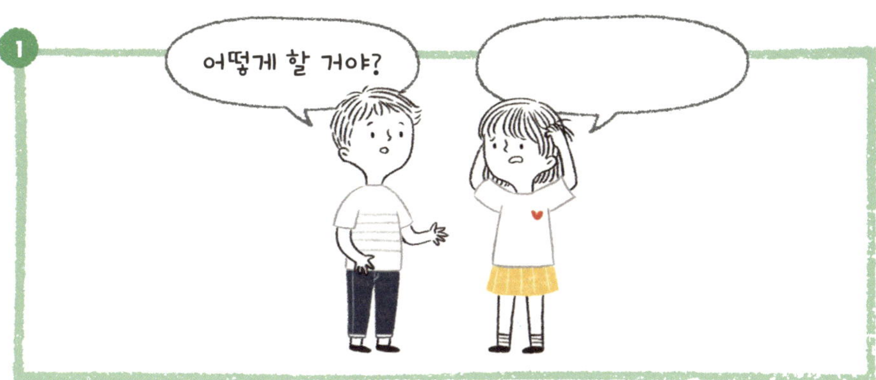


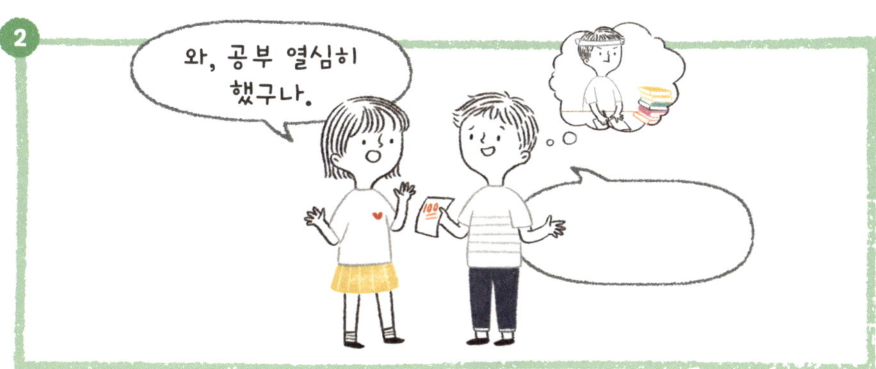


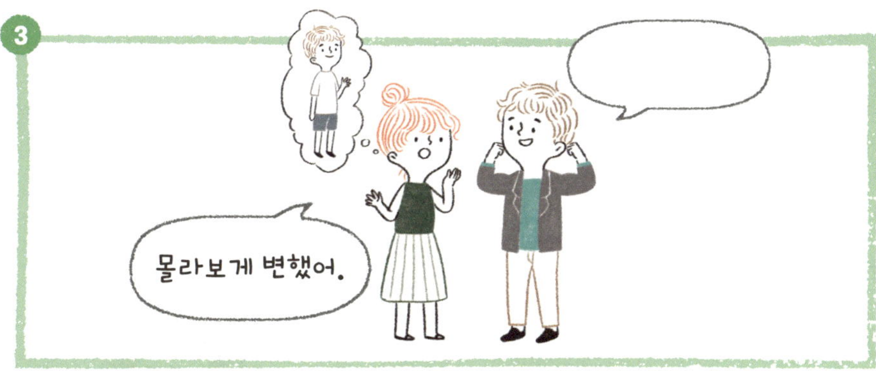


**몰라보게** totally (lit. to be hard to recognize) | **변하다** to change

# 온몸을 흔들어 봐.

Shake your whole body.

한번 해 봐.
Try it!

병원에 한번 가 봐.
Why don't you go to see a doctor?

이 옷 한번 입어 봐.
Try this on!

이 노래 한번 들어 봐.
Listen to this song!

이 화장품 한번 써 봐.
Try this cosmetic!

그 사람 한 번만 더 만나 봐.
Why don't you meet that person again?

조금만 더 기다려 봐.
Wait a little more!

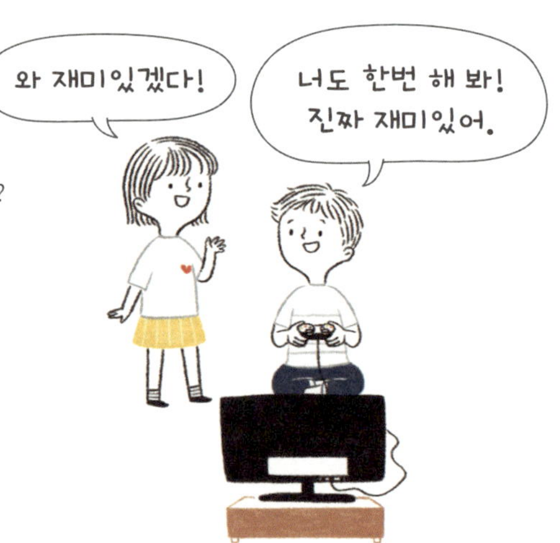

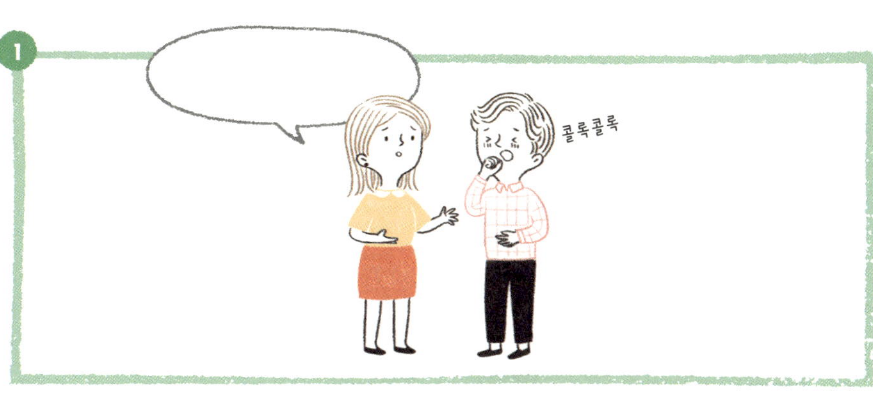
콜록콜록

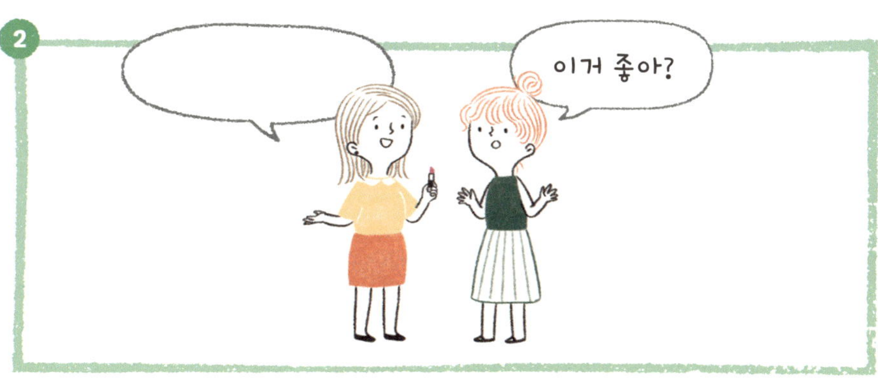
이거 좋아?

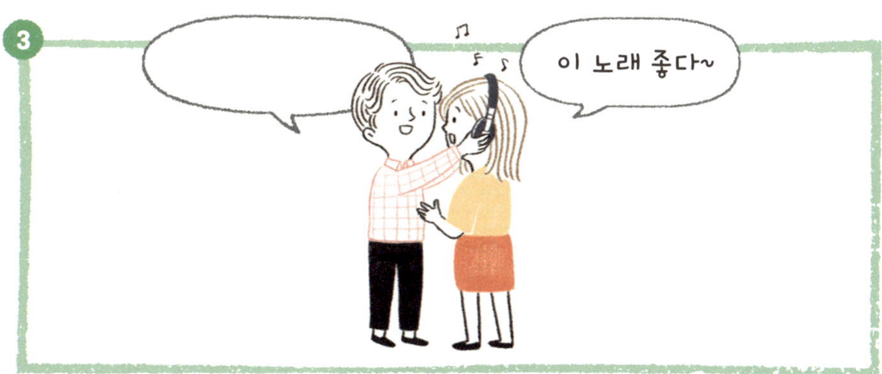
이 노래 좋다~

#  V-도록

**죽도록** 연습해도 안 돼.
I am practicing as hard as hell, but it's not working.

그 사람이 **미치도록** 그리워요.
I miss him to death.

심장이 **터지도록** 빨리 뛰어요.
 My heart is beating is so fast that it is likely to explode.

**심장이 터지도록 빨리 뛰어요. = 심장이 터질 정도로 빨리 뛰어요.**

**V-도록** is an expression used to exaggerate a current situation. It can be replaced with **V-(으)ㄹ 정도로**, which can describe the extent of something or the adverbs **너무** and **많이**.

#  V-아/어 보다

이 음식 한번 **먹어 봐**. 맛있어.
Try this food! It's delicious.

이거 한번 **써 보세요**. 좋아요.
Why don't you try this? It's good.

이 책 **읽어 봐 봐**. 재미있어.
Why don't you read this book? It's fun.

**V-아/어 봐** and **V-아/어 보세요** is used when you want to recommend something to someone with a soft tone. It is similar to "try -ing" and is often used after the adverb **한번** When it is used verbally, people often add **봐** right after **V-아/어 봐** like **V-아/어 봐 봐**.

울려 퍼지는 음악에 맞춰 / 온 세상이 함께 미쳐
[마처] ❶

볼륨을 높여 스피커 터지도록
[노펴] ❷

그리고 모두 함께 미쳐 정신 빠지도록
[미처] ❸

온 몸을 흔들어 봐 봐 아무 생각 안 나도록
[봐 봐] ❹

❶ 맞춰 is pronounced [마춰]. However, when you say it fast, it sounds like [마처].

❷ 높여 is pronounced [노펴]. But it sounds like [볼류믈로펴] when you say it with no pause, the last ㄹ affects the 노 sound.

❸ 챠, 쳐, 쵸, and 츄 are pronounced [차, 처, 초, 추].

❹ 봐 sounds like [봐] but it is often pronounced [바] since it is easier to pronounce that way.
**Ex** 흔들어 봐 봐 [흔드러 바 바]



볼륨을 높여 / 스피커 터지도록
⇨ 스피커 터지도록 볼륨을 높여.

The first and second phrases of a sentence are often switched like the above lyrics. This is done to emphasize the action in a sentence. The right order of the phrases is on the second line next to the arrow.

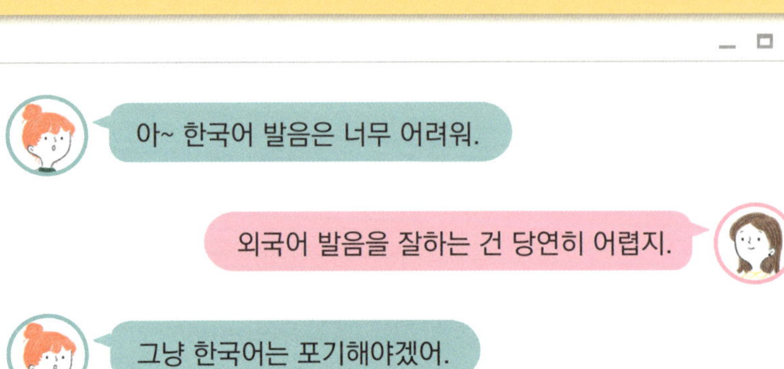


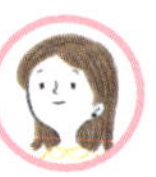

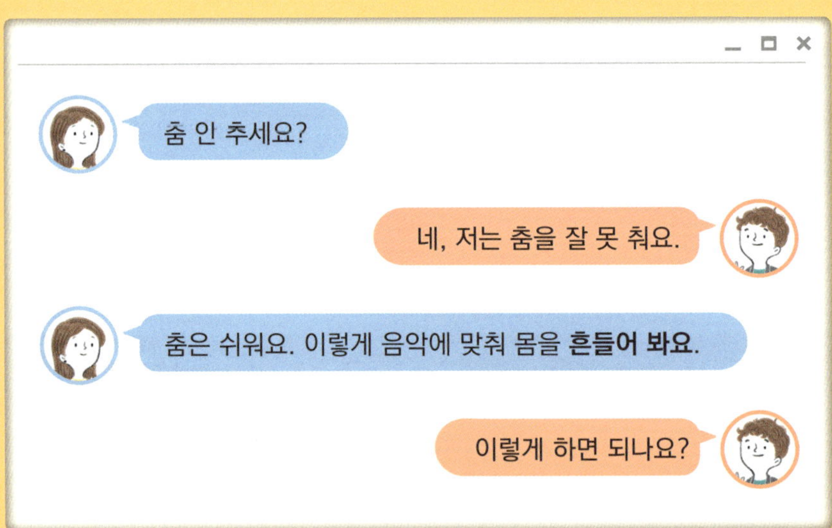


---

**당연히** of course | **포기하다** to give up | **노력하다** to try | **춤을 추다** to dance | **〜에 맞추다** to be along 〜

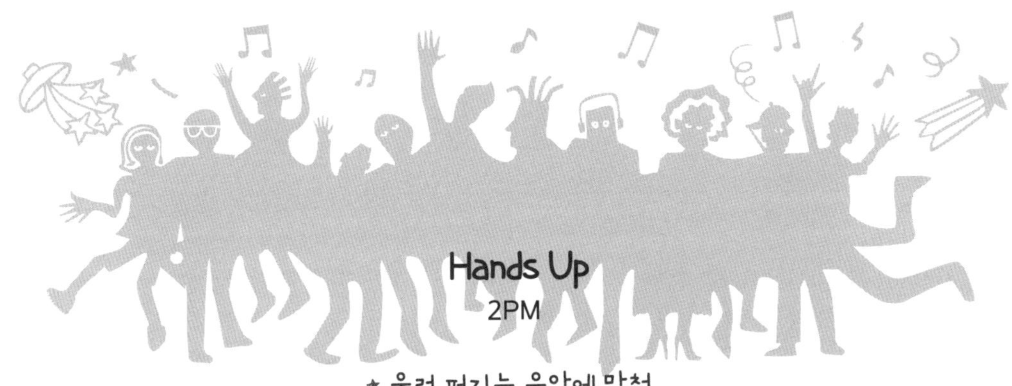

# Hands Up
## 2PM

★ 울려 퍼지는 음악에 맞춰
Everyone put your hands up and get your drinks up.
온 세상이 함께 미쳐.
Everyone put your hands up and get your drinks up.
Now, put your hands up. Put your hands up. Put, put, put, put, put.

볼륨을 높여 스피커 터지도록 그리고 모두 함께 미쳐 정신 빠지도록
온몸을 흔들어 봐 봐 아무 생각 안 나도록

오늘 모두 함께 밤 새 내 말에 동의하는 사람 만세 오늘 끝까지 계속 달려가세.
이랴! 이랴! You know what I'm sayin' 이건 귀로 듣는 피로 회복제 영양제
파티를 터트리는 기폭제 밤새 흔들리는 불빛에 딱 어울리지 내 말 맞제.

★ 반복

Here we go. Here we go. 계속 달리자고
이제 겨우 열두 시 아직 해 뜨려면 멀었다고
그러니 한 잔 더 마시고 다시 시작하자고

해가 뜨기 전에 절대 음악이 끊기는 일이 없게 DJ 오늘 밤을 부탁해.
"오빠 믿어도 되지 OK?" Yes Sir
나는 먼저 들어갈게 이런 말이 나오는 일이 없게
술 한 잔을 다 같이 들이킬게 one shot 다 같이 자 갈게.

★ 반복

Don't stop 오늘 밤은 떠오르는 모든 생각은 비워 버리고는 다 같이 즐겨 봐.

# Hands Up

2PM

★ To the beat as the music blares.
Everyone put your hands up and get your drinks up.
Go crazy with the whole world.
Everyone put your hands up and get your drinks up.
Now put your hands up. Put your hands up.
Put your hands up. Put your hands up.
Put your hands up. Put your hands up.
Put your hands up. Put your hands up.

Raise the volume until the speakers burst,
and all together go crazy until you lose your minds.
Shake your whole body and lose your minds.

Together all night,
all the people who agree with me mansei,
Come on up until the end of the day.

Giddy up! Giddy up! You know what I'm sayin'?
This is an energy-restoring tonic you hear with your ears.
The catalyst that explodes the party, dancing all night under the lights.
They go together exactly, aren't I right?

★ Repeat

Here we go. Here we go. Keep running.
Right now it's barely midnight. The sunrise is still far away.
So let's have one more glass and start again.

Before the sun rises, absolutely do not cut off the music.
DJ, take care of tonight. "Oppa I can trust you OK?"
Yes, sir, I won't say I'm leaving first.
Let's all have another glass together. One shot. Everyone's let's go.

★ Repeat

Don't stop. Tonight empty all thoughts, and everyone have fun together.

씨스타(SISTAR)

# Give It to Me

아무리 원하고 애원해도

눈물로 채워진 빈자리만

사랑을 달란 말이야

그거면 된다는 말이야

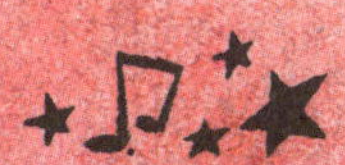

## About the singer and the song

The members of SISTAR have an image like they are your next-door girls. At the same time, they have unique and powerful voices which grabbed the attention of audiences soon after their debut. The song <Give It to Me> won first place on Korean music channels 11 times. It's about a girl who is constantly longing for her lover's heart.

# 아무리 원하고 애원해도

No matter how much I long and desire

아무리 애원해도 안 돼요.
No matter how much I long for it, it doesn't work.

아무리 애를 써도 안 돼요.
No matter how hard I try, it doesn't work.

아무리 먹어도 살이 안 쪄요.
No matter how much I eat, I don't gain weight.

아무리 운동해도 살이 안 빠져요.
No matter how hard I exercise, I'm not losing weight.

아무리 생각해도 이해가 안 돼요.
No matter how hard I try, I can't understand it.

아무리 연락해도 받지 않아요.
No matter how many times I call
her/him, she/he never answers.

아무리 찾아봐도 없어요.
No matter how hard I looked for it,
I couldn't find it.

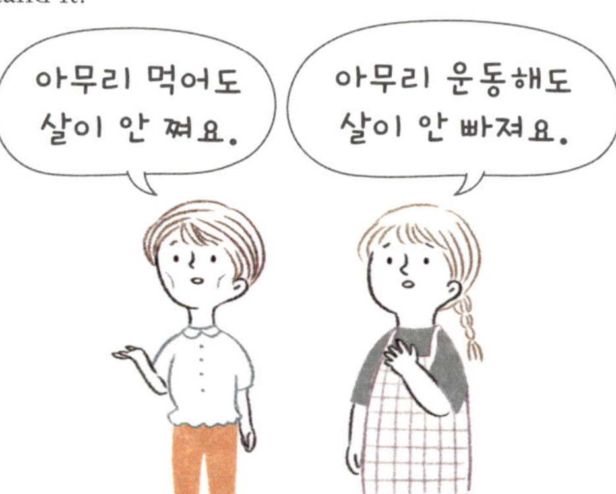

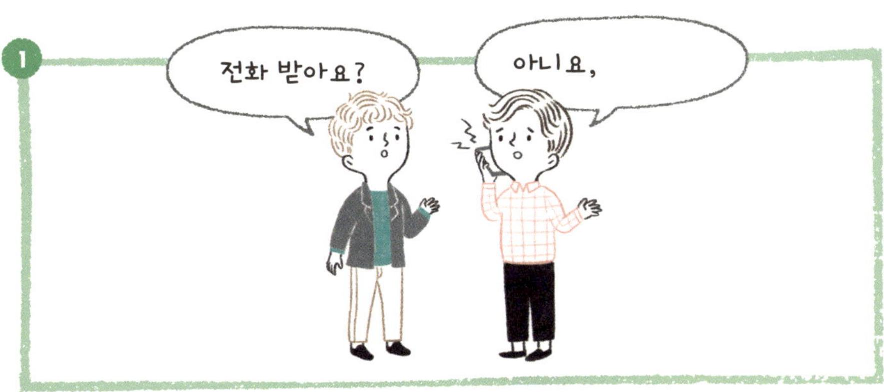


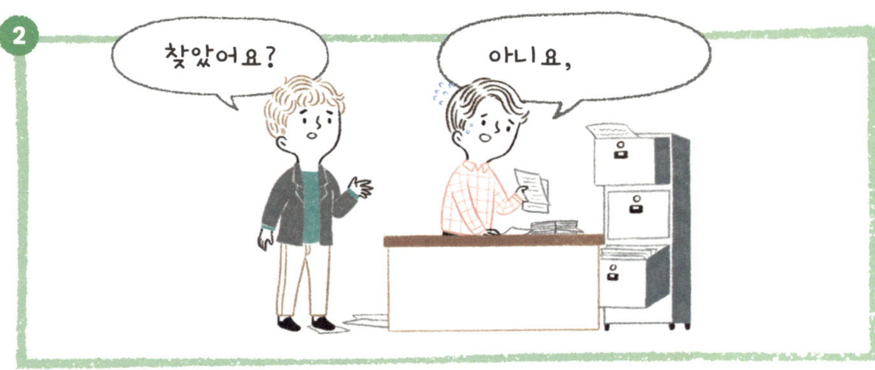


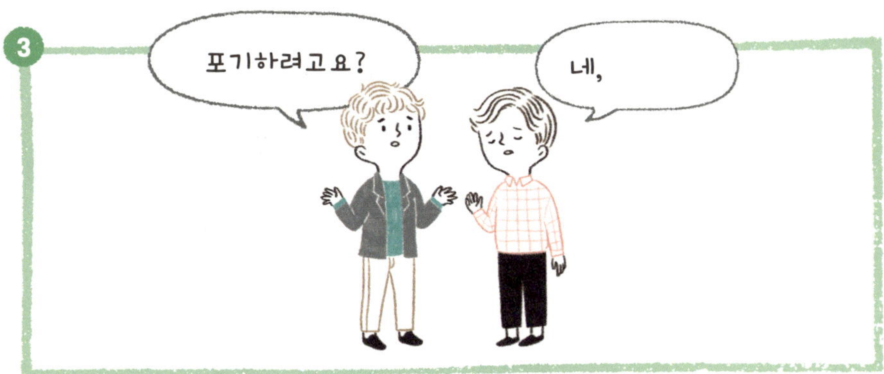


**전화를 받다** to answer the phone | **포기하다** to give up

# 사랑을 달란 말이야.

Give me love!


싫단 말이야.
I don't want it!


무섭단 말이야.
I'm scared!


나도 모른단 말이야.
I don't know either!


그게 아니란 말이야.
That's not true!


빨리 달란 말이야.
Give it to me quickly!


하지 말란 말이야.
Stop it!


손대지 말란 말이야.
Don't touch!

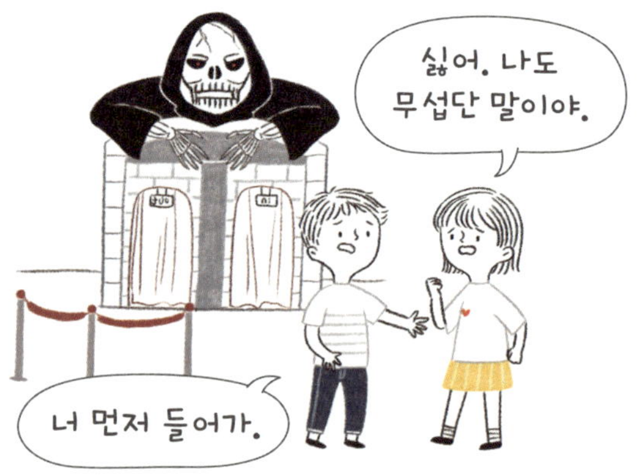

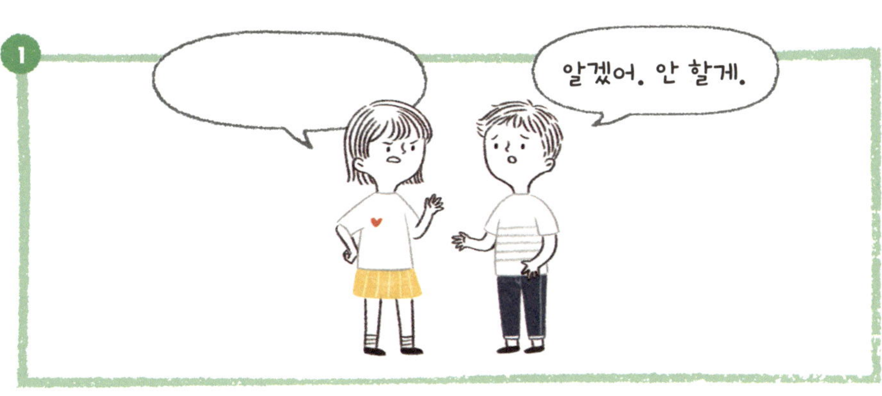
알겠어. 안 할게.

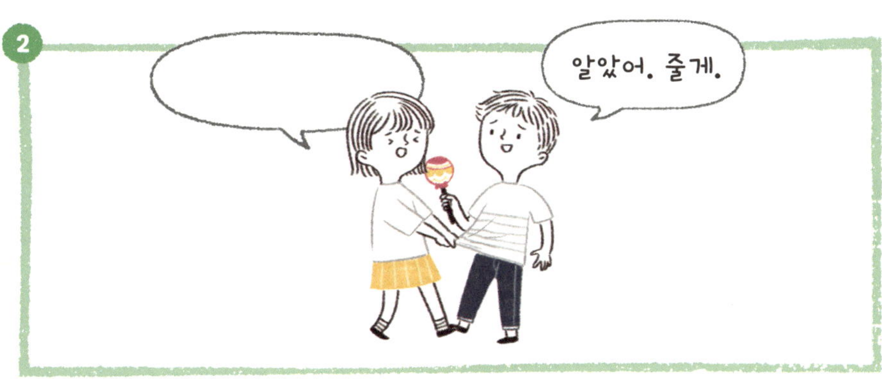
알았어. 줄게.

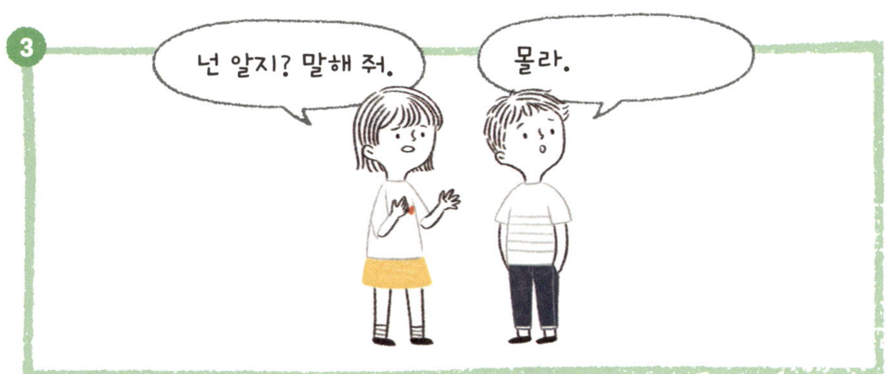
넌 알지? 말해 줘.
몰라.

# 그거면 된다는 말이야.

That's all I need.

너만 있으면 돼.
You are all I need.

이거 하나만 있으면 돼.
This is all I/we need.

노력하면 돼.
Just work hard.

다시 하면 돼.
Just try again.

다음에 실수 안 하면 돼.
Just don't make a mistake the next time.

내 말대로 하면 돼.
Just do as I tell you.

전자레인지에 넣고 3분만 돌리면 돼.
Just put it in the microwave and cook it for 3 minutes.

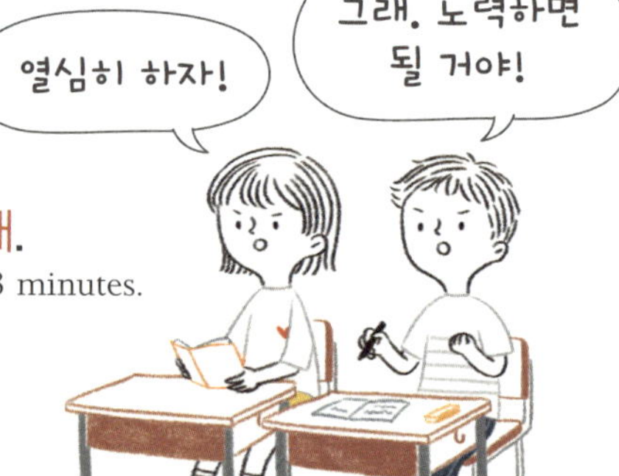

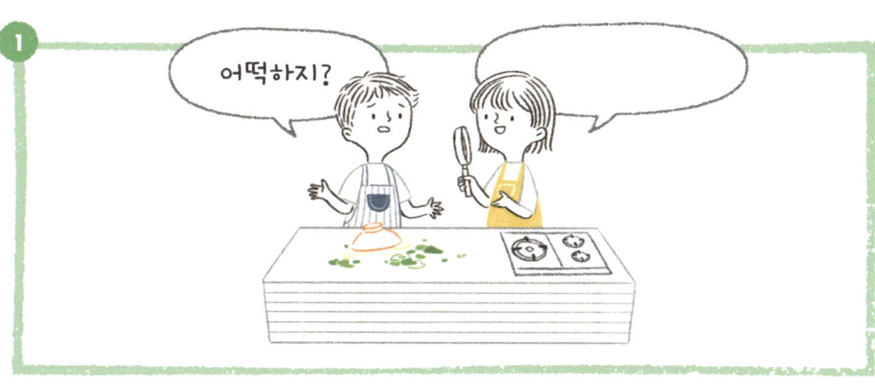
어떡하지?

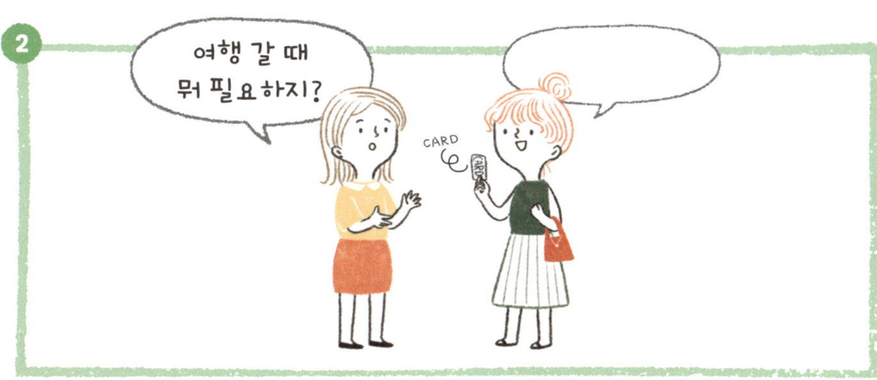
여행 갈 때
무 필요하지?
CARD

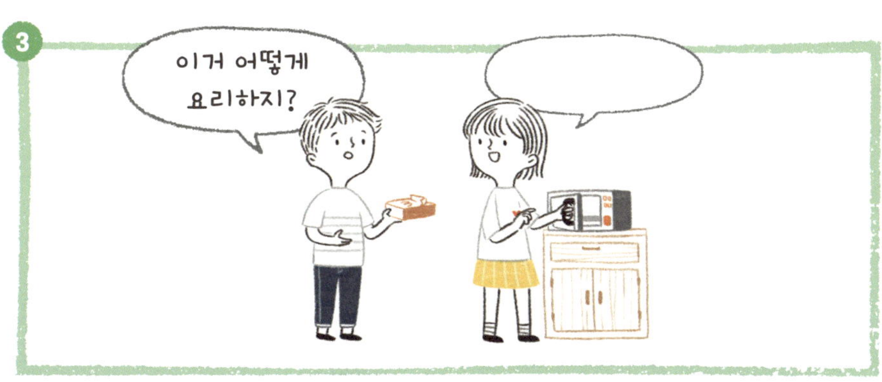
이거 어떻게
요리하지?

##  1 아무리 A/V-아도/어도

**아무리 힘들어도** 열심히 노력해야 돼요.
No matter how hard it is, we have to try hard.

그 사람이 **아무리 보고 싶어도** 참아야 해요.
No matter how much you miss him/her, you have to be patient.

**아무리** has to be combined with **A/V-아도/어도** all the time. It emphasizes the situation of **A/V-아도/어도**.

## 2 A-단 말이야, V-ㄴ단/는단 말이야, N(이)란 말이야

이거 진짜 **무겁단 말이야**.
This is really heavy. I mean it!

나도 남자**란 말이야**.
I'm a man, too. I mean it!

**A-단 말이야, V-ㄴ단/는단 말이야, N(이)란 말이야** are used to emphasize something to the person you are talking to. **-단 말이야** is used when you are emphasizing an adjective, **-ㄴ단/는단 말이야** is used when you are emphasizing a verb, and **(이)란 말이야** is used when you are emphasizing a noun.

##  3 A/V-(으)면 되다

국이 너무 짜면 물을 조금 더 **넣으면 돼**.
If the soup is salty, just add some water.

우리 집에 가려면 여기에서 10분만 **걸으면 돼요**.
We only have to walk 10 minutes from here to get to my house.

**A/V-(으)면 되다** means that a problem can be solved as long as the action suggested in the sentence is done. It can be literally translated as "it will be okay only if ~."

아무리 원하고 애원해도
[워나고]   [애워내도]

눈물로 채워진 빈자리만

사랑을 달란 말이야
[마리야/마랴] ★

그거면 된다는 말이야
[마리야/마랴] ★

★ If you pronounce 말이야 [마리야] quickly, it sounds like [마랴].

줄임말  **CONTRACTION**

사랑을 달란 말이야
달라는

그거면 된단 말이야
된다는

This is the most widely used contraction in Korea. –는 turns into ㄴ, which combines with the previous open syllable. Then, it becomes the open syllable's consonant.

**Ex** 저는 – 전 / 우리는 – 우린 / 한다는 – 한단

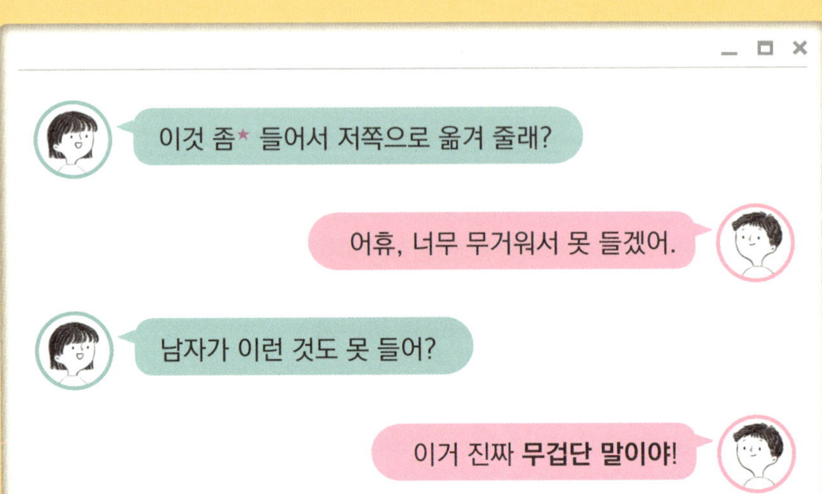


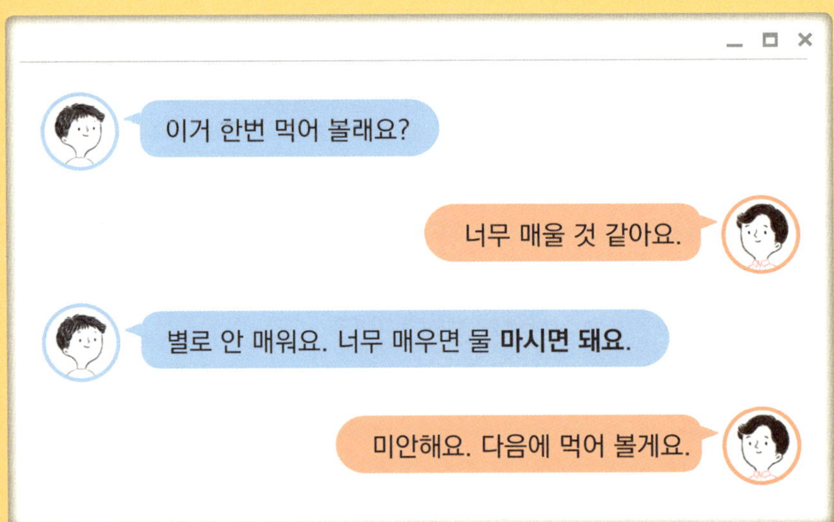


들다 to lift | 옮기다 to move | 진짜 really | 맵다 to be hot/spicy | 별로 not really | 다음에 next time

* 좀 is the contraction of 조금(little), but it is often used without any meaning, such as "You know," or "I mean" in English.

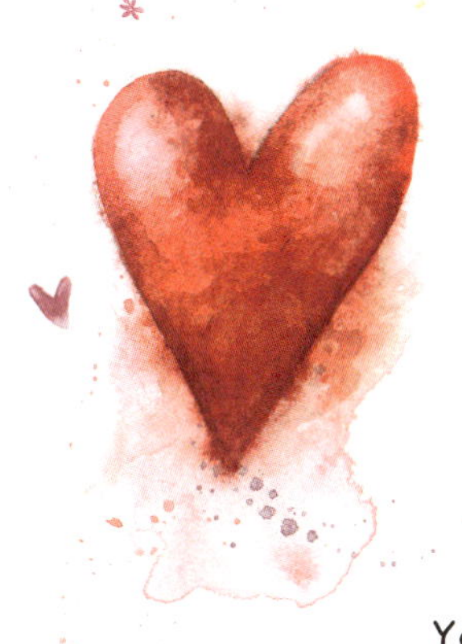

# Give It to Me

씨스타

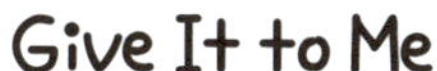

You see, I don't usually do this, but
I really need you tonight. Give it to me. Give it to me.
Give it to me. Give it to me. Give it to me. Give it to me.

서른이 넘기 전에 결혼은 할는지 사랑만 주다 다친 내 가슴 어떡해. oh
애꿎은 빗소리에도 가슴이 아파서 아직도 어리고 여려 순진하고 여려
눈물은 많은지

Give it to me. Oh, babe, give it to me. (Give it to me.)
Give it to me. Oh, babe, give it to me. (Oh, baby, give it to me.)
Oh oh oh oh oh ~ oh oh oh oh oh oh ~ oh

★ 아무리 원하고 애원해도 눈물로 채워진 빈자리만 사랑을 달란 말이야.
그거면 된다는 말이야 Oh, babe, give it to me.

아침이 오기 전에 그대가 올런지 바보같이 너 하날 보는 나 oh~

운다 하루 종일 울다 동이 튼다 저 해가 달인지 밤이 낮인지도 몰라.
Oh, babe, give it to me. I'm sorry. That's all I need~
Oh, babe, give it to me~ Oh, babe, give it to me~

Give it to me. Oh, babe, give it to me. (Give it to me.)
Give it to me. Oh, babe, give it to me. (Oh, baby, give it to me.)
Oh oh oh oh oh ~ oh oh oh oh oh oh ~ oh

★반복

# Give It to Me

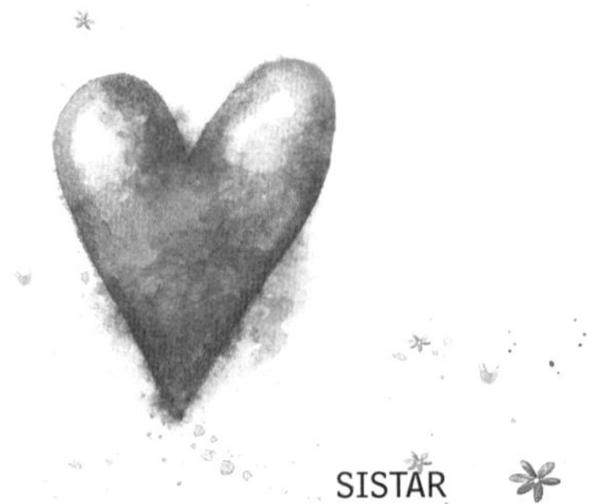

SISTAR

You see, I don't usually do this, but
I really need you tonight. Give it to me. Give it to me.
Give it to me. Give it to me. Give it to me. Give it to me.

I wonder if I would even get married before 30.
What do I do with my wounded heart after giving out so much love. Oh
Even the raindrops break my heart.
I'm still too naïve and young. Maybe that's why I'm full of tears.

Give it to me. Oh, babe, give it to me. (Give it to me.)
Give it to me. Oh, babe, give it to me. (Oh, baby, give it to me.)
Oh oh oh oh oh ~ oh oh oh oh oh oh ~ oh

★ No matter how much I long and desire,
My heart is empty, only filled with tears.
Give me love. That's all I need. Oh, babe, give it to me.

Wonder if you would come before morning.
Such a fool I am to wait for you. Oh~

I cry all day, and another day passes.
The sun becomes the moon, and the night becomes the day.
Oh, babe, give it to me. I'm sorry. That's all I need~
Oh, babe, give it to me~ Oh, babe, give it to me~

Give it to me. Oh, babe, give it to me. (Give it to me.)
Give it to me. Oh, babe, give it to me. (Oh, baby, give it to me.)
Oh oh oh oh oh ~ oh oh oh oh oh oh ~ oh

★ Repeat

갓세븐 (GOT7)

# A

에이 다 아는데 왜 자꾸 숨겨?

네가 날 좋아하는 게

이미 네 얼굴에 쓰여 있어.

에이 나를 보다 왜 눈을 돌려?

다 아는데 에이 에이

## About the singer and the song

GOT7 consists of seven members from Korea, Thailand, Hong Kong, and the U.S. GOT7 means that the members are as lucky as the number seven. The title of the song <A> is the sound of the Korean word 에이, which is a sound you make when you think the other person's behavior or words are not trustworthy or doubtful. The song is about a boy who tells a girl to be more honest with her feelings toward him instead of acting indifferently.

# 네 얼굴에 쓰여 있어.

It's written on your face.


## 스마트폰이 잠겨 있어.
My smartphone is locked.


## 창문이 닫혀 있어.
The windows are closed.


## 문이 열려 있어.
The door is opened.


## 사진이 벽에 걸려 있어.
There's a photo hanging on the wall.


## 책상 위에 놓여 있어.
It is on the desk.


## 일이 쌓여 있어.
My work is piled up.


## 여기에 뭐라고 쓰여 있어?
What's it written on here?

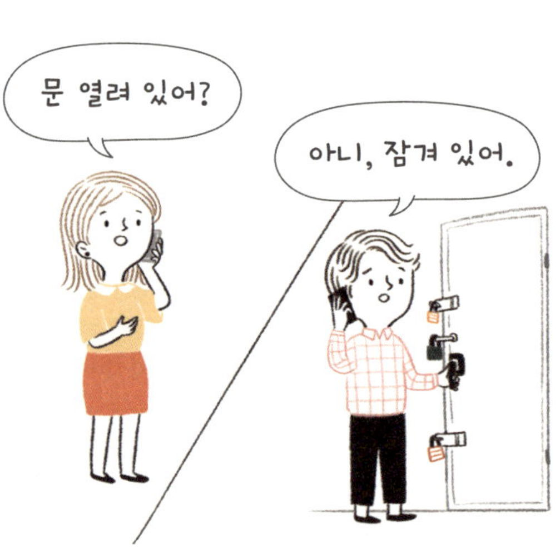

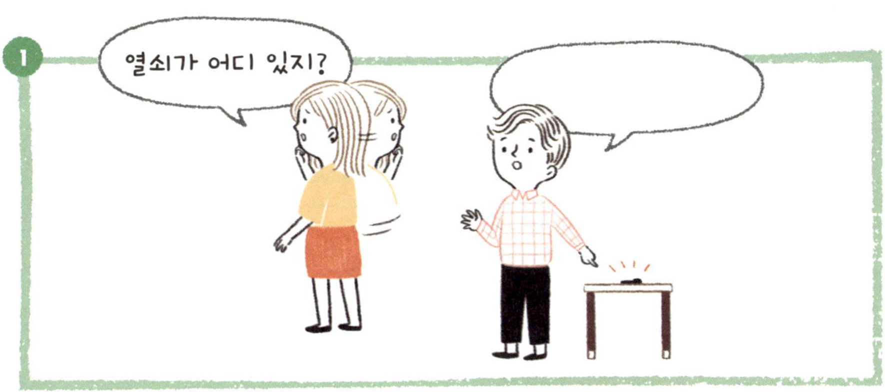


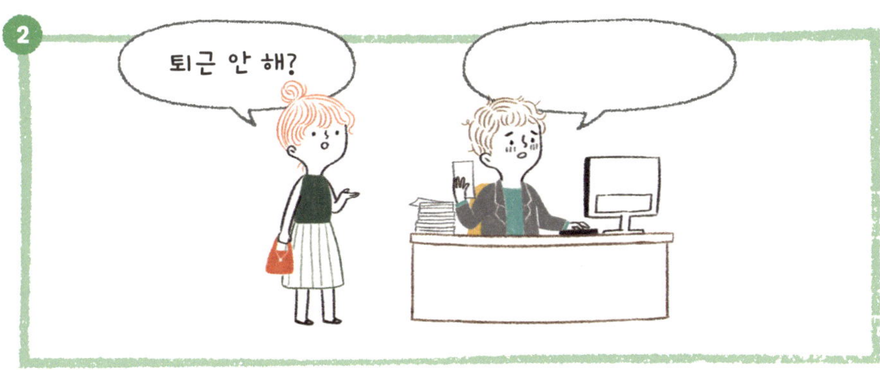


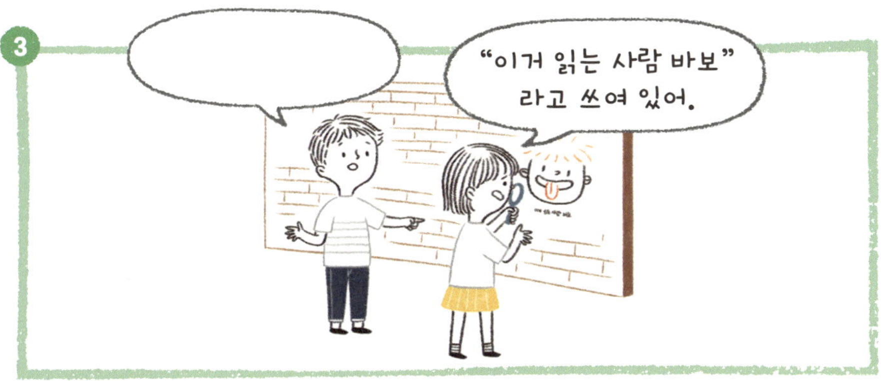


**열쇠** key | **퇴근하다** to finish work | **바보** stupid

# 나를 보다 왜 눈을 돌려?

Why do you turn your eyes away from me?

집에서 자다 나왔어.
I was sleeping at home and just came out.

공부하다 잠들었어.
I fell asleep while I was studying.

농구하다 다쳤어.
I got hurt while I was playing basketball.

딴생각하다 음식을 태웠어.
I burned the food while I got distracted.

밥을 급하게 먹다 체했어.
I had a digestion problem because
I was eating too fast.

집에 오다 친구를 만났어.
I met a friend on the way home.

길을 걷다 생각이 났어.
I thought of it while I was walking.

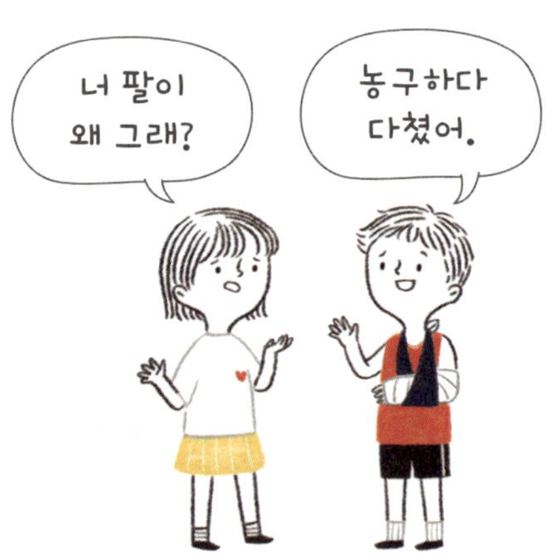

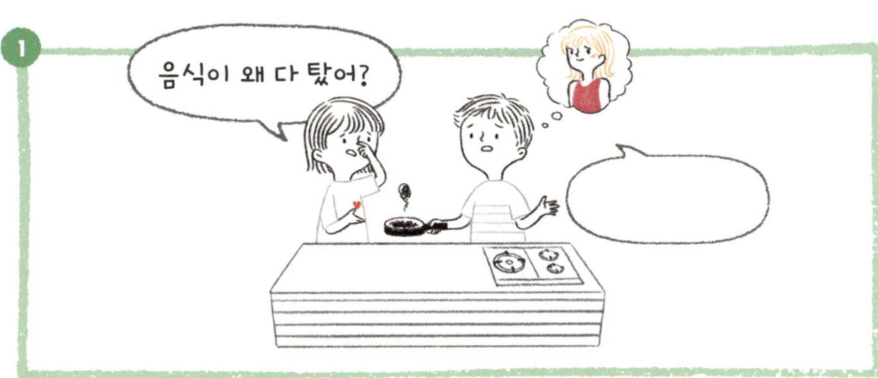


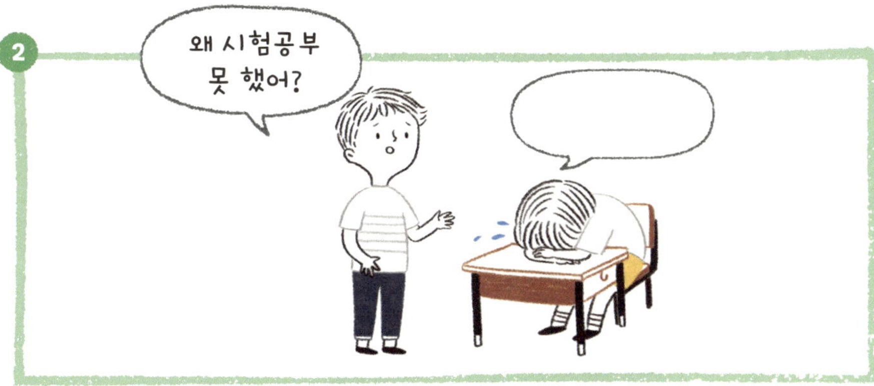


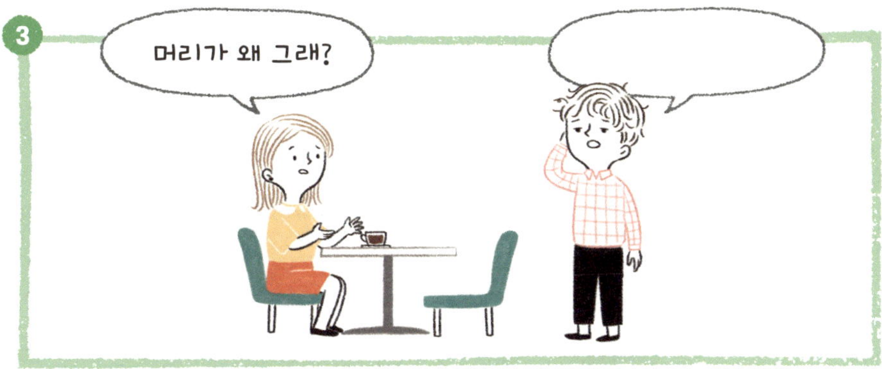


**타다** to be burned | **시험공부** study for an exam

#  피동사+아/어 있다

창문이 **열려 있어요**.
The window is opened.

아기가 엄마 품에 **안겨 있어요**.
The baby is in the mother's arms.

책상 위에 연필이 **놓여 있어요**.
There is a pencil on the desk.

**놓다-놓이다 / 닫다-닫히다 / 안다-안기다 / 열다-열리다**

When **V-아/어 있다** is combined with a passive verb, it means that the result of the previous action is continuing. Korean passive verbs are usually formed by adding **이/히/리/기** to transitive verbs.

# 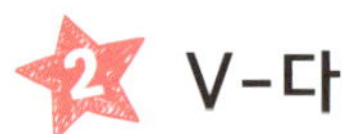 V-다(가)

일을 **하다** 전화를 받았어.
I picked up the phone while I was working.

옛날 여자 친구 얘기를 **하다** 싸웠어.
We had an argument while we were talking about my ex-girlfriend.

집에 **오다가** 대학교 때 친구를 만났어요.
I met a college friend on the way home.

**V-다(가)** is used when something happened while you were in the middle of doing something else. It has a nuance that you were not able to complete something because another thing occurred in the middle of it.

에이 다 아는데 왜 자꾸 숨겨

네가 날 좋아하는 게
[니]가 ❶　　[조아하는] ❷

이미 네 얼굴에 쓰여 있어
[니] ❶

에이 나를 보다 왜 눈을 돌려

다 아는데 에이 에이

❶ 네 means 너(you), and it sounds just like 내(my). To distinguish the pronunciation between 네(your) and 내(my), 네 is often pronounced [니].

❷ When the final consonant ㅎ comes right after a syllable that starts with a vowel, it becomes a silent ㅎ.

**Ex** 좋은 사람 [조은 사람]



얼굴에 쓰여 있어.

Koreans say, "Your feelings/thoughts are written on your face," to mean that your feelings/thoughts are obviously expressed on your face.

**Ex** 거짓말하지 마. 너 지금 거짓말한다고 얼굴에 쓰여 있어.

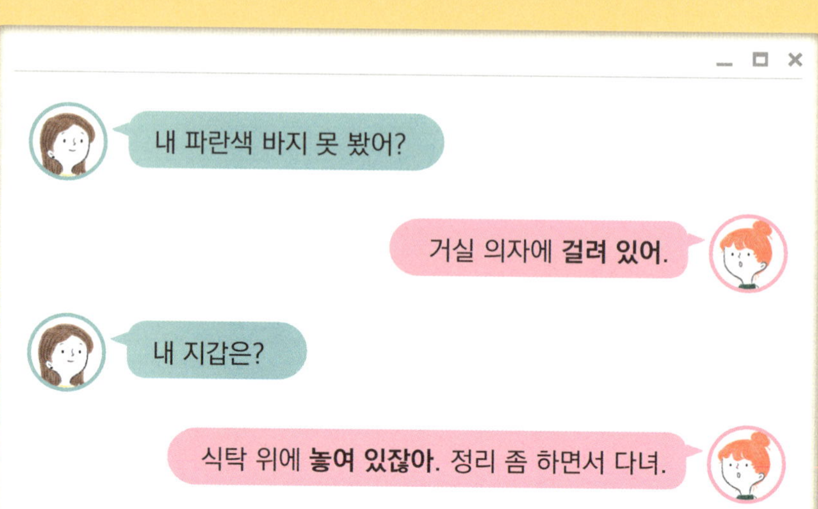


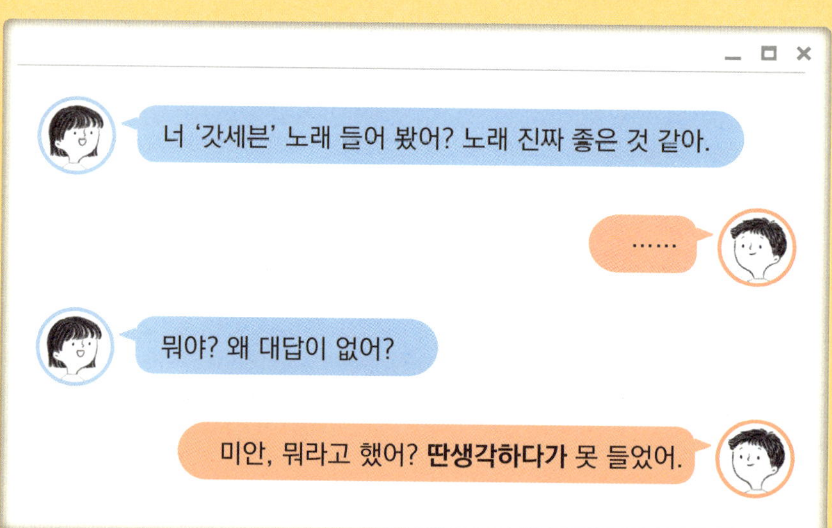


**파란색** blue | **거실** living room | **지갑** wallet | **식탁** table | **정리하다** to straighten up
**딴생각하다** to be distracted (lit. to think of something else)

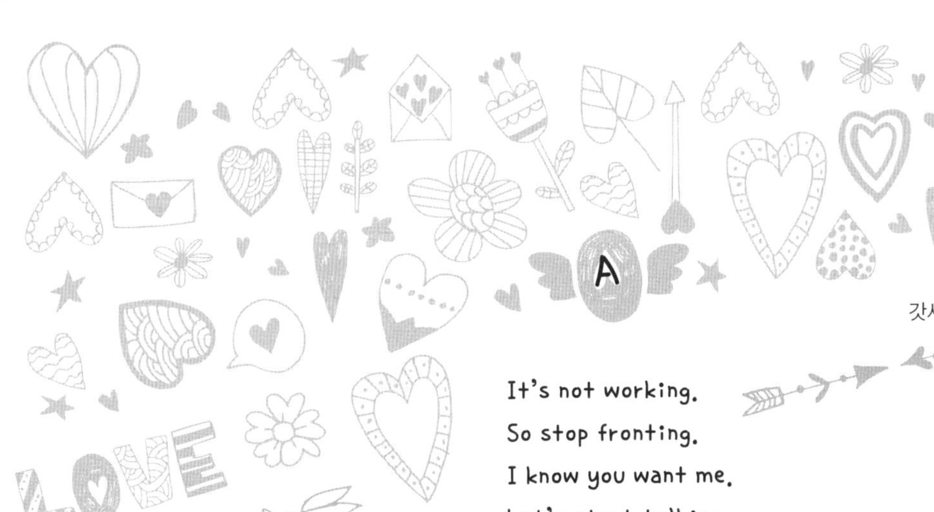


갓세븐

It's not working.
So stop fronting.
I know you want me.
Let's start talking.

★ 에이 다 아는데 왜 자꾸 숨겨?
네가 날 좋아하는 게
이미 네 얼굴에 쓰여 있어.
에이 나를 보다 왜 눈을 돌려?
다 아는데 에이 에이

날 바라보는 시선이 느껴질 때
돌아보면 언제나 네가 서 있어. (Hey, girl.)
고개 돌려 먼 곳을 봐도
놀라지 않은 척해 봐도
나는 알아 왜 네가 내 주위를 왜 맴도는지

★ 반복

날 좋아하는 마음을 모를 거라
믿고 있는 네 모습이 귀여워서 (So cute.)
모른 척해 주고 싶지만
더 이상은 못 참겠어 난
모두 알아 이리 와 봐.
더 이상 날 피하지 말고

★ 반복

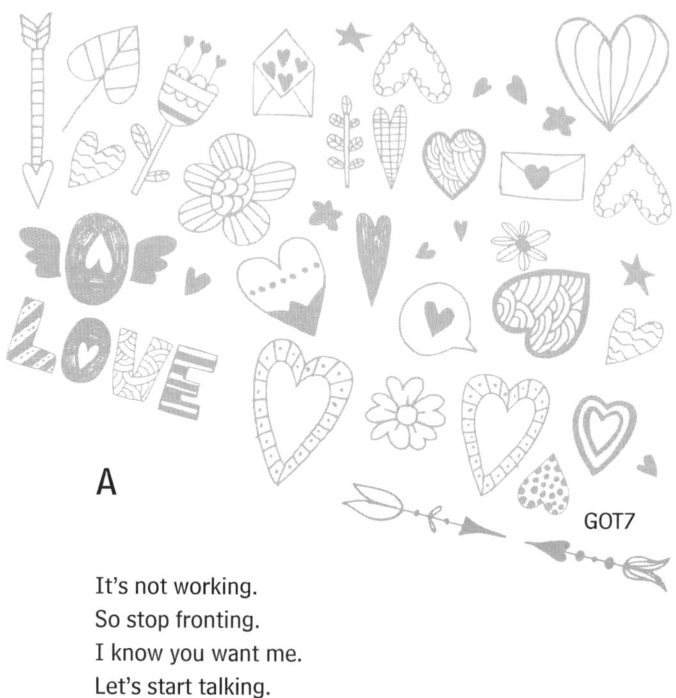

# A

GOT7

It's not working.
So stop fronting.
I know you want me.
Let's start talking.

★ A I know it all. Why do you keep hiding?
I know that you like me. It says on your face.
A Why do you turn your eyes away while looking at me?
I know it all. ∧∧

When I feel someone looking at me,
I glance back and you're always there. (Hey, girl.)
Even if you turn your head and look far away,
Even if you pretend not to be surprised,
I know why you hang around me.

★ Repeat

You think I don't know your mind.
That unawareness makes you look cute. (So cute.)
Though I wanna keep pretending that I don't know,
I can't go on like this any longer.
I know it all. Come on over here.
Don't run away anymore.

★ Repeat

소유&정기고(Soyou & Junggigo)

# 썸

연인인 듯 연인 아닌 연인 같은 너

나만 볼 듯 애매하게 날 대하는 너

때론 친구 같다는 말이

괜히 요즘 난 듣기 싫어졌어.

## About the singer and the song

The title of this song <썸 (Some)> means "something is going on between a man and a woman" in Korean. In other words, it means that there is chemistry between the two people. The song is about a man and a woman who are more than friends but are not in a relationship yet. SISTAR vocalist, Soyou and widely loved musician Junggigo sang this song as a duet.

# 친구 같다는 말

Saying that I'm like a friend

남자 같다는 말 많이 들어.
I often hear that I'm like a boy.

자매 같다는 말 많이 들어.
We often hear that we're like sisters.

쌍둥이 같다는 말 많이 들어.
We often hear that we're like twins.

어린애 같다는 말 많이 들어.
I often hear that I'm like a child.

바보 같다는 말 듣기 싫어.
I hate to hear that I'm like an idiot.

엄마 같다는 말 듣기 싫어.
I hate to hear that I'm like my mom.

아저씨* 같다는 말 듣기 싫어.
I hate to hear that I am like *Ajeossi*.

아줌마* 같다는 말 듣기 싫어.
I hate to hear that I am like *Ajumma*.

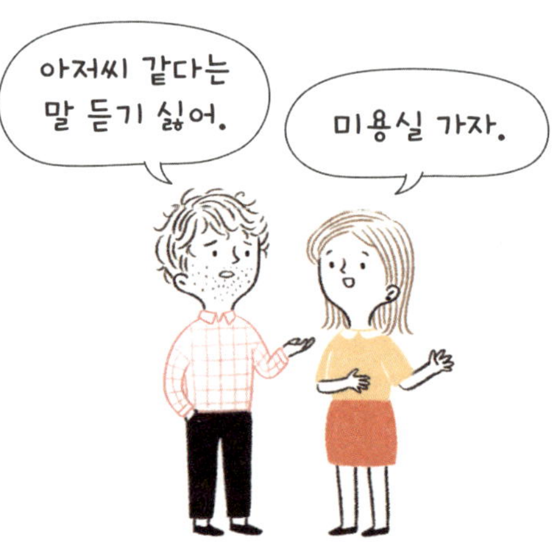


★ In Korea, when people say that you are like an 아저씨(uncle) or 아줌마(aunt), they mean that you look older than your age because you are not taking care of your style. It also means that you are old-fashioned.

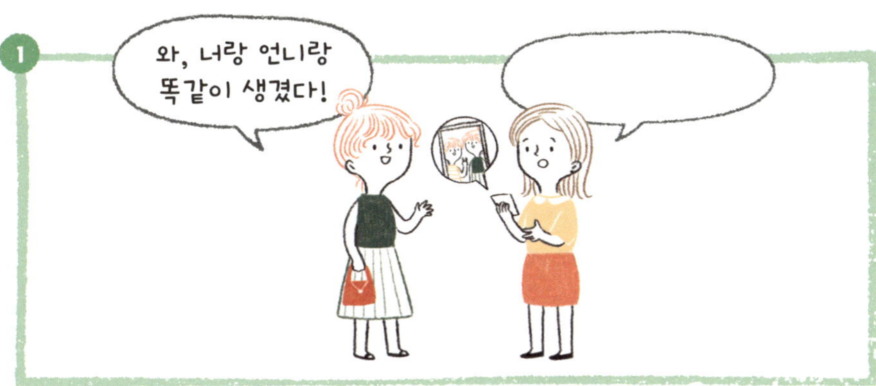


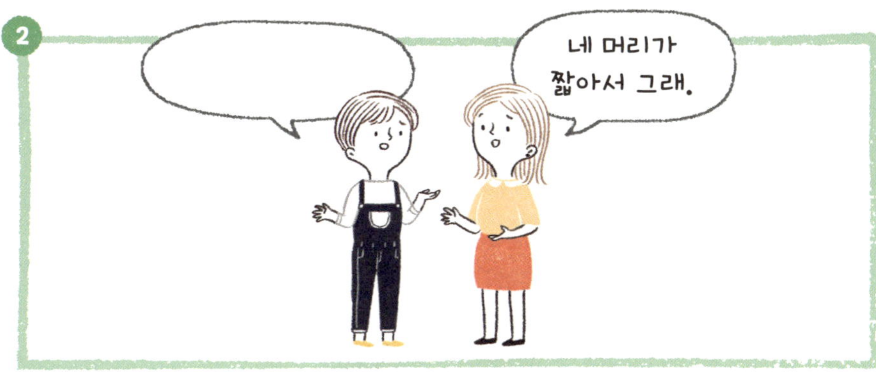


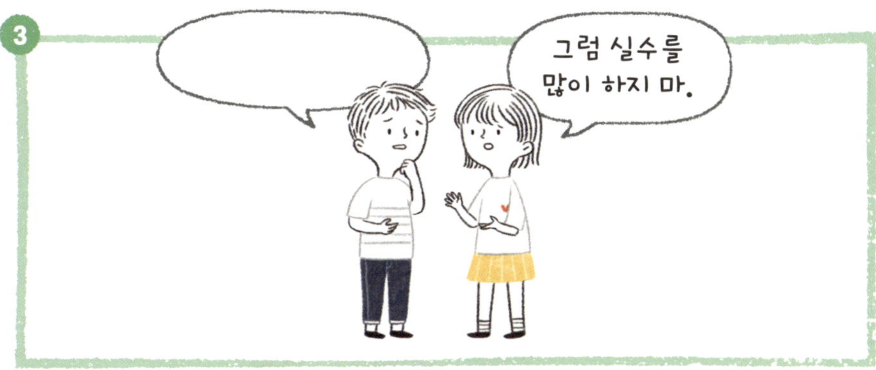


똑같이 생기다 to look just like ~ | 짧다 to be short | 실수 mistake

# 듣기 싫어졌어.

I don't want to hear that anymore.

## 공부하기 싫어졌어.

I don't want to study anymore.

## 말하기 싫어졌어.

I don't want to talk anymore.

## 밥 먹기 싫어졌어.

I don't want to eat anymore.

## 혼자 살기 싫어졌어.

I don't want to live by myself anymore.

## 거울 보기 싫어졌어.

I don't want to look in the
mirror anymore.

## 밖에 나가기 싫어졌어.

I don't want to go outside anymore.

## 모든 게 하기 싫어졌어.

I don't want to do anything.

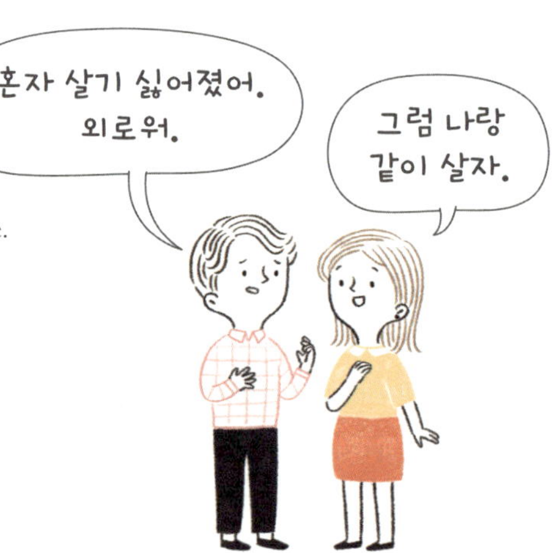

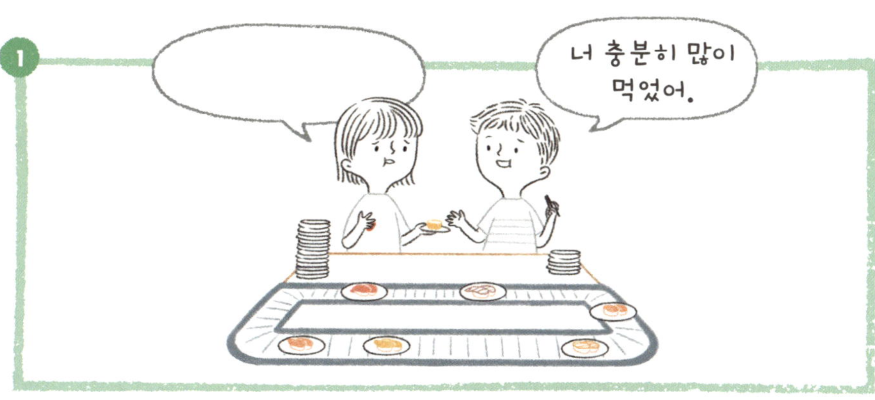


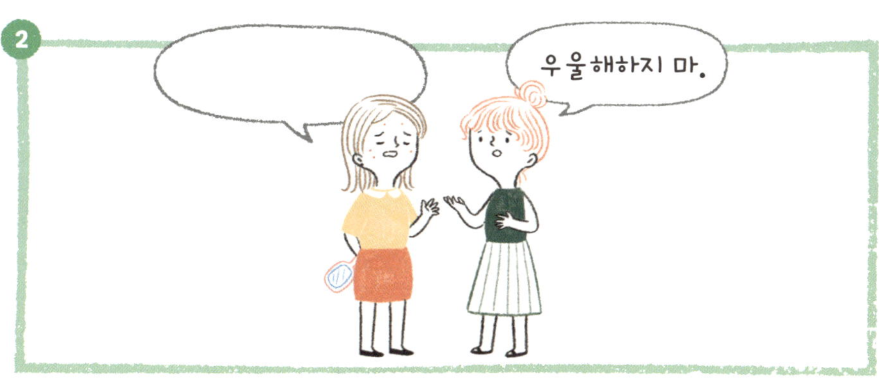


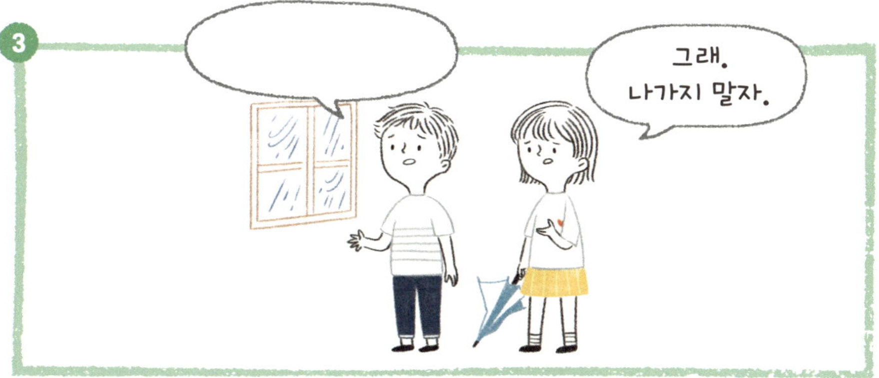


충분히 enough ｜ 우울하다 to be depressed

 ## N 같다는 말

**친구 같다는 말 듣기 싫어.**
I don't want her/him to say that I'm like a friend to him/her.

**한국 사람 같다는 말 많이 들어요.**
I often hear that I'm like a Korean.

**나한테 여자 같다는 말 하지 마.**
Don't tell me that I'm like a girl.

### N 같다

> **Ex** 너 여자 같다. You are like a girl.
> 내 남자 친구는 우리 아빠 같아. My boyfriend is like my dad.

**N 같다** is used when you think that one object is similar to another object. It is close to "~ be like ~." **N 같다는 말** is used when you quote another person by using the phrase **N 같다**.

 ## V-기 싫어지다

**집에 가기 싫어졌어요.**
I don't feel like going home.

**영화 보기 싫어졌어요.**
I don't feel like watching the movie.

**한국어 공부하기 싫어졌어.**
I don't want to study Korean anymore.

### V-고 싶어지다

> **Ex** 집에 가고 싶어졌어요. I want to go home now.
> 한국어 공부하고 싶어졌어요. I feel like studying Korean.

**V-기 싫어지다** means that you no longer want to continue doing something. It is similar to "don't want to ~ anymore" and "don't feel like -ing." In contrast, **V-고 싶어지다** means that you have become fond of doing something.

연인인 듯 연인 아닌 연인 같은 너
[여니닌][듣]❶ [여니나닌]

나만 볼 듯 애매하게 날 대하는 너
[볼 뜨 대매하게]❷❸

때론 친구 같다는 말이
[가따는]

괜히 요즘 난 듣기 싫어졌어.
[괜니] [드끼] [시러저써]

❶ When you read each syllable in ~ 듯 연인 ~ clearly, it sounds like [듣][여닌]. When you read the syllables fast, it sounds like [든녀닌]. (When the final consonant [ㄷ] is followed by a word that starts with 야, 여, 요, 유 or 이, [ㄷ] sounds like [ㄴ], and 야, 여, 요, 유 and 이 sound like [냐], [녀], [뇨], [뉴], and [니].)

❷ ㄷ in the phrase –(으)ㄹ 듯 sounds like [ㄸ]. (When the last syllable of a word contains the final consonant ㄹ that comes at the bottom, ㄱ, ㄷ, ㅂ, ㅅ and ㅈ followed by –(으)ㄹ make a tensed sound.)

❸ When you read 나만 볼 듯 애매하게 without a pause, it sounds like [나만볼뜨대매하게]. When you make pauses between the words, it sounds like [나만 볼 뜯 애매하게].



A — 오늘 저녁이나 같이 먹을까?

오늘 늦게 끝날 듯. — B

A — 엄청 바쁜 듯.

미안, 미안. — B

–(으)ㄴ/(으)ㄹ/는/인 듯하다 were originally used when people made assumptions. These days, young Koreans often use these phrases without adding '하다' in cell phone text messages.

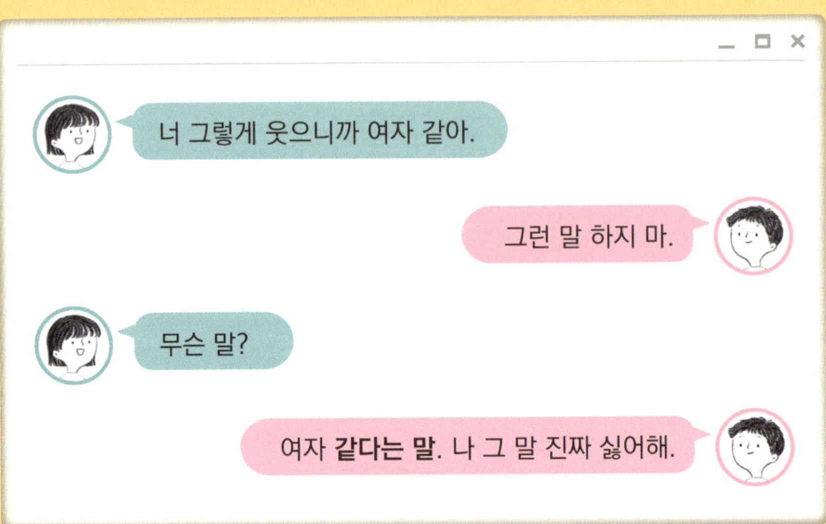


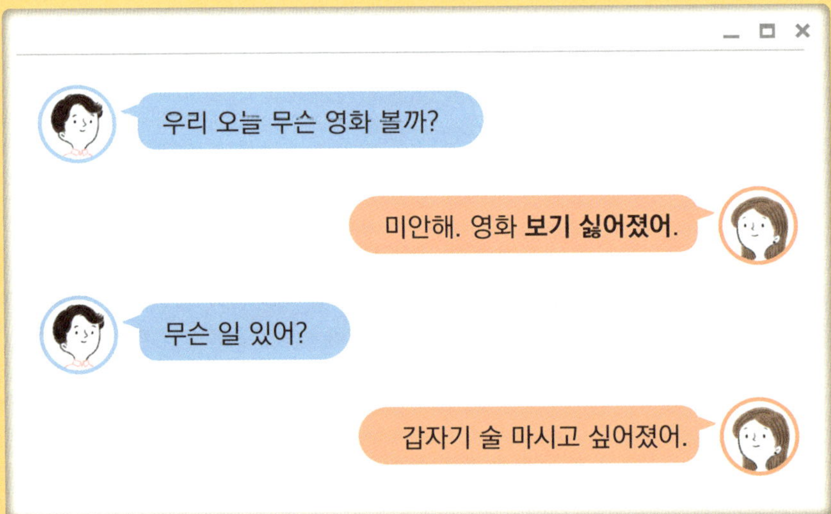


**웃다** to smile | **영화** movie | **갑자기** all of a sudden | **술** alcohol, liquor | **마시다** to drink

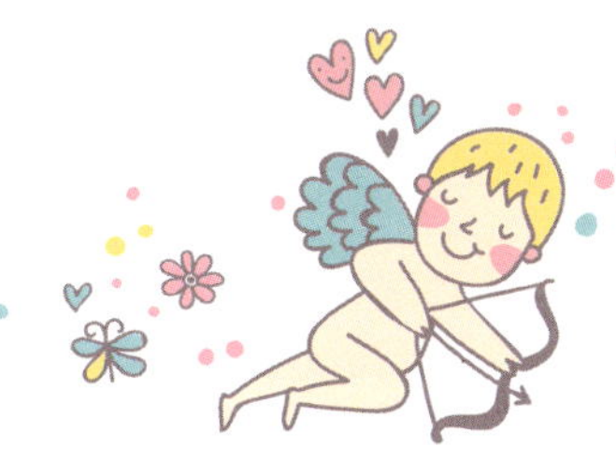

# 썸

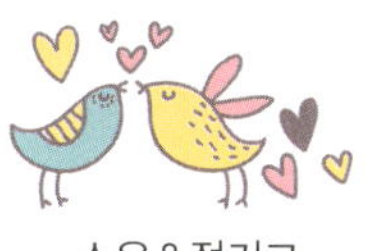

소유&정기고

가끔씩 나도 모르게 짜증이 나.
너를 향한 마음은 변하지 않았는데
혹시 내가 이상한 걸까 혼자 힘들게 지내고 있었어.

텅 빈 방 혼자 멍하니 뒤척이다
티브이에는 어제 본 것 같은 드라마
잠이 들 때까지 한 번도 울리지 않는 핸드폰을 들고

요즘따라 내 꺼인 듯 내 꺼 아닌 내 꺼 같은 너
네 꺼인 듯 네 꺼 아닌 네 꺼 같은 나
이게 무슨 사이인 건지 사실 헷갈려 무뚝뚝하게 굴지 마.
연인인 듯 연인 아닌 연인 같은 너
나만 볼 듯 애매하게 날 대하는 너
때론 친구 같다는 말이 괜히 요즘 난 듣기 싫어졌어.

매일 아침 너의 문자에 눈을 뜨고
하루 끝엔 네 목소리에 잠들고 파.
주말엔 많은 사람 속에서
보란 듯이 널 끌어 안고 싶어.

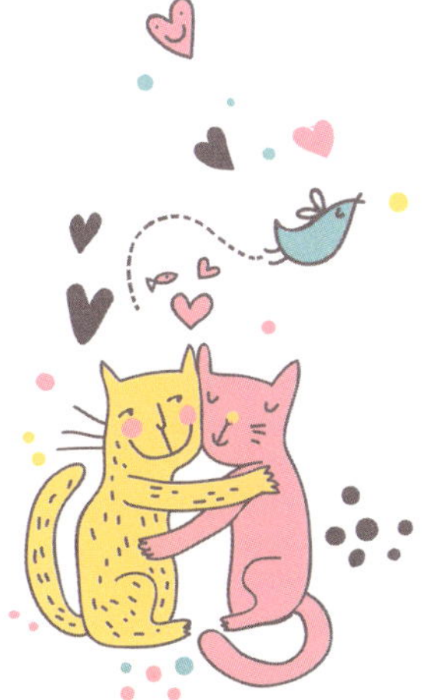

요즘따라 내 꺼인 듯 내 꺼 아닌 내 꺼 같은 너
네 꺼인 듯 네 꺼 아닌 네 꺼 같은 나
때론 친구 같다는 말이 괜히 요즘 난 듣기 싫어졌어.

너 요즘 너 별로야 너 별로야.
나 근데 난 너뿐야 난 너뿐야.
분명하게 내게 선을 그어 줘.
자꾸 뒤로 빼지 말고 날 사랑한다 고백해 줘.

# Some

Soyou & Junggigo

Sometimes I lose control and get annoyed.
My heart is still the same toward you, but
Is something wrong with me? I've been struggling all alone.

Tossing and toiling alone in an empty room,
Watching the same TV drama that is from yesterday,
My mobile phone in my hands never rings all day.

These days you are like mine, then not like mine and like mine again.
I'm like yours, then not like yours and like yours again.
Honestly, I'm getting confused about us, so don't be blunt to me.
You're like my lover, then not like my lover, and again like my lover.
You behave tricky as if I'm the one for you.
I don't want to hear that I'm like a friend to you anymore.

I want to wake up every morning to your messages,
Fall asleep while hearing your voice.
I want to hug you tightly in the middle of the crowd,
Showing that you are my only one.

These days you are like mine, then not like mine and like mine again.
I'm like yours, then not like yours and like yours again.
I don't want to hear that. I want to be more than your friend.

You're making me tired, so tired these days.
But you're the one, the only one for me.
Please be clear about us.
Stop being shy and tell me that you love me.

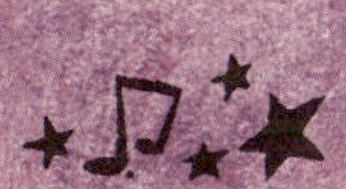

2AM

# 이 노래

줄 수 있는 게 이 노래밖에 없다.

가진 거라곤 이 목소리밖에 없다.

이게 널 웃게 만들 수 있을지 모르지만

그래도 불러 본다.

네가 받아주길 바래 본다.

**About the singer and the song**

2AM means that the group pursues music that would be nice to listen to at around 2:00 in the morning when you tend to relax and clear up your thoughts. The song <이 노래 (This Song)> was their debut song in 2008. It is a message from a guy who cannot offer much to his beloved girl because of his financial situation.

# 줄 수 있는 게 이 노래밖에 없다.

This song is all I can offer you.

## 살 수 있는 게 없어.
There is nothing I can buy.

## 입을 수 있는 게 없어.
There is nothing I can wear.

## 혼자서 할 수 있는 게 없어.
There is nothing I can do by myself.

## 할 수 있는 게 이것밖에 없어.
This is all I can do.

## 만들 수 있는 게 라면밖에 없어.
Instant noodles are the only thing I can make.

## 먹을 수 있는 게 김밥밖에 없어.
*Kimbab* is the only item I can eat
on the menu.

## 할 수 있는 게 뭐가 있어?
Is there anything you can do?

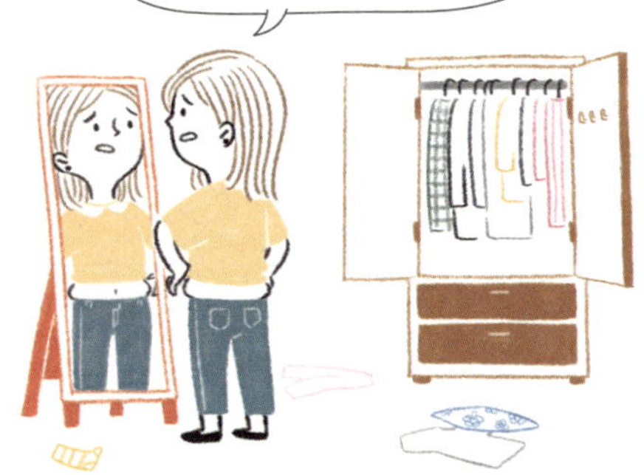

**1**

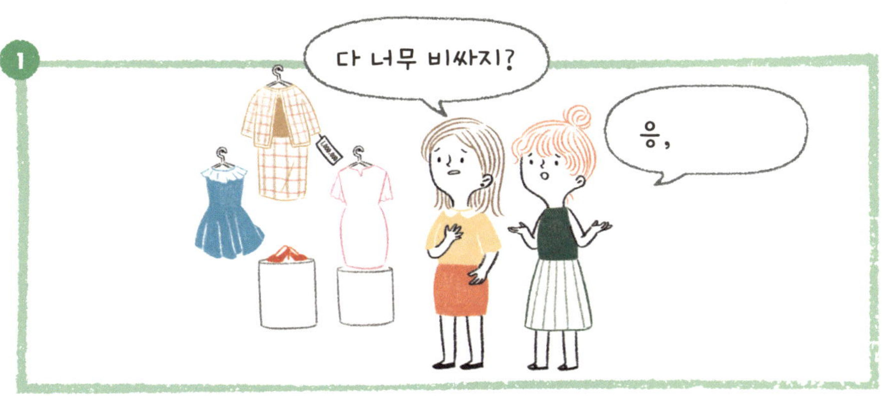


**2**

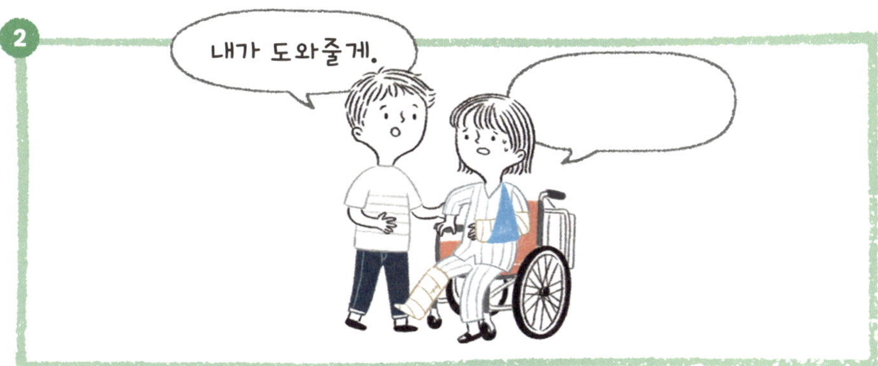


**3**

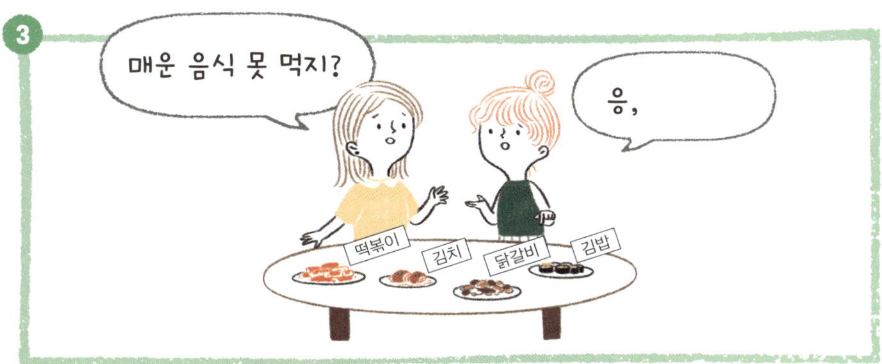


비싸다 to be expensive | 도와주다 to help | 맵다 to be spicy

# 이게 널 웃게 만들 수 있을지 모르지만

I don't know if this will make you smile.

잘할 수 있을지 모르겠어.
I don't know if I will be good at it.

내일 갈 수 있을지 모르겠어.
I don't know if I will be able to make it tomorrow.

잘 찾아갈 수 있을지 모르겠어.
I don't know if I will be able to find the right place.

언제 또 만날 수 있을지 모르겠어.
I don't know when we will be able to see each other again.

공부를 계속 할 수 있을지 모르겠어.
I don't know if I can continue studying.

제시간에 도착할 수 있을지 모르겠어.
I don't know if I can arrive on time.

오늘 안에 다 끝낼 수 있을지 모르겠어.
I don't know if I will be able to finish it by today.

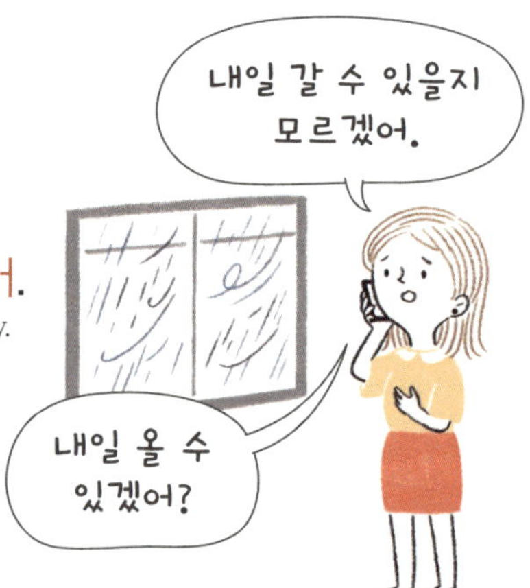

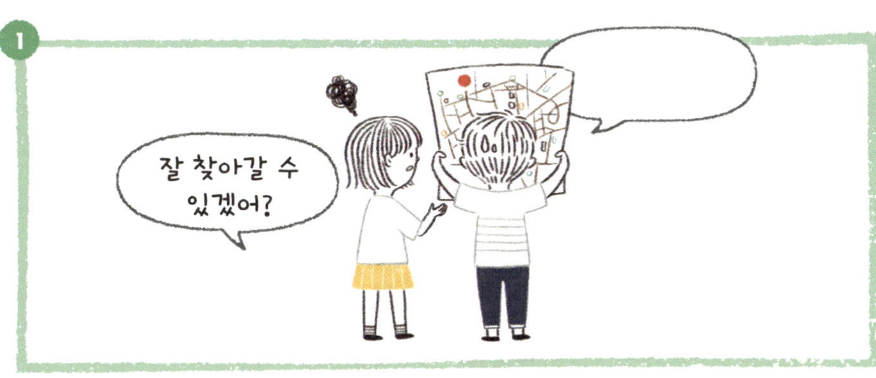
잘 찾아갈 수 있겠어?

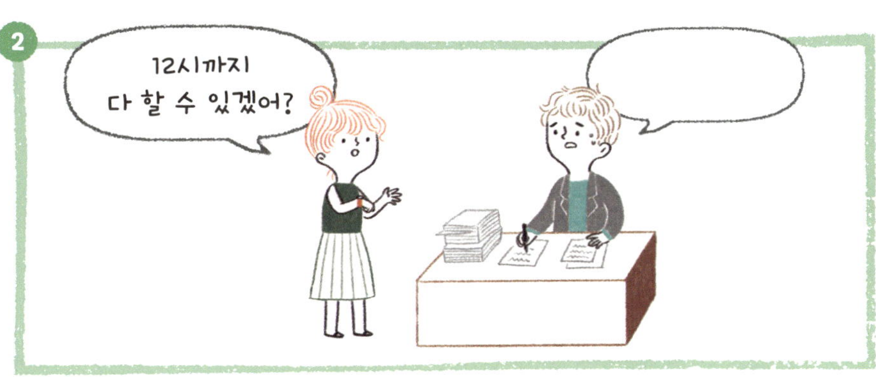
12시까지 다 할 수 있겠어?

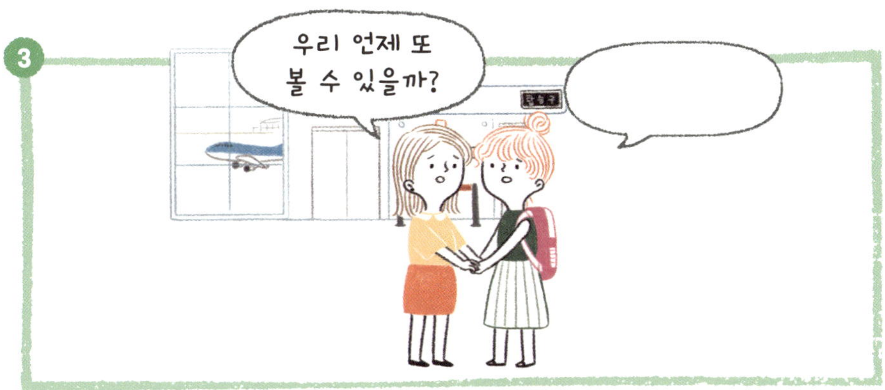
우리 언제 또 볼 수 있을까?

# 1. V-(으)ㄹ 수 있는 게 없다

**지금 할 수 있는 게 없어요.**
There is nothing I can do now.

**100원으로는 살 수 있는 게 없어요.**
There is nothing we can buy with 100 won.

**요리를 잘 못해서 만들 수 있는 게 라면밖에 없어요.**
I'm not good at cooking. Instant noodles are the only thing I can make.

**V-(으)ㄹ 수 있는 게 없다** means that there is nothing you can do. It is similar to "there's nothing one can do." The expression is often used with **밖에 없다** and becomes **V-(으)ㄹ 수 있는 게 N밖에 없다** It is used when you want to emphasize that there is only one choice you can make.


# 2. V-(으)ㄹ 수 있을지 모르겠다

**하고 싶은데 할 수 있을지 모르겠어.**
I want to do it, but I'm not sure if it is possible.

**또 오고 싶은데 또 올 수 있을지 모르겠어.**
I want to come again, but I'm not sure if that will happen.

**원피스가 예뻐서 샀는데 입을 수 있을지 모르겠어.**
I got this dress because it is pretty, but I'm not sure if I can wear it.

**V-(으)ㄹ 수 있을지 모르겠다** is used when you have doubts or worries about something. It is similar to "I doubt one can do something."

줄 수 있는 게 이 노래밖에 없다.
[줄 쑤]❶[인는]          [업따]

가진 거라곤 이 목소리밖에 없다.
          [목쏘리]바께]   [업따]

이게 널 웃게 만들 수 있을지 모르지만
        [우께] [만들 쑤]❶[이쓸찌]❷

그래도 불러 본다. 네가 받아 주길 바래 본다.


❶ ㅅ of –(으)ㄹ 수 sounds like [ㅆ].
  **Ex** 줄 수 있다 [줄 쑤 이따], 만들 수 있다 [만들 쑤 이따], 할 수 있다 [할 쑤 이따].

❷ ㅈ of –(으)ㄹ지 sounds like [ㅉ]. (When the last syllable includes the final consonant ㄹ and ㄱ, ㄷ, ㅂ, ㅅ, ㅈ comes after –(으)ㄹ, they sound like [ㄲ, ㄸ, ㅃ, ㅆ, ㅉ].)
  **Ex** –(으)ㄹ게 [–(으)ㄹ께], –(으)ㄹ 법하다 [–(으)ㄹ 뻐파다],
      –(으)ㄹ 수 있다 [–(으)ㄹ 쑤 이따], –(으)ㄹ지 모르겠다 [–(으)ㄹ찌 모르게따]




네가 받아 주길 바래 본다.

바라 ( O )

When 바라다 is combined with –아/어, it becomes 바라. However, most Koreans say 바래 instead of 바라. Moreover, when 바라다 combines with 아/어 보다, it becomes 바라 보다. However, 바라보다 also means "to stare" so people usually say 바래 보다 instead.

(Reference: 95p)

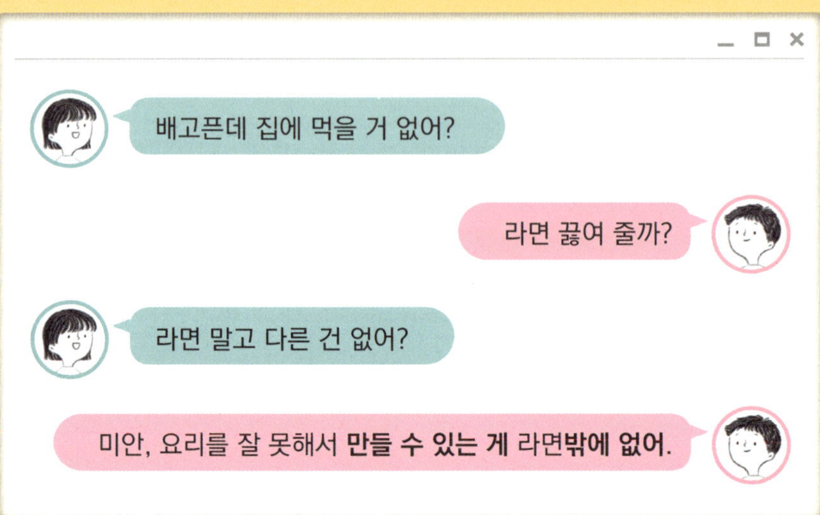


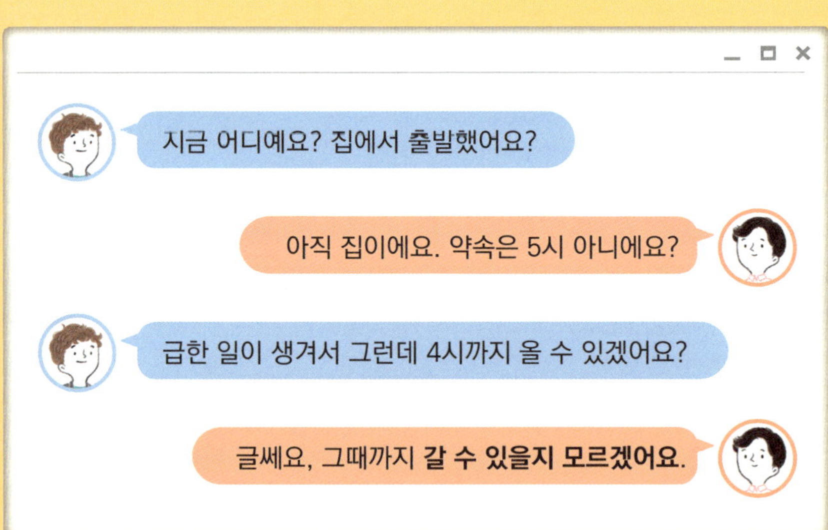


**라면** Ramyeon, instant noodles | **요리** cooking | **출발하다** to leave | **약속** appointment
**급한 일이 생기다** something urgent happens

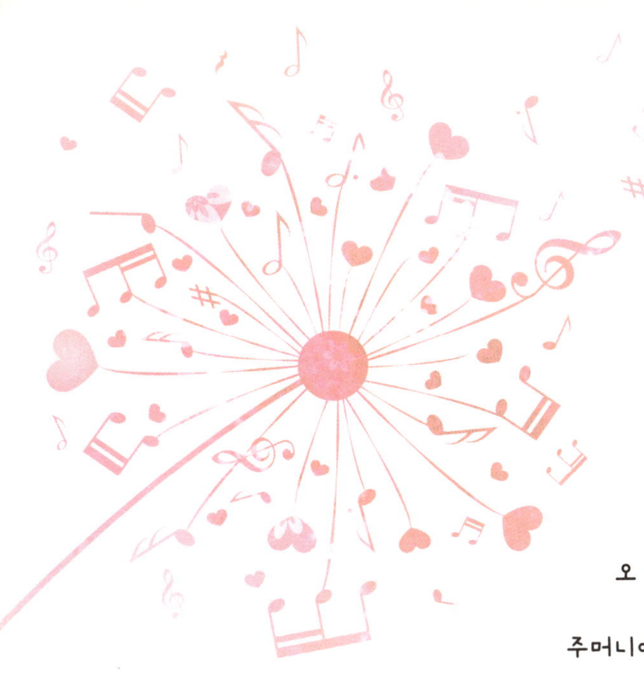

# 이 노래

2AM

예쁜 목걸일 사 주고 싶지만
멋진 차를 태워 주고 싶지만
예쁜 옷을 입혀 주고 싶지만
오 난 좋은 곳에 데려가고 싶지만

주머니에 넣은 손엔 잡히는 게 없는데
어떻게 널 잡을 수가 있어.
내 생활은 너에게 어울리질 않는데
그래도 내 곁에 있어 주겠니?

★ 줄 수 있는 게 이 노래밖에 없다.
가진 거라곤 이 목소리밖에 없다.
이게 널 웃게 만들 수 있을진 모르지만
그래도 불러 본다 네가 받아 주길 바래 본다.

너는 괜찮다고 말을 하지만
나만 있으면 된다고 하지만
행복하다고 늘 말해 주지만
너는 더 바라는 게 없다고 하지만

예쁘고 좋은 것들 재밌고 멋진 일들
너도 분명히 하고 싶잖아 Baby
내 곁에 있어 주면 못 하는 걸 알잖아.
그래도 내 곁에 있어 주겠니?

★ 반복

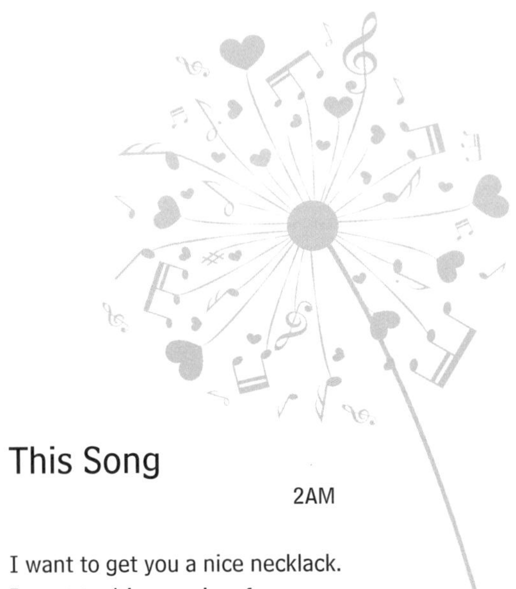

# This Song

2AM

I want to get you a nice necklack.
I want to drive you in a fancy car.
I want to get you beautiful dresses.
Oh, I want to show you around wonderful places.

But I found nothing in my hands.
How can I ask you not to leave me?
My life is not good enough for you.
Will you still be next to me?

★ All I can give you is this song.
  All I possess is this voice.
  But if that can still make you smile,
  I'd carefully call your name, hoping that you will accept me.
  You say that you are okay.
  You say that all you need is me.
  You always say that you are happy.
  And say that you need nothing else.

There are pretty things, fun things.
You would like to try, baby.
You know I can't offer such things to you.
Will you still be next to me?

  ★ Repeat

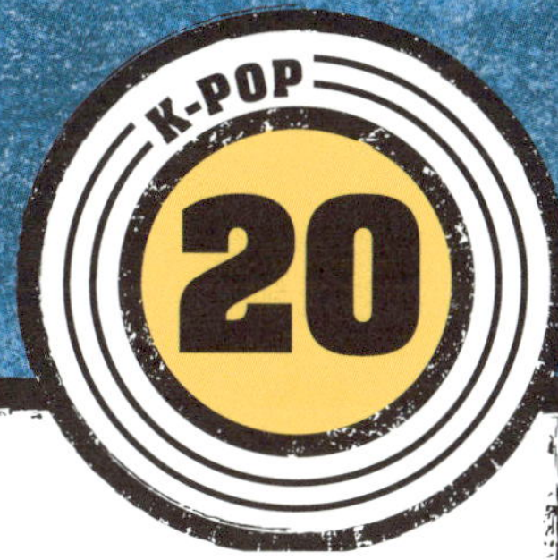

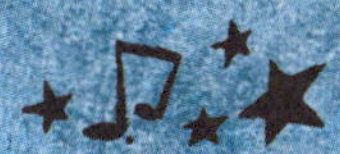

빅스(VIXX)

# Error

나를 놓치기 싫어. 나를 더 망치기 싫어.

끝나도 끝나지 않는 기억에

이길 자신이 난 없어.

사랑 같은 건 결국 한 사람에겐 거짓말

이젠 널 잊는 나를 지켜봐.

두 눈 똑바로 뜨고서

넌 절대 날 잊지 마. (Ah)

넌 나를 지우지 마. (Ah)

## About the singer and the song

VIXX debuted in 2012 as a six-member boy group. They performed with a vampire look for their hit song <I'm Ready to Get Hurt>. VIXX is popular for performing in unique outfits for each song. In their <Error> music video, they turn into cyborgs. The song is about a boy who becomes a cyborg to keep himself from feeling pain after a breakup. Sadly, he fails to stay away from the painful memories even after he becomes a cyborg.

# 넌 절대 날 잊지 마.

Don't ever forget me.

절대 안 돼.
No, never.

절대 못 해.
It is impossible.

절대 용서 못 해.
I will never forgive you.

절대 질 수 없어.
We should never lose.

절대 참을 수 없어.
I cannot stand it.

절대 아무한테도 말하지 마.
Don't ever tell anyone.

절대 따라하지 마세요.
Don't ever follow it.

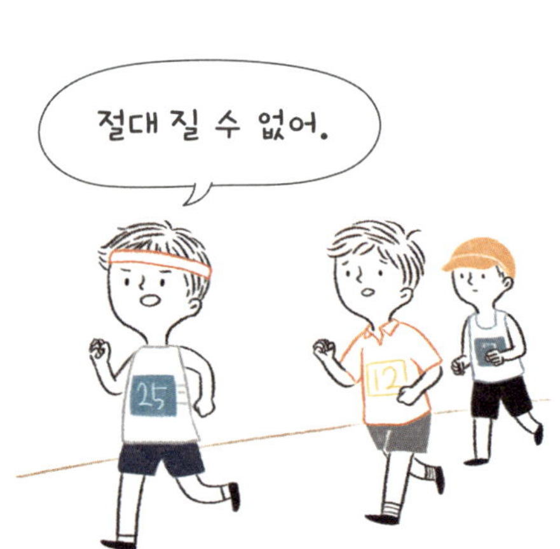

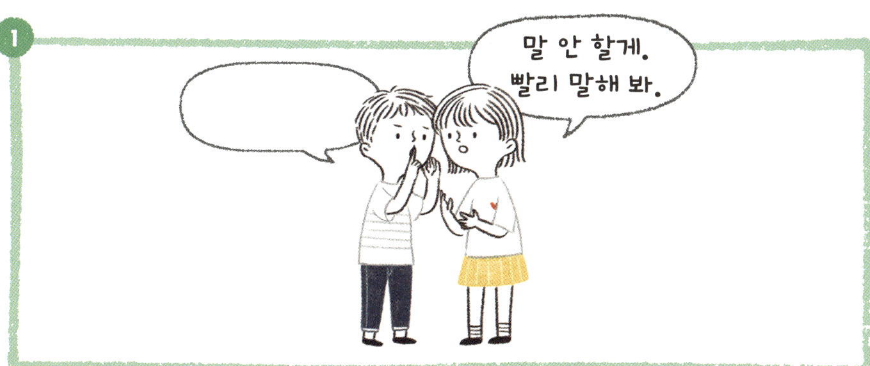


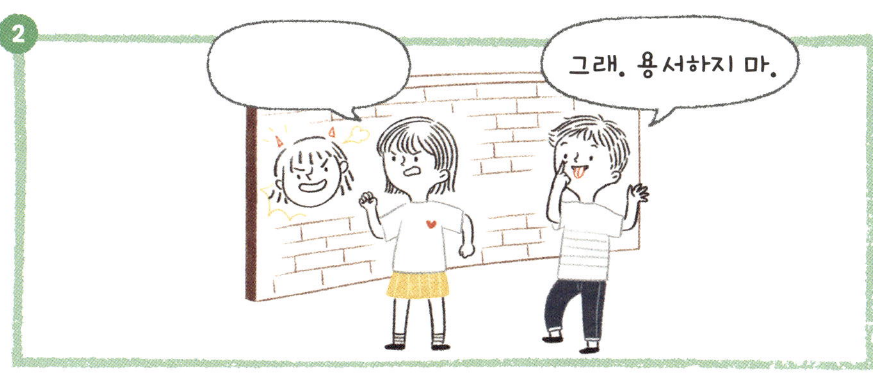


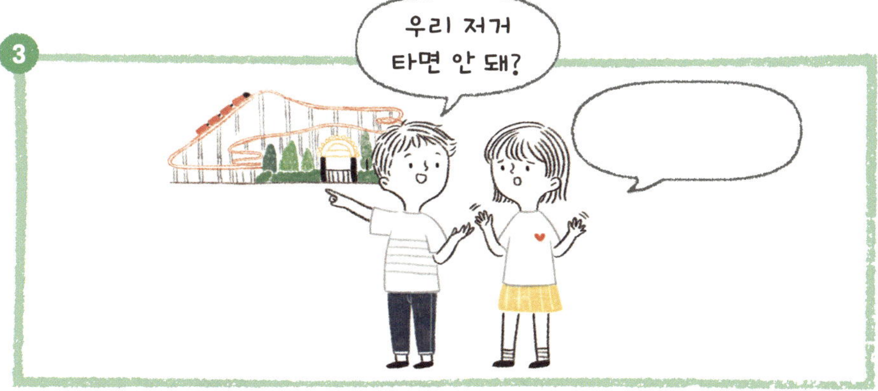


**빨리** quickly | **저거** that | **타다** to ride

# 이길 자신이 난 없어.

I'm not confident I will win.


이길 자신이 있어.
I'm confident I will win.

잘할 자신이 있어.
I'm confident to be good at it.

후회 안 할 자신이 있어.
I'm confident that I won't regret it.

너를 기다릴 자신이 없어.
I'm not confident to wait for you.

부모님을 볼 자신이 없어.
I'm not confident to see my parents.

강아지를 잘 키울 자신이 없어.
I'm not confident to raise a dog.

좋아하는 사람에게 고백할 자신이 없어.
I'm not confident to tell my feelings to the
person I like.

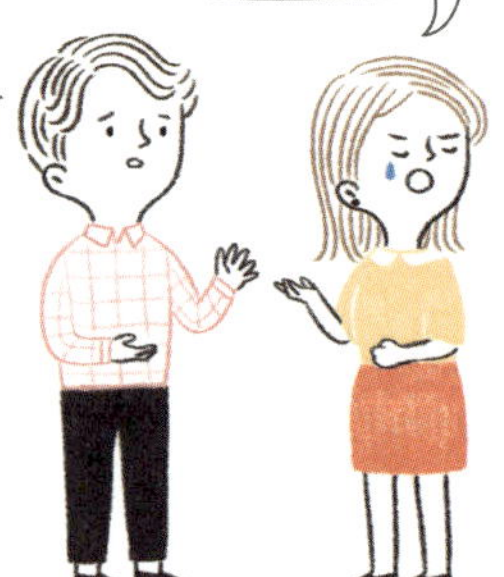

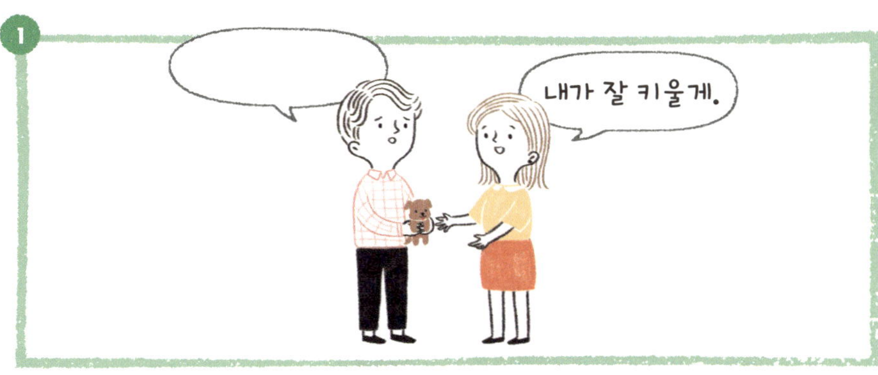


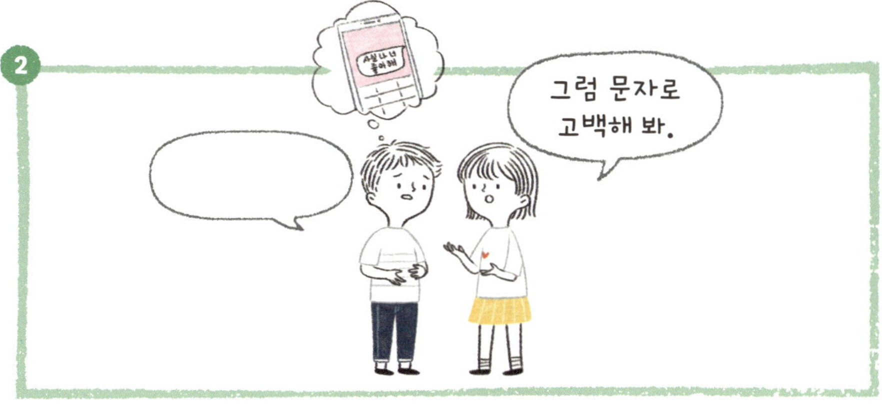


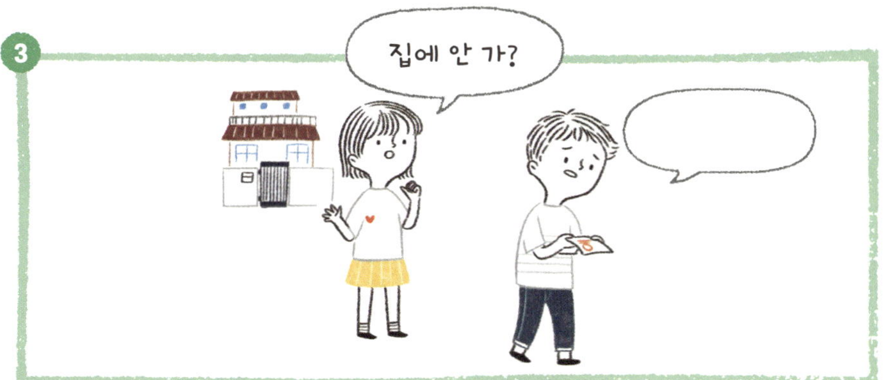


**문자** text message

 ## 절대 + 부정 A/V

**내일까지 이 일은 절대 못 끝내.**
It is impossible to finish this work by tomorrow.

**이제부터 너랑 절대 연락 안 할 거야.**
I will never talk to you again.

**다음부터는 나한테 절대 거짓말하지 마.**
Don't ever lie to me again.

절대 is an adverb which is used to emphasize the impossibility in any cases. It is always used with 안, 못, 아니다, 없다 or –지 말다 in sentences. It is the same as "never."

 ## V–(으)ㄹ 자신이 있다/없다

**열심히 할 자신이 있어요.**
I'm confident that I will work hard.

**잘할 자신이 없어요.**
I'm not confident that I will do it well.

**양이 많아서 다 먹을 자신이 없어요.**
I'm not confident to eat such a huge amount of food.

V–(으)ㄹ 자신이 있다 means that the speaker is confident to do a certain thing. V–(으)ㄹ 자신이 없다 means that the speaker is afraid to do a certain thing.

나를 놓치기 싫어 나를 더 망치기 싫어
[노치기] [시러]　　　　　　　　[시러]

끝나도 끝나지 않는 기억에 이길 자신이 난 없어
[끈나도]❶ [끈나지]❶ [안는]　　　　　　　　[업써]

사랑 같은 건 결국 한 사람에겐 거짓말
[거진말]❷

이젠 널 잊는 나를 지켜 봐 두 눈 똑바로 뜨고서
[인는]❶

넌 절대 날 잊지 마 (Ah) 넌 나를 지우지 마 (Ah)
[절때]❸　　[나 리찌]

❶ When you read the word 끝 it sounds like [끋]. However, when it's followed by a syllable that starts with ㄴ, the final consonant 끝 sounds like [ㄴ] instead of [ㄷ].

🗯 **Ex** 끝 [끋] – 끝나도 [끈나도], 잊 [읻] – 잊는 [인는]

❷ When the final consonant [ㄷ] is followed by a syllable that starts with ㅁ, [ㄷ] sounds like [ㄴ].

🗯 **Ex** 거짓 [거짇] – 거짓말 [거진말]

❸ ㄷ, ㅅ, and ㅈ have a tensed sound when they come after the final consonant ㄹ.

🗯 **Ex** 일등 [일뜽], 일상 [일쌍], 일주일 [일쭈일]

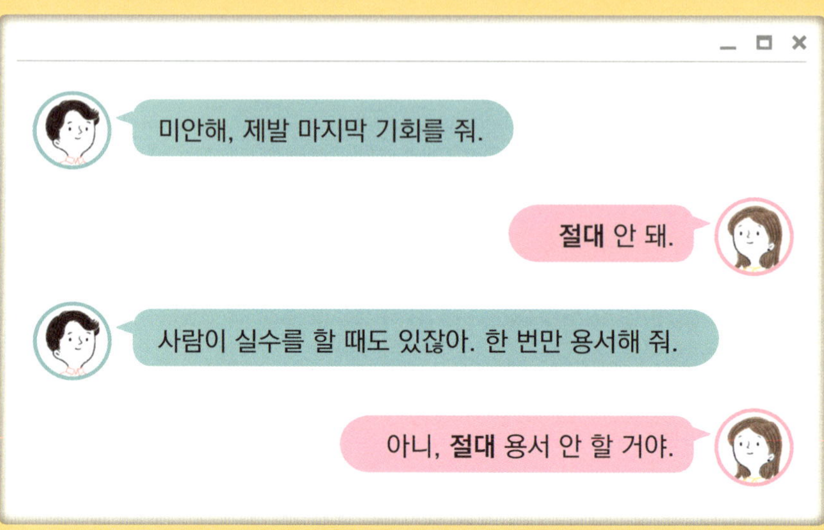


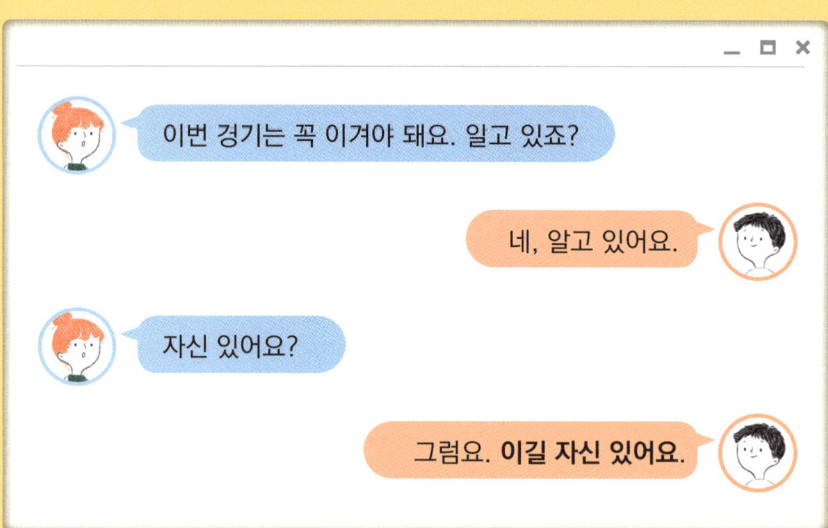


기회 opportunity | 실수 mistake | **용서하다** to forgive | **경기** game | **이기다** to win

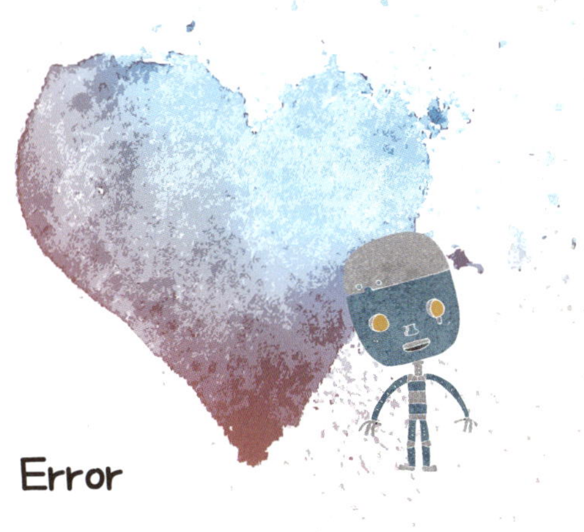

# Error

빅스

어쩔 수 없어서 버렸어 모든 감정을 지웠어.
널 애써 지울 수 없어서 (Let me free)
내 맘이 안쓰러워서 (Let me breathe)

이대로 살면 돼 숨 쉬면 돼.
살아 있기만 하면 돼 왜 안 돼.
내가 괜찮다는데 (Let me free)
내가 이게 더 나은데 (Let me breathe) oh

(Ye) 칼날 같은 네 말에 베일까 두려웠어 난
숨 쉬고 밥을 먹는 채로 그냥 버티기만 해.

나는 비겁했어 버티고 싶었어.

내 손에 내 가슴을 쥐고
나를 위하는 삶을 선택했어 난

★ 나를 놓치기 싫어 나를 더 망치기 싫어.
끝나도 끝나지 않는 기억에 이길 자신이 난 없어.

사랑 같은 건 결국 한 사람에겐 거짓말
이젠 널 잊는 나를 지켜 봐 두 눈 똑바로 뜨고서
넌 절대 날 잊지 마 (Ah) 넌 나를 지우지 마. (Ah)

# Error

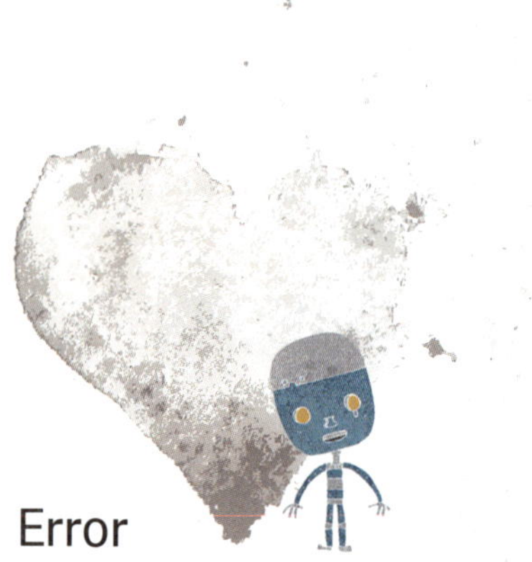

VIXX

I couldn't help it, so I let go of all my feelings.
But I couldn't let go of you. (Let me free.)
And my heart is in agony. (Let me breathe.)

I just have to live like this, breathe like this.
I only have to be alive. Why can't I?
Because it is fine with me. (Let me free.)
It is better for me this way. (Let me breathe.) Oh.

(Ye) I was afraid to be torn by your edgy words.
I breathe and eat, but I am barely alive.

I was a coward. I wanted to carry on.
Grasping my heart with my own fist,
I chose a life for myself.

★ I don't want to lose myself. Don't want to destroy myself.
I'm not confident to get over the endless memories.

Love is eventually a lie to one side.
Now watch me how I dump you from my mind.
Don't you ever forget me. (Ah) Don't you ever erase me. (Ah)

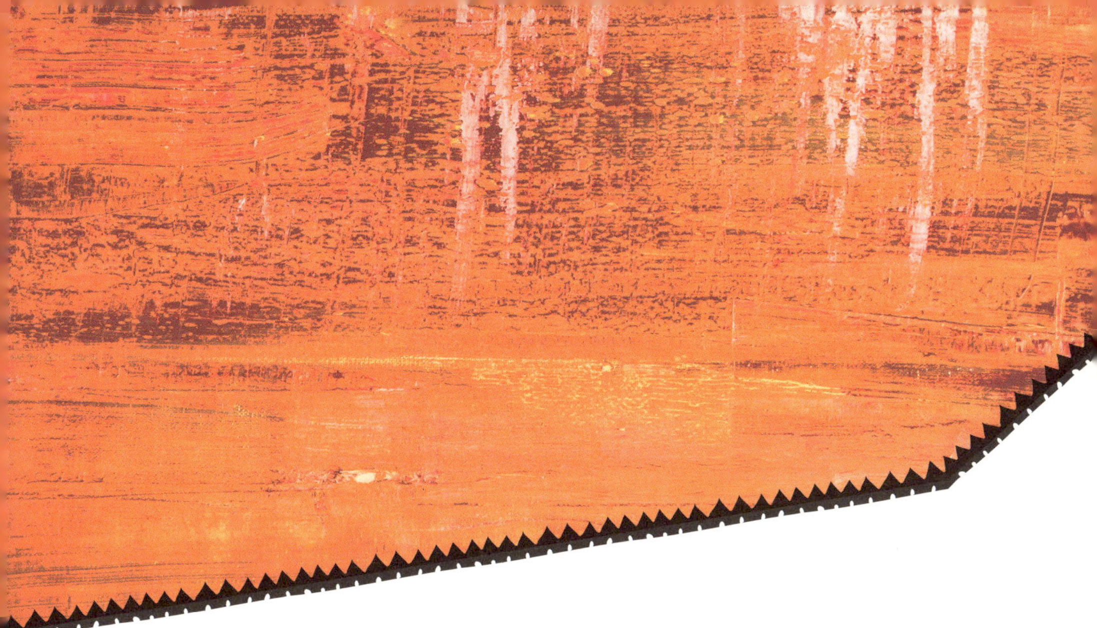

# Appendix

## 01 오늘부터 우리는

### Exercise 1
1 언제부터 한국어를 공부했어요?
2 1시부터 2시까지 점심시간입니다.
3 어제부터 담배 끊었어요.

### Exercise 2
1 하루 종일 서서 일해.
2 케이크를 만들어서 남자 친구에게 줄 거야.
3 소파에 누워서 텔레비전을 봐.

## 02 Honey

### Exercise 1
1 괜찮니?
2 언제 오니?
3 다 했니?

### Exercise 2
1 네가 행복하기를 원해.
2 가벼운 노트북을 원해요.
3 빠른 답변 원해요.

## 03 벚꽃 엔딩

### Exercise 1
1 우리 같이 커피 마셔요.
2 우리 같이 놀아요.
3 우리 같이 한국어 공부해요.

### Exercise 2
1 한국 음식 어떤가요?
2 이 노래 어떤가요?
3 거기 날씨 어떤가요?

## 04 남자 없이 잘 살아

### Exercise 1
1 그 식당은 예약 없이 못 가.
2 신분증 없이 못 들어가.
3 눈물 없이 못 보겠어.

### Exercise 2
1 거짓말하지 마.
2 울지 마.
3 걱정하지 마.

## 05 결혼해 줄래

### Exercise 1
1 화장실 좀 갔다 올게.
2 여기서 기다릴게.
3 앞으로 안 할게.

### Exercise 2
1 눈물이 나.
2 열이 나.
3 겁이 나.

## 06 No No No

### Exercise 1
1 부러워하지 마.
2 우울해하지 마.
3 부끄러워하지 마.

### Exercise 2
1 농담이 아니야.
2 남의 일이 아니야.
3 예전의 내가 아니야.

## 07 너뿐이야

### Exercise 1
1 지갑에 1,000원밖에 없어.
2 냉장고에 물밖에 없어.
3 5분밖에 안 걸려.

### Exercise 2
1 가진 것이 돈뿐이야.
2 이걸 아는 사람은 오직 우리 둘뿐이야.
3 힘들 때 곁에 있는 사람은 가족뿐이야.

## 08 하루만

### Exercise 1
1 떡볶이를 만들 수 있다면 좋겠다.
2 매일 이렇게 먹을 수 있다면 좋을 텐데.
3 돈 걱정 안 하고 살 수 있다면 좋을 텐데.

### Exercise 2
1 운전 조심하기를 바랍니다.
2 연락 주시길 바랍니다.
3 성공하기를 바랍니다.

## 09 Be My Baby

### Exercise 1
1 잊어버릴 것 같아.
2 혼자서 다 먹어 버릴 것 같아.
3 돈을 다 써 버릴 것 같아.

### Exercise 2
1 내가 빌려줄게.
2 나중에 보여 줄게.
3 아침에 깨워 줄게.

## 10 노래가 늘었어

### Exercise 1
1 비가 오고 나서 날씨가 추워졌어.
2 남자 친구와 헤어지고 나서 너무 힘들어.
3 화장품을 바꾸고 나서 피부가 좋아졌어.

### Exercise 2
1 너 오늘 연예인 같아!
2 나 정말 바보 같아.
3 학교가 감옥 같아.

## 11 남자가 사랑할 때

### Exercise 1
1 우울할 때 단 음식을 먹어요.
2 여행갈 때 선글라스를 가지고 갈 거예요.
3 목이 아플 때 따뜻한 물을 많이 드세요.

### Exercise 2
1 물어보고 싶은 게 있어요.
2 갖고 싶은 게 있어요.
3 보여 주고 싶은 게 있어요.

## 12 Ah-Choo

### Exercise 1
1 자나 봐.
2 길이 많이 막히나 봐.
3 싸우나 봐.

### Exercise 2
1 바빠서 얼굴 보기가 힘들어.
2 혼자 하기가 힘들어.
3 시끄러워서 집중하기가 힘들어.

## 13 사랑 사랑 사랑

### Exercise 1
1 힘들어도 포기 안 할 거야.
2 피곤해도 씻고 자.
3 재미없어도 끝까지 들어 주세요.

### Exercise 2
1 기분이 나빠졌어.
2 지갑이 없어졌어.
3 날씨가 추워졌어.

## 14 너의 모든 순간

**Exercise 1**
1 생각만 해도 떨려.
2 생각만 해도 끔찍해.
3 생각만 해도 눈물이 나.

**Exercise 2**
1 집에 음식이 없으면 시켜 먹곤 해.
2 주말에는 늦잠을 자곤 해.
3 일할 때 음악을 듣곤 해.

**Exercise 3**
1 내 남자 친구였으면 좋겠다.
2 몸이 10개였으면 좋겠다.
3 여기가 우리 집이었으면 좋겠다.

## 15 Hands Up

**Exercise 1**
1 머리 터지도록 고민하고 있어.
2 코피가 터지도록 공부만 했어.
3 죽도록 운동했어.

**Exercise 2**
1 병원에 한번 가 봐.
2 이 화장품 한번 써 봐!
3 이 노래 한번 들어 봐.

## 16 Give It to Me

**Exercise 1**
1 아무리 연락해도 받지 않아요.
2 아무리 찾아봐도 없어요.
3 아무리 애를 써도 안 돼요.

**Exercise 2**
1 하지 말란 말이야.
2 빨리 달란 말이야.
3 나도 모른단 말이야.

**Exercise 3**
1 다시 하면 돼.
2 이거 하나만 있으면 돼.
3 전자레인지에 넣고 3분만 돌리면 돼.

## 17 A

**Exercise 1**
1 책상 위에 놓여 있어.
2 일이 쌓여 있어.
3 여기 뭐라고 쓰여 있어?

**Exercise 2**
1 딴생각하다 음식을 태웠어.
2 공부하다 잠들었어.
3 집에서 자다 나왔어.

## 18 썸

**Exercise 1**
1 쌍둥이 같다는 말 많이 들어.
2 남자 같다는 말 많이 들어.
3 바보 같다는 말 듣기 싫어.

**Exercise 2**
1 먹기 싫어졌어.
2 거울 보기 싫어졌어.
3 밖에 나가기 싫어졌어.

## 19 이 노래

**Exercise 1**
1 살 수 있는 게 없어.
2 혼자서 할 수 있는 게 없어.
3 먹을 수 있는 게 김밥밖에 없어.

**Exercise 2**
1 잘 찾아갈 수 있을지 모르겠어.
2 오늘 안에 다 끝낼 수 있을지 모르겠어.
3 언제 또 만날 수 있을지 모르겠어.

## 20 Error

**Exercise 1**
1 절대 아무한테도 말하지 마.
2 절대 용서 못 해.
3 절대 안 돼.

**Exercise 2**
1 강아지를 잘 키울 자신이 없어.
2 좋아하는 사람에게 고백할 자신이 없어.
3 부모님 볼 자신이 없어.

## 01 Starting from Today

### Expression 1

W1: Would you be my girlfriend from today on?

W2: Okay. Then today is our first day.

### Exercise 1

❶ M: Since when have you studied Korean?

W: I studied Korean since January of last year.

❷ W1: Is the doctor not in the office?

W2: No, it is lunch hour from 1 p.m. to 2 p.m.

❸ M1: Oh, you don't smoke?

M2: Nope. I quit as of yesterday.

### Expression 2

W1: What did you get from the store?

W2: I got some milk.

### Exercise 2

❶ W1: Do your legs hurt a lot?

W2: Yes, I work while standing all day.

❷ W1: Wow! Is that a cake you are making?

W2: Yes, I am making one for my boyfriend.

❸ W: What's up?

M: I'm just watching TV on the sofa.

### Conversation

M: Didn't you say you will start working out every evening starting from today?

W: Yeah, but I want to rest today and start tomorrow.

M: Don't put off until tomorrow. Start today.

W: I'm too tired. I cannot possibly start today......

.....................................................................

M: Do you have any plans for this weekend?

W: I'm going to catch up with a friend and go shopping.

M: What about after shopping?

W: I will probably go to my friend's for dinner.

## 02 Honey

### Expression 1

M1: Did you sleep well?

M2: Yes, good morning.

### Exercise 1

❶ W: Are you alright?

M: Yes, I'm alright.

❷ W1: When are you coming?

W2: I'm on my way.

❸ M: Did you finish your homework?

W: No, not yet.

### Expression 2

W1: What do you want?

W2: I want something cheaper.

### Exercise 2

❶ W1: Mom, what do you want me to be?

W2: I just want you to be happy.

❷ M1: What kind of laptop are you looking for?

M2: I want something light.

❸ W1: I want an answer, soon.

W2: Yes, ma'am. I will get back to you within 5 minutes.

### Conversation

W1: Did you finish your assignment?

W2: Not yet.

W1: How long will it take? You're going to be late for the appointment.

W2: It's going to be around an hour from now. You can go first.

.....................................................................

M1: Have you gone out with your girlfriend for a long time?

M2: Yeah, it's been around 5 years.

M1: Do you guys plan to get married?

M2: I want to but I don't know if she feels the same way.

## 03 Cherry Blossom Ending

### Expression 1

M: Let's go for the cherry blossom picnic together.

W: I will take a test tomorrow.

### Exercise 1

1. M1: Let's have coffee together.
   M2: Wow, coffee time!

2. M: Let's hang out together.
   W: Sorry, I'm busy this weekend

3. M: Let's study Korean together.
   W: Sure! When shall we start?

### Expression 2

W: I have a new hair style. What do you think?

M: Pretty!

### Exercise 2

1. W: How do you like Korean food?
   M: I think it's a bit spicy.

2. M: How do you like this song?
   W: I like the lyrics very much.

3. M1: How's the weather there?
   M2: It's really hot.

### Conversation

W: Let's go for the Cherry Blossom Picnic together.

M: What? You mean, just the two of us?

W: No, I mean altogether with our friends.

M: Ha-ha, cool!

----

M: How do you like this song?

W: Good! What is it called?

M: It's called 'Cherry Blossom Ending' by Busker Busker.

W: It's absolutely my type of music. Let's play it one more time.

## 04 I Don't need a Man

### Expression 1

W: I can't sleep without a pillow.

### Exercise 1

1. M: Look how crowded it is!
   W: Yeah, you don't want to go there without a reservation.

2. W1: Do we need an ID?
   W2: Yes, we cannot enter without an ID.

3. W1: This movie is so sad.
   W2: I know. I can't watch it without sobbing.

### Expression 2

W: We're over. Don't ever call me again.

M: Don't leave me. I'll do better.

### Exercise 2

1. M: I promise I didn't drink.
   W: Don't lie to me.

2. W: Don't cry.

3. M: What do I do now?
   W: Don't worry. Everything's going to be alright.

### Conversation

W: Where do we go for dinner on Saturday?

M: What about the Thai restaurant in downtown?

W: That place is really crowded on weekends. You don't want to go there without a reservation.

M: Is that so? Then I'll make a reservation later today.

----

M: I have a presentation tomorrow.

W: Really? Have you prepared a lot?

M: I have but I'm still so worried.

W: Don't worry so much. You are going to do just fine.

## 05 Will You Marry Me?

### Expression 1

W1: What would you like?

W2: I will get this one.

W3: I will look around and be back.

### Exercise 1

❶ W1: Where are you going?

W2: I will use the restroom and be back.

❷ W1: Are you coming as well?

W2: No, I will wait for you here.

❸ W: Will you always lie to me?

M: I won't ever again.

### Expression 2

W: Your nose is bleeding!

### Exercise 2

❶ W: I can't help crying.

M: Me, too.

❷ W: Are you not feeling well?

M: I'm running a fever.

❸ W: I'm getting scared.

M: You can do it! Go for it!

### Conversation

W1: I will be back after catching up with a friend.

W2: Are you going to be late?

W1: Well, I'm not sure. I will call you when it gets late.

W2: Okay.

----

W: Are you not feeling well?

M: I have been coughing and running a fever since yesterday.

W: I think you caught cold. You'd better see the doctor.

M: Okay, I will after work.

## 06 No No No

### Expression 1

W: I'm sorry. What do I do?

M: It's alright. Don't be too sorry.

### Exercise 1

❶ M: Don't be envious.

❷ M: Don't be depressed.

❸ M: Don't be shy.

W: I'm shy.

### Expression 2

W: This is too small.

M: What you see is not what all you see.

### Exercise 2

❶ W: Stop joking.

M: I'm not joking.

❷ W: Flu is going around these days.

M: It's happened to me.

❸ M: Wow! You got so pretty!

W: I'm not the one I used to be.

### Conversation

W1: What's wrong? Why are you crying?

W2: My boyfriend started his military service yesterday.

W1: Don't be so sad. Time flies.

W2: But I already miss him so much.

----

M1: Do I have to finish this in one day?

M2: Yes. You have to finish it by tomorrow.

M1: No way, you are joking.

M2: No, I'm not joking.

## 07 You Are the Only One

### Expression 1

W: Do you speak Korean?

M1: '안녕하세요' is all I know in Korean.

M2: Wow! You are good!

### Exercise 1

❶ W1: Can you just lend me 10,000 won?

  W2: I only have 1,000 won in my wallet.

❷ M: Is there anything to eat at your house?

  W: There's only some water in the fridge.

❸ M: Is the market far from here?

  W: It only takes 5 minutes.

### Expression 2

W1: Are you okay?

W2: Yes, I'm okay. See, you are the only one who is worried about me.

### Exercise 2

❶ M: Money is all that I have.

❷ W: Is this a secret just between you and me?

  M: We are the only ones who know about this.

❸ W: Family is the only ones who stay next to me in my hardship.

### Conversation

M: Is there anything to eat at your house?

W: Open the fridge.

M: There's only some water.

W: Really? Then you can get something to eat from the market.

...................................................

M: Have some. It's vitamin.

W: Why all of a sudden?

M: It looks like you are having a hard time these days.

W: You are the only one who worries about me.

## 08 Just One Day

### Expression 1

M: Don't you know how I feel?

W: I wish I knew how you feel.

### Exercise 1

❶ W1: Is there any Korean food you want to make?

  W2: I wish I knew how to make tteokbokki (spicy rice cake).

❷ W: I wish we could eat like this every day.

  M: I know. I wish the same.

❸ W: I wish I could live without worrying about money.

  M: Do you need a lot of money?

### Expression 2

W: I wish you a happy new year.

### Exercise 2

❶ M: I hope you drive safely.

❷ M: We are looking for a 5-year old boy who's lost. Please call us if you find a boy crying all alone.

❸ M1: I will definitely quit smoking this year!

  M2: I wish it goes successful.

### Conversation

W1: Is there anywhere you wished to go?

W2: Yes, I've always wished to go to Paris.

W1: I wish to go to Paris, too.

W2: Ah, won't it be wonderful if we could go to Paris right now?

...................................................

M1: Since when did you start smoking?

M2: I started smoking when I was 21. I'm trying to quit this year.

M1: That's a good idea. I hope you would make it.

M2: Thanks. I will do my best.

## 09  Be My Baby

### Expression 1

W1: I think he's going to leave me.

W2: What are you talking about? You know how much he loves you.

### Exercise 1

❶ M: I think I might forget it.

W: Than write it down here.

❷ M: I think I'll eat them all.

W: No, you can't. Wait till the guests come.

❸ W1: I think I'm going to spend all the money.

W2: Then keep in your savings!

### Expression 2

M: I will make you happy. Marry me!

### Exercise 2

❶ W: I want to get that cloth but don't have money.

M: I will lend you some.

❷ W1: When will you show me your boyfriend?

W2: I will show you later.

❸ M: I don't think I can wake up early tomorrow.

W: I will wake you in the morning.

### Conversation

W1: Let's eat this ice cream together.

W2: No thanks. I already had some.

W1: Please, I think I'll eat them all if you don't have some.

W2: Alright then, I'll have some.

..............................................................

W: Wow, this pair of shoes is so pretty!

M: Really? Then go ahead.

W: No, it looks expensive. I don't have money.

M: I'll get them for you.

## 10  My Singing Got Better

### Expression 1

W: It looks so delicious!

M: You are going to regret after eating. Don't.

### Exercise 1

❶ W: It's so cold all of a sudden.

M: It's become cold after the rain.

❷ M: What's wrong? Are you okay?

W: It's really hard after breaking up with my boyfriend.

❸ W1: Wow! Your skin has become so fair!

W2: My skin got so much better after using the product.

### Expression 2

W: I felt like I was dreaming today.

M: It was like a hell to me.

### Exercise 2

❶ M: You look like a celebrity today!

W: You think so?

❷ W: Why are your shoes unmatched?

M: I feel like a jerk.

❸ W: I don't want to go to school.

M: Our school is like a prison.

### Conversation

M: What's going on? You are leaving so early after work.

W: Actually, I'm learning Korean after work.

M: Oh, that's why you are listening to K-Pop songs these days!

W: Yeah, I'm getting more interested in K-Pop since I started to take Korean classes.

..............................................................

W1: You should throw away the trash after having cookie, not leave it on the table.

W2: Oh, alright. Sorry.

W1: And clean up the leftovers. Don't do it later.

W2: Okay, I got it but don't push me. You are just like my mom.

## 11 Man in Love

### Expression 1

M: Do you wear skirt even when you are at home?

W: No, I wear shorts at home.

### Exercise 1

❶ M: Why are you eating so much chocolates and candies?

W: I eat sweets when I get depressed.

❷ M: Why did you get new sunglasses?

W: I'm going to bring them when I travel.

❸ W: What do you do when you have sore throat?

M: Drink a lot of warm water when you have sore throat.

### Expression 2

M: What do you want to eat?

W: I'm hungry but there's nothing I want to eat.

### Exercise 2

❶ M: There's something I want to ask.

W: What is it? Go ahead!

❷ W: There's something I want to have.

M: Tell me. I'll get you one.

❸ W1: There's something I want to show you.

W2: What is it? Show me quickly!

### Conversation

M: What does 'chi-mek' mean in Korean?

W: It's an abbreviation of '(fried) chicken and beer' in Korean.

M: What's the relevance between chicken and beer?

W: Koreans usually have beer with chicken.

.................................................

W1: It's my birthday next week.

W2: Congrats! Is there anything you want to get on your birthday?

W1: What do I want to get? Well, I can't come up with one right now.

W2: Yeah? Then let me know when you can think of one. I'll get it for you.

## 12 Ah-Choo

### Expression 1

M: She/He went to get some pizza an hour ago but is not coming back.

W: I guess she/he is making it herself/himself. (I'm just joking.)

### Exercise 1

❶ W1: Isn't he picking up the phone?

W2: I think he is sleeping.

❷ W: Why aren't they here, yet?

M: I guess the traffic is heavy.

❸ W: The atmosphere looks pretty serious over there.

M: I think they are in a fight.

### Expression 2

W1: Isn't it hard to get a job?

W2: It is really hard to get a job these days.

### Exercise 2

❶ W1: Do you see your boyfriend often lately?

W2: He's so busy that we can't catch up so often.

❷ W: It's hard to do by myself.

M: I will help you.

❸ W: Isn't it noisy here?

M: It's so noisy that it's hard to concentrate.

### Conversation

W: I think it's raining outside.

M: Really?! But the weather is so sunny!

W: Look! People are carrying umbrellas.

M: Really! I didn't bring my umbrella...

.................................................

W1: There's a movie I want to watch. Do you want to go and watch with me?

W2: I have an appointment... Why don't you go and watch with your boyfriend!

W1: My boyfriend is so busy with work these days that it's hard to see him.

W2: Well, that's what happens when you get a job.

## 🔢 Love Love Love

### Expression 1

W1: Eat before you leave even if you are busy.

W2: Sorry, I'm late.

### Exercise 1

❶ M: You can give up if it's too hard.

 W: I'm not going to even if it's hard.

❷ W1: I'm so tired. I'm going to sleep.

 W2: Wash before you sleep even if you are tired.

❸ M: Please listen till I finish even if it's not fun.

### Expression 2

M: I like you.

W: What are you talking about? We are friends.

### Exercise 2

❶ W: I'm upset.

❷ W: I lost my wallet.

 M: Take a careful look.

❸ W: It became cold.

 M: Yes, it's truly fall now.

### Conversation

M1: Are you not feeling well?

M2: I caught cold, but I don't have time to see the doctor.

M1: You'd better see the doctor even if you are busy.

M2: Right, thank you.

.......................................................

W: What are you trying to say?

M: In fact… I like you.

W: What? What are you saying all of a sudden? Stop joking.

M: I'm not joking. I'm very serious.

## 🔢 Every Moment of You

### Expression 1

W1: You are thinking of your boyfriend!

W2: Yes, I feel so good even when I just think of him.

### Exercise 1

❶ W1: You are driving for the first time tomorrow, right?

 W2: Yes, I'm so nervous to even think of it.

❷ M: I stepped on the cockroach yesterday.

 W: It's awful to even to think of it.

❸ W1: You must be missing your mom.

 W2: Yes, I burst into tears even just thinking of her.

### Expression 2

W: Sometimes I wonder 'What if we haven't met?'

M: Don't think of such things.

### Exercise 2

❶ W: Do you often order delivery food?

 M: Yes, I order delivery food when there's no food at home.

❷ W: Do you wake up early even on weekends?

 M: No, I usually oversleep on the weekends.

❸ W: When do you usually listen to music?

 M: I usually listen to music when I work.

### Expression 3

W1: It's already Monday tomorrow. I have to go to work.

W2: I wish it was Friday today.

### Exercise 3

❶ W1: He's awesome!

 W2: I wish he were my boyfriend.

❷ W: Are you busy?

 M: I wish there were more hours in a day.

❸ W: It's amazing here!

 M: I wish this was our home.

## Conversation

W1: Oh, I wish I were an office worker.

W2: Why all of a sudden?

W1: Then I won't have to take tests.

W2: Office workers don't take test, but their work is harder.

- - - - - - - - - - - - - - - - - - - -

M1: Do you like to watch soccer?

M2: Of course. I used to go to the soccer stadium with my dad on weekends when I was young.

M1: Really? Then would you like to go to watch a soccer match with me this Saturday?

M2: Absolutely! I am excited even to think of it.

## 15 Hands Up

### Expression 1

M: I was sick to death yesterday.

W: It's because you worked so hard.

### Exercise 1

❶ M: What are you going to do?

W: I am trying to think that my brain is nearly exploding.

❷ W: Wow, you studied really hard!

M: I studied so hard that my nose bled.

❸ W: You have changed so much that I could hardly recognize!

M: I exercised so hard that I nearly passed out.

### Expression 2

W: Wow, it must be fun!

M: Try yourself! It's really fun.

### Exercise 2

❶ W: Why don't you go and see the doctor?

❷ W1: Hey, try this cosmetic!

W2: Is it nice?

❸ M: Hey, try this song!

W: It's good~

## Conversation

W1: Oh, it is so hard to pronounce Korean.

W2: Of course it is hard to pronounce a foreign language.

W1: I should just give up on Korean.

W2: Don't give up before you try so hard.

- - - - - - - - - - - - - - - - - - - -

W: Aren't you going to dance?

M: No, I don't dance well.

W: It's easy to dance. Just shake with the music!

M: Is this how you do it?

## 16 Give It to Me

### Expression 1

W1: No matter how much I eat, I don't gain weight.

W2: No matter how hard I exercise, I don't lose weight.

### Exercise 1

❶ M1: Does she/he answer the phone?

M2: No. No matter how many times I call him/her, she/he would never answer.

❷ M1: Have you found it?

M2: No matter how hard I looked for it, I couldn't find it.

❸ M1: Are you giving up?

M2: Yes. No matter how hard I try, it doesn't work.

### Expression 2

M: You can go first.

W: No. I'm scared, too!

### Exercise 2

❶ W: Stop it. Stop it!

M: Okay. I won't.

❷ W: Hurry, give it to me!

M: Okay. Here you go.

❸ W: You know that, don't you? Just tell me.

M: I don't know, either!

## Expression 3

W: Let's work hard!

M: Sure. It will be fine as long as we work hard!

## Exercise 3

❶ M: What am I going to do?

　W: Just try again.

❷ W1: What do I need when I go traveling?

　W2: This is all we need.

❸ M: How do we cook this?

　W: Just put it in the microwave and run it for 3 minutes.

## Conversation

W: Would you please move this to that side?

M: Oh no, it is too heavy to lift it.

W: Be a man. Can't you even lift this?

M: It is really heavy. I mean it!

M1: Would you like to try some?

M2: It looks very spicy.

M1: Not really. Drink a lot of water if it's too spicy.

M2: Sorry. I'll try next time.


## 17  A

## Expression 1

W: Is the door opened?

M: No, it's locked.

## Exercise 1

❶ W: Where's the key?

　M: It's on the desk.

❷ W: Aren't you off work?

　M: I have work piled up.

❸ M: What's it written on here?

　W: It says, "Anyone reads this is stupid."

## Expression 2

W: What happened to your arm?

M: I got hurt while I was playing basketball.


## Exercise 2

❶ W: Why are the food all burnt?

　M: I burnt them while I got distracted.

❷ M: Why couldn't you study for the exam?

　W: I fell asleep while I was studying.

❸ W: What happened to your hair?

　M: I was sleeping at home and just came out.

## Conversation

W1: Have you seen my blue pants?

W2: They are on the chair in the living room.

W1: What about my wallet?

W2: It's on the table. Will you organize your stuff?

W: Have you heard GOT7's song? I think the song is really cool

M: ........

W: What's wrong? Why aren't you saying anything?

M: Sorry, what did you just say? I got distracted and didn't hear you.


## 18  Some

## Expression 1

M: I hate to hear that I look like a bum.

W: Let's go to the hair shop.

## Exercise 1

❶ W1: Wow, you look just like your sister!

　W2: We hear that many times.

❷ W1: People often say that I look like a boy.

　W2: It's because your hair is short.

❸ M: I don't like people saying that I'm like an idiot.

　W: Than stop making so many mistakes!

## Expression 2

M: I don't want to live by myself anymore. I feel lonely.

W: Then why don't we live together!

## Exercise 2

**①** **W:** I don't want to eat anymore.
**M:** You had plenty enough.

**②** **W1:** I don't want to see the mirror anymore.
**W2:** Don't be depressed.

**③** **M:** I don't want to go outside anymore.
**W:** That's fine. Let's not go out.

## Conversation

**W:** You're like a girl when you smile that way.
**M:** Don't say that.
**W:** What do you mean?
**M:** That I'm like a girl when I smile! I really hate to hear that.

........................................................................

**M:** What movie shall we watch tonight?
**W:** Sorry. I don't feel like watching a movie.
**M:** Is there something wrong?
**W:** I just feel like drinking alcohol all of a sudden.

## 19 This Song

### Expression 1

**W:** I gained too much weight that there is nothing I can wear.

### Exercise 1

**①** **W1:** Aren't they all very expensive?
**W2:** There is nothing I can buy.

**②** **M:** Let me help you.
**W:** There is nothing I can do by myself.

**③** **W1:** You can't eat spicy food, right?
**W2:** Kimbab is the only item I can eat on the menu.

### Expression 2

**M:** Will you be able to come tomorrow?
**W:** I don't know if I would be able to make it tomorrow.

## Exercise 2

**①** **W:** Will you be able to find it?
**M:** I don't know if I would be able to find the place right.

**②** **W:** Will you be able to finish it by midnight?
**M:** I don't know if I would be able to finish it within today.

**③** **W1:** When will we be able to see again?
**W2:** I don't know when that is going to be.

## Conversation

**W:** I'm hungry. Do you have anything to eat?
**M:** Do you want me to make some ramyun?
**W:** Is there anything else?
**M:** Sorry, I'm not good at cooking. Ramyeon is the only thing I can make.

........................................................................

**M1:** Where are you? Have you left home?
**M2:** I'm still at home. Wasn't our appointment at 5 p.m.?
**M1:** Something urgent happened. Can you come out by 4 p.m.?
**M2:** Well, I'm not sure if I can make it by then.

## 20 Error

### Expression 1

**M:** We should never lose.

### Exercise 1

**①** **M:** Don't ever tell anyone.
**W:** I won't. Tell me, quickly!

**②** **W:** I will never forgive you.
**M:** Okay, don't forgive me.

**③** **M:** Can we just ride that?
**W:** No, never.

### Expression 2

**M:** I'm going to study overseas.
**W:** Then let's break-up. I'm not confident to wait for you.

## Exercise 2

**❶ M:** I'm not confident to raise the dog well.

　**W:** I will take good care of it.

**❷ M:** I'm not confident to tell my feelings to her/him in person.

　**W:** Then why don't you tell her/him by texting?

**❸ W:** Aren't you going home?

　**M:** I'm not confident to see my parents.

## Conversation

**M:** I'm sorry. Please give me the last chance.

**W:** No, never.

**M:** People make mistakes. Please forgive me this time.

**W:** No, I will never forgive you.

.........................................................................................

**W:** We need to win this game. You know it, right?

**M:** Sure, I do.

**W:** Are you confident?

**M:** Absolutely! I'm confident to win.

## 01 오늘부터 우리는

### 가수 및 노래 소개

〈오늘부터 우리는〉은 '여자친구'의 두 번째 앨범 타이틀곡으로 발표 후 많은 주목을 받지 못했다. 그러던 중 비가 온 무대 위에서 멤버들이 여덟 번이나 넘어지면서도 이 곡을 끝까지 부르는 영상이 유튜브에 공개되어 세계적으로 큰 화제를 모으게 되었다. 이후 이 곡은 음원 차트에 재진입하는 데 성공하였고 오랜 기간 팬들의 큰 사랑을 받게 되었다.

### 표현 1

'N부터'는 선행하는 명사가 어떤 일이나 시간의 시작점이라는 것을 나타내며 'from'과 같은 의미이다. 단 시작점이 되는 곳이 어떤 장소라면 명사 뒤에 '부터'가 아닌 '에서'를 붙인다.

### 표현 2

'V₁-아/어서 V₂'는 일어나는 사건의 순서를 연결할 때 사용한다. 이때 앞선 행위의 결과가 뒤의 행위로 연결되는 것으로 두 행위는 서로 연관성이 있어야 한다.

### 발음

① 천천히 발화 시, 문자 그대로 [널 향한]으로 발화한다. 그러나 빠르게 발화 시, 첫음절에 놓이지 않은 'ㅎ'은 약화되어 [ㅇ]에 가깝게 발화되고, 받침 'ㄹ'의 영향을 받는다.

② '빛'이 다른 명사의 뒤에 붙어 한 단어를 이루면 '빛'의 초성 'ㅂ'은 경음회되어 [ㅃ]로 발음된다.

③ '빛'의 단독 발음은 [빋]이나 뒤의 음절 '내'의 초성 'ㄴ'로 인해 받침 [ㄷ]는 [ㄴ]로 비음화되어, '빛 내'는 [빈 내]로 발음된다.

### 맞춤법

'설레다'는 기분 좋게 가슴이 두근거리는 것을 의미한다. '설레다'의 의미로 '설레이다'를 쓰기도 하나 '설레다'만 표준어로 인정한다. 그러므로 '설레다'의 명사형은 '설렘'이고 '설레임'은 표준어가 아니지만 일상생활에서나 노래 가사에서 많이 접할 수 있다.

## 02 Honey

### 가수 및 노래 소개

지금의 '카라'는 한국을 대표하는 걸그룹 중에 하나이지만 데뷔 후 1~2년간은 대중들에게 큰 주목을 받지 못했다. 〈Honey〉는 그런 '카라'에게 처음으로 음악 방송 1위를 선물한 곡으로 짝사랑을 하고 있는 소녀의 마음을 잘 표현한 곡이다. 예전 '카라'의 모습이 궁금하다면 〈Honey〉 뮤직 비디오를 통해 풋풋한 '카라'의 모습을 만날 수 있을 것이다.

### 표현 1

'A/V-니?'는 질문을 할 때 사용하는 반말 표현으로 상대방에게 친근한 느낌을 표현하며 질문할 때 사용한다. 거의 동일한 표현으로 'A/V-냐?'라는 표현도 있는데 'A/V-니?'보다는 좀 더 강한 표현이다.

### 표현 2

'N을/를 원하다'는 어떤 대상을 소유하고 싶다는 의미로 'want'와 같은 의미이다. 그러나 'A/V-기를 원하다'는 'want'와 'wish'의 의미를 모두 가지며 주어가 자신의 원하는 것을 말하거나 다른 대상이 어떤 행위를 하거나 어떤 상태가 되기를 희망함을 나타낼 때도 사용된다.

### 발음

① 'of'의 의미를 가지는 조사 '의'는 주로 [에]로 발음된다.

② 받침 [ㄴ]이나 [ㄹ] 뒤에 'ㅎ'가 있는 경우, 휴지를 두지 않고 발화하면 'ㅎ'는 발음되지 않고 받침에 있던 자음 [ㄴ], [ㄹ]이 연음되어 발음된다.

## 03 벚꽃 엔딩

### 가수 및 노래 소개

'버스커 버스커'는 2011년 한국의 대표적인 오디션 프로그램 '슈퍼스타K 3'에 참가해 준우승을 차지한 3인조 밴드이다. 〈벚꽃 엔딩〉은 2011년 1집 앨범 '버스커 버스커'의 수록곡으로 해마다 벚꽃이 피는 3, 4월이 되면 한국의 길거리 어디에서나 들을 수 있는 한국의 봄 캐롤이라고 불리는 노래이다.

### 표현 1

'V-아요/어요' 상대방에게 어떤 행위를 제안하는 표현으로 'let's~'와 비슷하다. '아요/어요'는 친근하지만 예의가 필요한 관계의 사람들에게 사용하고 '-(으)ㅂ시다'는 '-아요/어요'보다 좀 더 예의 있고 격식적인 표현이다. '-자'는 아주 가까운 사람이나 어린 사람에게 쓰는 반말이다.

### 표현 2

'N이/가 어떤가요?' 어떤 대상의 상태가 어떤지를 직접 물어볼 때나 어떤 대상에 대한 상대방의 의견이나 생각을 물을 때 사용하는 표현이다. 같은 의미의 표현으로 'N이/가 어때요?'를 쓸 수 있는데 'N이/가 어떤가요?'가 더 부드러운 느낌이다.

### 발음

① 종성 'ㅌ'는 'ㅣ' 모음 앞에서 [ㅊ]로 소리 난다.

② 종성 'ㅂ'는 자음 'ㄴ' 앞에서 [ㅁ]로 소리 난다.

**어순**

한국 어순은 주어 – 목적어 – 서술어 순이다. 그러나 노래 가사에서는 이 어순이 뒤바뀌기도 한다.

## 04 남자 없이 잘 살아

### 가수 및 노래 소개

'미쓰에이'는 중국인 '페이', '지아'와 한국인 '민', '수지'로 구성된 'JYP'의 다국적 4인조 걸 그룹이다. 〈Bad Girl Good Girl〉이란 곡으로 데뷔와 동시에 각종 음악 방송에서 1위를 차지하며 가장 성공적인 데뷔를 한 걸그룹으로 평가받는다. 데뷔곡을 통해 남성에게 끌려 다니는 착한 여자의 이미지를 거부하던 '미쓰에이'는 〈남자 없이 잘 살아〉에서는 남자가 없어도 된다고 말하는 더욱 당당하고 독립적인 여성상을 표현하고 있다.

### 표현 1

'N 없이'는 N이 없는 상태를 나타내는 표현으로 'without'과 같은 의미이다. 'N 없이 못 V'의 형태로도 많이 쓰이는데 'cannot do something without somebody/ something'과 비슷한 표현이 된다. '못 V' 대신에 'V-(으)ㄹ 수 없다'를 사용하는 경우도 많으며 상황을 좀 더 강조하고자 할 때는 'N 없이' 뒤에 '는'을 덧붙여 쓰기도 한다.

### 표현 2

'V-지 말다'는 금지를 나타내는 표현으로 'do not'과 같은 표현이다. 'V-지 마'는 가까운 관계에서 사용하는 반말 표현이고, 'V-지 마세요'는 예의가 필요한 사이에서 사용하는 존대 표현이다.

### 발음

'없'은 단독으로 읽으면 [업]으로 발음되나 뒤에 모음이 오면 겹받침의 두 자음 [ㅂ], [ㅅ]이 모두 소리 난다. 이 때, [ㅂ]으로 인하여 자연스레 [ㅅ]은 [ㅆ]으로 소리 난다. 그러나 '없이'의 경우, [업씨] 혹은 [업시]로 발음해도 괜찮다.

### 유용한 표현

'need'는 한국어로 '필요하다'이다. 그러나 'do not need'는 한국어로 '필요 없다'이다.

## 05 결혼해 줄래

### 가수 및 노래 소개

한국에서는 모든 영역에서 뛰어난 남자를 표현할 때 '엄마 친구의 아들'이라는 말을 줄여 '엄친아'라고 부른다. '이승기'는 한국의 대표적인 '엄친아' 이미지의 가수로 노래뿐만 아니라 예능과 연기 모든 영역에 걸쳐 좋은 모습을 보여 주고 있다. 〈결혼해 줄래〉는 2009년 발표된 곡이지만, 한국에서 결혼식 축가로 인기가 많아 지금도 한국의 결혼식장에 가면 많이 들을 수 있다.

### 표현 1

'V-(으)ㄹ게요'는 화자가 자신의 의지를 나타내는 표현으로, 약속을 하거나 허락을 구하는 의미를 담고 있기도 한다. 'will'과 비슷한 표현이다.

### 표현 2

'N이/가 나다'는 없던 것이 생겨났음을 의미하는 표현으로, 감정 혹은 신체 변화를 나타낼 때 많이 사용된다. 말을 할 때는 조사 '이/가'가 생략되는 경우가 많다.

### 발음

① 받침 'ㄹ'을 포함한 어미의 경우, '-(으)ㄹ' 뒤의 'ㄱ'은 [ㄲ]로 발음된다.
② '눈물이'는 발음 나는 대로 [눈무리]로 발음하면 된다. 다만 [눈무리]를 [눙무리]로 발음하지 않도록 주의한다.
③ 받침 'ㅎ'은 뒤에 모음이 오는 경우에 발음하지 않는다.

## 06 No No No

### 가수 및 노래 소개

'에이핑크'는 2011년 데뷔한 6인조 걸그룹으로 〈No No No〉는 그들의 세 번째 앨범에 수록된 곡이다. 이 노래는 '에이핑크'에게 처음으로 지상파 음악 방송 1위를 안겨 준 곡이며 일본 무대 진출 데뷔곡이기도 하다. 힘들어하고 있는 이성에게 힘이 되어 주겠다는 밝은 내용으로, '에이핑크' 특유의 소녀적인 발랄함이 잘 묻어나는 곡이다.

### 표현 1

'A-아하지/어하지 말다'는 금지의 표현으로 'don't be'와 비슷한 표현이다. 앞서 배운 'V-지 마'는 동사에 결합하여 사용하지만 'A-아하지/어하지 마'는 형용사 뒤에 결합하여 사용한다.

### 표현 2

'(N₁은/는) N₂이/가 아니다'는 'N₁ ≠N₂'임을 나타낸다. 이때 N₁이 화자와 청자가 모두가 알고 있는 상황이나 사실이면 문장에서 생략되는 경우가 많다. '아니야'는 친구나 가까운 관계에서 쓰는 반말 표현이고 '아니에요'는 예의 있게 말하는 표현이다.

### 발음

'-(으)ㄹ게'는 [(으)ㄹ께]로 발음한다.

### 줄임말

한국어에는 발음을 좀 더 간편하고 빠르게 하기 위해 짧은 형태로 줄여 쓰는 말들이 많다.

### 07 너뿐이야

**가수 및 노래 소개**

'박진영'은 가수, 작곡가, 프로듀서이자 'JYP 엔터테인먼트'의 대표이다. 'JYP 엔터테인먼트'는 한국의 3대 기획사 중의 하나로 '원더걸스', '2PM', '2AM', '갓세븐', '트와이스' 등의 아이돌 그룹이 소속되어 있다. 〈너뿐이야〉는 2012년 발표한 곡으로, 사랑이 깨질까 봐 걱정하는 여자를 안심시키는 남자의 사랑 노래이다.

**표현 1**

'N밖에'는 대상을 한정해서 말할 때 사용하는 조사로 'only, just' 와 같은 의미이지만 한국어에서는 명사 뒤에 붙여 사용한다. 또한 부정을 나타내는 '안, 못, 아니다, 없다, 모르다' 등의 말과 항상 함께 사용해야 한다.

**표현 2**

'N뿐이다'는 대상을 한정해서 말할 때 사용하면 표현1의 'N밖에'와 같은 의미의 표현이다. 그러나 'N밖에'는 뒤에 '안, 못, 아니다,없다, 모르다' 등의 부정 표현을 같이 사용해야 하지만 'N뿐이다'는 문장을 바로 끝낼 수 있다.

**발음**

'너뿐이야'는 발음 나는 대로 [너뿌니야]로 읽으면 되는데, 빨리 발음하는 경우 [너뿌냐]로 발음된다.

**줄임말**

한국 사람들은 간편하고 빠르게 말하기 위해 줄임말을 쓰기를 좋아한다. 이러한 줄임말을 단어에서도 많이 찾아볼 수 있다.

### 08 하루만

**가수 및 노래 소개**

'방탄소년단'은 남성 7인조 그룹으로 짧게 줄여 BTS라고도 부른다. 한국보다는 오히려 해외의 K-Pop 팬들에게 높은 인지도를 가지고 있으며 강렬한 랩핑과 군무가 특징이다. 이 곡 〈하루만〉은 바쁜 스케줄 중에 사랑하는 사람과 단 하루의 시간이라도 같이 보냈으면 한다는 멤버들의 진심 어린 희망을 부드러운 힙합 선율에 실어 전하고 있는 곡이다.

**표현 1**

'V-(으)ㄹ 수 있다면'은 어떤 일의 가능성에 대해서 가정하면서 말할 때 사용하는 표현이다. 주로 뒤에 '좋겠다, 좋을 텐데, 얼마나 좋을까?' 등의 표현과 결합하여 자신의 희망을 나타낼 때 많이 사용된다.

**표현 2**

'V-기를 바라다'는 주어의 희망을 나타낼 때 사용하는 표현으로 'I wish'와 비슷한 표현이다. 주로 화자가 다른 대상의 행위나 상태를 희망하거나 요구할 때 주로 사용되며 'V-기를 원하다'와 의미와 쓰임이 거의 동일하다.

**발음**

받침 'ㄹ'로 끝나는 어미의 경우, '-(으)ㄹ' 뒤의 'ㅅ'는 [ㅆ]로 발음된다.

**맞춤법**

'바라다'는 '-아/어'와 결합 시 '바라'가 되어야 하나 거의 모든 한국 사람들이 '바래'로 사용한다. '바라'라고 말하면 어색하게 여기니 주의해야 한다.

### 09 Be My Baby

**가수 및 노래 소개**

2007년 데뷔한 '원더걸스'는 한국 가요 시장의 걸그룹 전성 시대를 연 선두 주자라고 할 수 있다. 데뷔 당시 '4minute'의 '현아'가 초창기 멤버였으나 건강상의 문제로 탈퇴하고 '유빈'이 합류하였으며 2015년에는 다시 '선예'와 '소희'가 차례로 탈퇴하고 현재는 '유빈', '예은', '선미', '혜림' 4인 체제로 활동하고 있다. 〈Be My Baby〉는 사랑하는 사람을 향한 달콤한 사랑 고백의 노래이다.

**표현 1**

'V-아/어 버릴 것 같다'는 하면 안 되는 행동을 하거나 그렇게 되면 안 되는 상태가 될까 봐 걱정할 때 사용하는 표현으로 'V-아/어 버리다'와 'A/V-(으)ㄹ 것 같다'의 두 가지 문법이 결합된 표현이다. 'V-아/어 버리다'는 그렇게 되면 안 된다고 생각하는 상황이 되었음을 나타낼 때 사용하며 'A/V-(으)ㄹ 것 같다'는 'I think'와 같이 자신의 생각을 나타낼 때 쓰는 표현이다.

**표현 2**

'V-아/어 줄게'는 상대방을 위해 어떤 행동을 할 것임을 약속할 때 사용하는 표현이다. 영어의 'I will'과 비슷한 표현으로 주어에는 항상 '나'만 사용할 수 있다.

**발음**

① '것'의 받침 'ㅅ'은 [ㄷ]로 발음나는데 뒤에 'ㄴ'이나 'ㅁ'이 오면 받침의 발음은 비음화되어 [ㄴ]으로 발음된다.
② 'ㄹ' 받침 뒤의 'ㄷ, ㅅ, ㅈ'는 경음으로 발음되는 경우가 많다.

### 10 노래가 늘었어

**가수 및 노래 소개**

'에일리'는 2012년 싱글 〈Heaven〉이라는 곡으로 데뷔하였다. 데뷔 전 NBC TV SHOW '머레이쇼'의 경연 코너에서 2위를 차지한 바 있으며 비슷한 시기 유튜브에 올린 노래하는 동영상의 조회 수가 1000만 건에 달해 '천만 소녀'로 불리었다. 〈노래가 늘었어〉는 노래를 통해 이별의 아픔을 극복해 나가는 어느 여성의 이야기를 담고 있다.

### 표현 1

'V-고 나서'는 어떤 행위나 사건에 대한 결과를 순서에
따라 기술할 때 사용하는 표현으로 'after ~ing 동명사구'
정도의 의미이다. '나서'를 생략하고 'V-고'만 사용해도
의미적으로 큰 차이가 없지만 '나서'를 사용하면 순서를
정확히 강조해 주는 느낌이다.

### 표현 2

'N 같다'는 동일하지 않은 두 대상이 비슷하게 느껴지는
기분을 나타낼 때 사용하는 표현으로 'look like, seem
like'와 비슷한 표현이다. '꼭, 마치' 등의 표현과 같이
사용하는 경우가 많다.

### 발음

'ㅊ'는 '차, 처, 초, 추'와 '챠, 쳐, 쵸, 츄'의 발음이 같다.

### 어순

'-고 나서'는 ①동작을 나타내는 선행절과 결합하여 쓰인다.
'-고 나서' 뒤에 ②변화된 상태나 다음 동작을 서술하는
후행절이 온다.

## 11 남자가 사랑할 때

### 가사 및 노래 소개

'인피니트'는 2010년 데뷔한 7인조 남성 그룹으로
80~90년대의 리듬을 현대적인 감각에 맞게 바꾸어 절도
있는 안무와 함께 표현하는 것이 특징이며 대표곡으로는
〈내꺼하자〉 등이 있다. 〈Man in Love〉는 사랑에 빠진
남자라면 한 번쯤 겪어 봤을 공감 가는 이야기를 경쾌한
멜로디에 실어 전달하고 있는 중독성 있는 곡이다.

### 표현 1

'A/V-(으)ㄹ 때'는 어떤 일을 하는 순간이나 어떤 일이
생기는 경우 등을 가리키는 표현으로 'when~, in case
of'와 비슷한 의미이다. 어떤 일을 하는 순간이나 상황을
강조하고 싶을 때 '에는'을 붙여 쓸 수 있다.

### 표현 2

'V-고 싶은 게 있다'는 하고 싶은 무언가가 있다는 것을
나타낼 때 사용한다. 만약 희망하는 무언가가 장소라면
'V-고 싶은 곳'으로, 사람이라면 'V-고 싶은 사람', 말이라면
'V-고 싶은 말' 등으로 바꾸어 쓰면 된다.

### 발음

① '때엔'은 'ㅐ'와 'ㅔ'의 발음이 같으므로 빨리 발화 시
1음절로 [땐]으로 발음된다.
② '삶'은 단독으로 읽으면 [삼]으로 발음되나 뒤에 모음이
오면 받침 발음이 모두 발음된다.
③ '단 하나'는 문자 그대로 [단 하나]로 읽으나 빨리
발음하면 'ㅎ'이 약화되어 [다나나]로 발음된다.

### 줄임말

보조사 '는'은 앞의 음절에 받침이 없는 경우, '는'을 'ㄴ'으로
줄여 사용하기도 한다. 위의 경우, '에는' → '엔'으로 줄여
사용하였다.

## 12 Ah-Choo

### 가수 및 노래 소개

'러블리즈'는 '걸리쉬팝(Girlish-Pop)'을 컨셉으로 하는
8인조 여성 아이돌 그룹으로 2015년 발표한 〈Ah-Choo〉가
큰 성공을 거두면서 인지도를 높였다. 〈Ah-Choo〉는
재채기를 할 때 나오는 소리로 재채기를 참기 힘들 때처럼
사랑하는 사람 앞에서 마음을 숨기기 힘들어하는 소녀의
수줍은 마음을 잘 표현한 곡이다.

### 표현 1

'V-나 보다'는 현재 상황을 보고 다른 대상의 상태나
행동에 대해 추측하여 말할 때 사용한다. 과거 일에 대해서
추측해서 말할 때는 'V-았나/었나 보다'를 사용한다. 'V-는
것 같다'와 비슷한 표현이지만 'V-나 보다'를 사용하려면
자신의 추측에 대한 근거가 있어야 한다.

### 표현 2

'V-기 힘들다'는 어떤 일을 하는 것이 쉽지 않다는
의미로 'It's hard to ~'와 같은 표현이다. '힘들다' 대신에
'어렵다(difficult)' 등의 표현으로 바꿔 쓸 수도 있다.

### 발음

어간 말 받침 비음 'ㅁ', 'ㄴ' 뒤에 오는 평음 'ㄱ,ㄷ,ㅅ,ㅈ'는
[ㄲ, ㄸ, ㅆ, ㅉ] 경음으로 소리 난다.

### 줄임말

'V-고프다'는 'V-고 싶다'의 줄임말로, 어떤 행동을 하기를
원한다는 의미를 가지고 있다. 'V-고 싶다'는 일반적으로
일상생활에서 많이 쓰이고 'V-고프다'는 시나 노래 가사에
많이 쓰인다.

## 13 사랑 사랑 사랑

### 가수 및 노래 소개

'FT아일랜드'는 2007년에 데뷔한 5인조 아이돌 그룹으로
댄스 위주의 다른 아이돌 그룹과 달리 밴드의 형태를
취하고 있다. 메인 보컬 이홍기의 뛰어난 가창력과
멤버들의 탄탄한 연주로 실력 있는 밴드로 인정받고
있다. 〈사랑 사랑 사랑〉은 2010년 발표한 곡으로, 연인과
이별하는 남자의 절제된 감정을 가사로 표현하고 있다.

### 표현 1

'-아도/어도'는 어떤 일의 결과나 해야 되는 행위가
기대하는 바와 상반될 때 사용하는 표현으로 'even if',
혹은 'even though'의 의미이다.

**표현 2**

'A-아지다/어지다'는 상태의 변화를 나타낼 때 사용하는 표현으로 'get + 형용사, become + 형용사'와 비슷한 의미의 표현이다. 일반적으로 어떤 대상이 변화한 뒤의 상태를 말할 때 사용하므로 'A-아졌어요/어졌어요'와 같이 과거형으로 말하는 경우가 많다.

**발음**

① '사랑'은 발음 나는 대로 [사랑]으로 발음하면 된다. 다만 [사랑]을 [싸랑]으로 발음하지 않도록 주의한다.
② '눈물이'는 발음 나는 대로 [눈무리]로 발음하면 된다. 다만 [눈무리]를 [눙무리]로 발음하지 않도록 주의한다.
③ '네'는 '내'와 발음이 같아 이를 구분하기 위해 '네'를 [니]라고 많이 발음한다.

**유용한 표현**

헤어질 때 쓰는 인사말은 위와 같다. 친구 사이에 주로 쓰는 반말 인사말이다.

## Ⅰ 너의 모든 순간

**가수 및 노래 소개**

발라드는 한국에서 가장 인기 있는 음악 장르 중의 하나로 '성시경'은 '발라드의 왕자'라 불릴 만큼 이 장르에서 확고한 위치를 차지하고 있다. 〈너의 모든 순간〉은 아시아 지역에서 많은 인기를 끌었던 한국 드라마 '별에서 온 그대'의 O.S.T 수록곡으로 성시경의 감미로운 음색을 통해 한국의 발라드 감성이 무엇인지를 잘 보여 주고 있는 곡이다.

**표현 1**

'생각만 해도'는 어떤 일을 직접 하지 않고 생각만으로도 직접 그 일을 한 것 같은 기분이 든다는 것을 나타내는 말로 'just to think'의 의미이다.

**표현 2**

'V-곤 하다'는 화자가 일정 기간 계속했던 반복적인 행동을 나타낼 때 사용한다. '하다'의 시제 변화에 따라 현재까지 계속하고 있는 행동을 나타내기도 하며 과거에 반복했던 행동을 나타내기도 한다.

**표현 3**

'N이었으면/였으면 좋겠다'는 화자의 희망이나 바람을 나타낼 때 쓰이는 말로 'I wish'와 비슷한 표현이다. 주어 자리에는 '나'만 사용할 수 있는데 보통 말할 때는 '나'를 생략하고 말한다.

**발음**

① 받침의 발음이 [ㄱ], [ㄷ], [ㅂ]로 나는 음절 뒤에 'ㄴ', 'ㅁ'가 오면 받침의 발음은 비음화되어 각각 [ㅇ]([ŋ]), [ㄴ], [ㅁ]로 발음된다.
② 어미 '-(으)ㄹ' 뒤의 'ㅅ'는 [ㅆ]로 발음된다.

**어순**

한국어는 다른 언어에 비해서 어순이 비교적 자유로운 편이며 노래에서는 이런 현상이 더욱 심하게 나타난다. 그러나 일반적인 발화에서 주어는 제일 앞에, 동사나 형용사는 가장 뒤에 온다.

## ⅠⅤ Hands Up

**가수 및 노래 소개**

2PM은 2008년 〈10점 만점에 10점〉이라는 곡으로 데뷔하였으며 아크로바틱 안무와 넘치는 남성미가 그룹의 특징으로 '야수돌'이라는 별명을 가지고 있다. 오후 2시에 활력을 줄 수 있는 노래를 하겠다는 2PM이라는 그룹명에 알맞게 신나는 댄스 음악을 위주로 한다. 〈Hands Up〉은 정신없이 몸을 흔들라는 가사의 신나는 클럽 음악이다.

**표현 1**

'V-도록'은 현재의 상태가 어느 정도라는 것을 다소 과장하여 비유해서 말할 때 사용하는 표현이다. 정도를 나타내는 'V-(으)ㄹ 정도로'의 표현으로 바꿔 쓸 수 있으며 간단하게는 '너무, 많이' 등의 부사와 바꿔 쓸 수도 있다.

**표현 2**

'V-아/어 봐'와 'V-아/어 보세요'는 시도를 권하고 추천하거나 명령을 완곡하게 할 때 쓰는 표현으로 'try -ing' 와 같은 표현이다. '한번'이라는 부사와 함께 쓰는 경우가 많으며 말할 때는 'V-아/어 봐' 뒤에 습관적으로 '봐'를 한 번 더 붙여 말하기도 한다.

**발음**

① '맞춰'는 [마춰]로 발음하지만 발음의 편의상 빠르게 발화 시 [마처]로 발음할 수도 있다.
② '높여'는 [노펴]로 발음함. 다만, '볼륨을 높여'는 휴지를 두지 않고 붙여서 [볼류믈로펴]로 발음된다.
③ '쟈, 쳐, 쵸, 츄'는 [자, 처, 초, 추]로 발음한다.
④ '봐'는 [봐]로 발음하지만 발음의 편의상 [바]로 많이 발음한다.

**어순**

행위를 강조하기 위해 위의 가사와 같이 앞절과 뒷절의 순서를 바꾸기도 하는데 바른 어순의 문장은 이와 같다.

## ⅠⅥ Give It to Me

**가수 및 노래 소개**

'씨스타'는 이웃집 누나와 언니 같은 이미지와 특색 있는 보컬을 강조하는 그룹으로 데뷔 후 얼마 지나지 않아 대중들에게 실력으로 빠르게 인정받은 그룹이다 〈Give It to Me〉는 한국의 음악 방송에서 열한 번이나 1위를 차지한 곡으로 이성에게 사랑을 갈구하는 애절한 마음을 잘 표현하고 있는 곡이다.

### 표현 1
'아무리'는 'A/V-아도/어도'와만 결합되어 사용하는
표현으로 'A/V-아도/어도'의 상황을 강조해서 나타낸다.

### 표현 2
'A-단 말이야, V-ㄴ/는단 말이야, N-(이)란 말이야'는
어떤 사실을 다시 한 번 강조해서 상대에게 각인시켜 말할
때 사용하는 표현이다. 강조하는 말이 형용사일 때 '-단
말이야' 동사일 때 '-ㄴ/는단 말이야' 명사일 때 '-(이)란
말이야'의 형태로 사용한다.

### 표현 3
'-(으)면 되다'는 앞의 상황이 되거나 그런 행동만 하면
문제가 해결됨을 의미한다. 'It will be okay if ~'와 비슷한
의미이다.

### 발음
말이야[마리야]는 빨리 발음하면 [마랴]가 된다.

### 줄임말
한국어에 나타나는 줄임말 중에서 가장 대표적인 형태로,
'-는'이 'ㄴ'로 줄어 앞의 모음으로 끝나는 음절에 받침으로
결합된다.

## 17 A

### 가수 및 노래 소개
'GOT7'은 한국, 태국, 홍콩, 미국의 다국적 멤버 7명으로
구성된 아이돌 그룹으로 행운을 가진 7명이라는 의미이다.
곡명인 〈A〉는 한국어로 '에이'라고 발음하는데 상대방이
하는 행동이나 말이 사실인지 의심하거나 사실이 아니라고
생각할 때 내는 소리이다. 이 노래는 자신에게 관심 없는
척하는 소녀에게 솔직하게 마음을 고백해 보라고 말하고
있는 노래이다.

### 표현 1
'V-아/어 있다'는 피동사의 뒤에 결합하여 앞선 행위가
일어난 뒤에 그 상태가 지속되고 있음을 나타낼 때
사용한다. 한국어의 피동사(passive verb)는 타동사에
'이/히/리/기'를 붙여 만드는 경우가 많다.

### 표현 2
'V-다(가)'는 어떤 일을 하는 도중에 다른 일을 하게
되었거나 어떤 상태가 되었음을 나타낼 때 사용한다.
처음에 시작한 그 일은 중간에 일어난 일 때문에 완료되지
않은 것 같은 느낌을 준다.

### 발음
① '너(you)'를 의미하는 '네'는 '내(my)'와 발음이 같아 이를
구분하기 위해 보통 [니]라고 발음한다.
② 받침 'ㅎ'은 뒤에 모음으로 시작하는 음절이 오는 경우,
발음하지 않는다.

### 유용한 표현
감정이나 생각이 얼굴에 드러날 때 위와 같이 표현한다.

## 18 썸

### 가수 및 노래 소개
노래의 제목 〈썸〉은 영어의 '썸씽(somthing)'에서 온 말로
한국에서는 연인이 아닌 남녀 사이에 연애 기류가 흐르는
것을 보고 '썸을 타다'라고 말한다. 이 곡은 이렇게 친구와
연인 중간에 있는 남녀 사이의 묘한 감정을 이야기하는
노래로 '씨스타'의 보컬 '소유'와 실력파 뮤지션 '정기고'가
함께 불러 대중들에게 많은 사랑을 받았다.

### 표현 1
'N 같다'는 한 대상이 다른 대상과 비슷하다는 생각이 들
때 사용하는 표현으로 'look like~'와 비슷한 표현이다. 'N
같다는 말'은 다른 사람에게 그런 이야기를 듣고 다시 그
말을 옮겨 쓸 때 사용한다.

### 표현 2
'V-기 싫어지다'는 어떤 일을 하는 것이 싫어졌음을
얘기하는 표현으로 'don't want to ~ anymore, don't feel
like ~ing' 비슷한 표현이다. 반대로 어떤 일을 하는 것이
좋아졌음을 나타낼 때는 'V-고 싶어지다'를 사용한다.

### 발음
① '- 듯 연인?'은 띄어 읽으면 [듣] [여닌], 붙여 읽으면
[든녀닌]으로 읽는다. (받침 발음[ㄷ] 뒤에 새로운 단어로
시작하는 '야, 여, 요, 유, 이'가 오면 [ㄷ]는 [ㄴ]로 '야, 여, 요,
유, 이'는 [냐], [녀], [뇨], [뉴], [니]로 발음한다.)
② '-(으)ㄹ 듯'의 'ㄷ'는 [ㄸ]로 발음한다. (받침 'ㄹ'을
포함한 어미의 경우, '-(으)ㄹ' 뒤의 'ㄱ, ㄷ, ㅂ, ㅅ, ㅈ'는
경음으로 발음된다.)
③ '나만 볼 듯 애매하게'를 휴지 없이 읽는 경우
[나만볼뜨대매하게]로 읽는다. 휴지를 지켜 읽으면 [나만 볼
뜯 애매하게]로 읽는다.

### 유행어
원래 '-(으)ㄴ/(으)ㄹ/는/인 듯하다'는 자신의 생각이나
추측을 나타내는 글을 쓸 때 많이 사용하던 표현인데
최근에는 한국의 젊은 사람들이 문자를 보낼 때 '하다'를
생략한 '-(으)ㄴ/(으)ㄹ/는/인 듯'의 형태로 많이 사용한다.

## 19 이 노래

### 가수 및 노래 소개

'2AM'이라는 그룹명은 하루 동안의 여러 감정이 차분히 정리되는 시간인 새벽 2시에 듣기 좋은 음악을 부르겠다는 그룹의 음악적 색깔을 잘 나타내고 있다. 〈이 노래〉는 2008년 발표된 2AM의 데뷔곡으로 사랑하는 연인에게 많은 것을 해 줄 수 없는 가난한 남자의 마음을 담고 있다.

### 표현 1

'V-(으)ㄹ 수 있는 게 없다'는 가능한 일이 없다는 의미로 'there's nothing one can do'과 비슷한 의미의 표현이다. '밖에 없다'와 같이 써서 'V-(으)ㄹ 수 있는 게 N밖에 없다'의 형태로도 많이 쓰이며 가능한 일이 단 하나만 있음을 강조하여 말할 때 사용한다.

### 표현 2

'V-(으)ㄹ 수 있을지 모르겠다'는 어떤 일이 가능한지에 대한 의심이나 걱정 등을 나타낼 때 사용하는 표현으로 'I doubt one can to something'과 비슷한 의미의 표현이다.

### 발음

① '-(으)ㄹ 수'의 'ㅅ'는 [ㅆ]로 발음한다.
② '-(으)ㄹ지'의 'ㅈ'는 [ㅉ]로 발음한다 (받침 'ㄹ'을 포함한 어미의 경우, '-(으)ㄹ' 뒤의 'ㄱ,ㄷ,ㅂ,ㅅ,ㅈ'는 [ㄲ,ㄸ,ㅃ,ㅆ,ㅉ]로 경음으로 발음된다.)

### 맞춤법

'바라다'는 '-아/어'와 결합 시 '바라'가 되어야 하나 거의 모든 한국 사람들이 '바래'로 사용한다. 게다가 '아/어 보다'와 결합 시 '바라 보다'가 되는데 '바라보다'라는 어휘는 'stare'의 의미를 가지고 있기 때문에 의미 혼동이 우려가 있어 '바래 보다'라고 말하는 게 더 낫다.

## 20 Error

### 가수 및 노래 소개

'빅스'는 2012년에 데뷔한 6인조 아이돌 그룹으로 대표곡으로는 뱀파이어 컨셉으로 인기를 얻은 〈다칠 준비가 돼 있어〉라는 곡이 있다. 발표하는 곡마다 컨셉을 정해서 활동하는 컨셉돌로 인기를 끌고 있으며 〈Error〉는 사이보그 컨셉의 뮤직비디오가 인상적이다. 실연의 상처를 느끼지 않기 위해 사이보그가 되지만 이후에도 연인을 그리워하며 아파한다는 내용의 가사이다.

### 표현 1

'절대'는 어떤 경우에도 그렇게 될 수 없다는 것을 강조하는 부사로 항상 부정을 나타내는 '안, 못, 아니다, 없다, -지 말다' 등과 함께 사용해야 하며 'never'와 같은 의미의 표현이다.

### 표현 2

'V-(으)ㄹ 자신이 있다'는 어떤 일을 할 수 있다는 화자의 의지를 나타내는 표현이며 'V-(으)ㄹ 자신이 없다'는 어떤 일을 할 수 없을 것 같다는 두려움을 나타내는 표현이다.

### 발음

① '끝'은 단독 발음 시 [끋]으로 발음되는데, 뒤에 'ㄴ'로 시작하는 음절이 오는 경우 받침 발음 [ㄷ]는 [ㄴ]로 변한다.
② 받침 발음 [ㄷ]은 뒤에 'ㅁ'으로 시작하는 음절이 오는 경우 [ㄷ]→[ㄴ]으로 변한다.
③ 'ㄹ' 받침 뒤의 'ㄷ, ㅅ, ㅈ'는 경음으로 발음되는 경우가 많다.

## Vocabulary

### ㄱ



### ㄴ



### ㄷ



### ㄹ



### ㅁ



### ㅂ

**01** 오늘부터 우리는 (Starting from Today)
Music by 이기(IGGY) / 용배(SYB)
Words by 이기(IGGY) / 용배(SYB)
(C) SOURCEMUSIC Inc. All rights reserved. Used by permission.

**02** Honey
Music by 한재호(Han Jae-Ho) / 김승수(Kim Seung-Soo)
Words by 한재호(Han Jae-Ho) / 김승수(Kim Seung-Soo) /
송수윤(Song Soo-Yoon)
(C) Sweetune. All rights reserved. Used by permission.

**03** 벚꽃 엔딩 (Cherry Blossom Ending)
Music by 장범준(Jang Beom-June)
Words by 장범준(Jang Beom-June)

**04** 남자 없이 잘 살아 (I Don't Need a Man)
Music by J.Y. Park "The Asiansoul"
Words by J.Y. Park "The Asiansoul"
(C) 2013 JYP Publishing Corp (KOMCA). All rights reserved.
Used by permission.

**05** 결혼해 줄래 (Will You Marry Me?)
Music by 김도훈(Kim Do-Hoon) / 이상호(Lee Sang-Ho)
Words by 김도훈(Kim Do-Hoon) / 황성진(Hwang Sung-Jin)
(C) 2009 Music Cube, Inc. All rights reserved. Used by permission.

**06** No No No
Music by 신사동호랭이(Shinsadong Tiger) / KUPA
Words by 신사동호랭이(Shinsadong Tiger) / KUPA

**07** 너뿐이야 (You Are the Only One)
Music by J.Y. Park "The Asiansoul"
Words by J.Y. Park "The Asiansoul"
(C) 2012 JYP Publishing Corp (KOMCA). All rights reserved.
Used by permission.

**08** 하루만 (Just One Day)
Music by RAP MONSTER / J-HOPE / SUGA / PDOGG
Words by RAP MONSTER / J-HOPE / SUGA / PDOGG

**09** Be My Baby
Music by J.Y. Park "The Asiansoul" / Rainstone
Words by J.Y. Park "The Asiansoul"
(C) 2011 JYP Publishing Corp (KOMCA). All rights reserved.
Used by permission.

**10** 노래가 늘었어 (My Singing Got Better)
Music by 휘성(WHEESUNG) / 문하(MOONHAKIM)
Words by 휘성(WHEESUNG)
(C) 2016 Music Cube, Inc. All rights reserved. Used by permission.

**11** 남자가 사랑할 때 (Man in Love)
Music by 한재호(Han Jae-Ho) / 김승수(Kim Seung-Soo) /
이창현(Lee Chang-Hyun)
Words by 한재호(Han Jae-Ho) / 김승수(Kim Seung-Soo) /
송수윤(Song Soo-Yoon) / 이호원(Lee Ho-Won) /
장동우(Jang Dong-woo)
(C) Sweetune. All rights reserved. Used by permission.

**12** Ah-Choo
Music by One piece (Yoonsang, Davink, Spacecowboy),
Words by 서지음(Seo Ji-Eum)

**13** 사랑 사랑 사랑 (Love Love Love)
Music by 김도훈(Kim Do-Hoon) / 이상호(Lee Sang-Ho)
Words by 김도훈(Kim Do-Hoon) / 이상호(Lee Sang-Ho) /
정한림(Jung Han-Rim)
(C) 2010 Music Cube, Inc. All rights reserved. Used by permission.

**14** 너의 모든 순간 (Every Moment of You)
Music by 성시경(Sung Si-Kyung)
Words by 심현보(Shim Hyun-bo)

**15** Hands Up
Music by J.Y. Park "The Asiansoul"
Words by J.Y. Park "The Asiansoul"
(C) 2011 JYP Publishing Corp (KOMCA). All rights reserved.
Used by permission.

**16** Give It to Me
Music by 이단옆차기 (Kim Michael Chung, Ham Joon-Seok,
Lee Yong-Hwan, Park Jang-Geun, PKA Duble Sidekick),
Words by 이단옆차기 (Kim Michael Chung, Ham Joon-Seok,
Lee Yong-Hwan, Park Jang-Geun, PKA Duble Sidekick),

**17** A
Music by J.Y. Park "The Asiansoul"
Words by J.Y. Park "The Asiansoul"
(C) 2014 JYP Publishing Corp (KOMCA). All rights reserved.
Used by permission.

**18** 썸 (Some)
Music by eSNa / 김도훈(Kim Do-Hoon) / Xepy
Words by 오승택(Lil Boi) / eSNa / Junggigo / 민연재(Min Yeon-Jae )
/ Xepy
(C) 2014 Music Cube, Inc. All rights reserved. Used by permission.

**19** 이 노래 (This Song)
Music by J.Y. Park "The Asiansoul"
Words by J.Y. Park "The Asiansoul"
(C) 2008 JYP Publishing Corp (KOMCA). All rights reserved.
Used by permission.

**20** Error
Music by 황세준 (Hwang Sei-Joon) / 멜로디자인 (MELODESIGN)
Words by 김원식 (RAVI) / 김이나 (Kim Eana)